COLLECTED POEMS

COLLECTED POEMS

John Fuller

Chatto & Windus
LONDON

First published in 1996

1 3 5 7 9 10 8 6 4 2

Copyright © John Fuller 1996

John Fuller has asserted his right under the Copyright,
Designs and Patents Act, 1988 to be identified as the author
of this work

First published in Great Britain in 1996 by
Chatto & Windus Limited
Random House, 20 Vauxhall Bridge Road,
London SW1V 2SA

Random House Australia (Pty) Limited
20 Alfred Street, Milsons Point, Sydney
New South Wales 2061, Australia

Random House New Zealand Limited
18 Poland Road, Glenfield
Auckland 10, New Zealand

Random House South Africa (Pty) Limited
Endulini, 5a Jubilee Road, Parktown 2193, South Africa

Random House UK Limited Reg. No. 954009

Papers used by Random House UK Limited are natural, recyclable
products made from wood grown in sustainable forests. The
manufacturing processes conform to the environmental
regulations of the country of origin

A CIP catalogue record for this book
is available from the British Library

ISBN 0 7011 6612 6

Typeset by Deltatype Ltd, Birkenhead, Merseyside
Printed in Great Britain by
Mackays of Chatham PLC, Chatham, Kent

for Prue

Look at this: after one glance,
A guarded pair standing akimbo
Are just about to dance!

We too, with what spirit of play
Did we eagerly follow the droning pipe
And tread the day away?

From sunlight into the dark wood
Of the required extemporised life
We have wandered where we could.

Now there are paths, and they are ours:
Like lost children we have slept a little
But woken to the stars.

Author's note

I have resisted the temptation to include in this volume any early, uncollected, occasional or unpublished poems. It does not include poems written for children, nor poems from *Partingtime Hall*, written with James Fenton. It does contain the majority of poems from the following collections: *Fairground Music, The Tree that Walked, The Grey Among the Green, The Mechanical Body, Stones and Fires* (Chatto and Windus); *Waiting for the Music* (Salamander Press); *Cannibals and Missionaries, Epistles to Several Persons, The Mountain in the Sea, The Illusionists*, and *The Beautiful Inventions* (Secker and Warburg). The poems have been somewhat rearranged in terms of period and theme.

Contents

I
1954–1965

Fairy tale

Blushing, she fled: no one was on her side.
She could not bear the whistle and the slap,
The fustian prospect of a farmer's lap.
Her father moped. Her sisters swore. She cried,
Dreamed of the Prince, neglected all her tasks
And now had run away, but not for long:
The wood was frightful as a wig, as wrong
As her own hearth. Soon she returned, through masks
Of mist. Her heart jumped at the stir that took
Her eye: the royal hounds sagged in the porch,
Their tongues like shoehorns. Someone waved a torch.
Hardly believing, breathless, she ran to look –
But worse than all the sniggers of the wood,
The waiting Prince was ugly, pale and good.

Girl with coffee tray

Slipping, she fell into the sitting-room,
For one gay second noticed what was there:
The salmon cushion on the lashed cane chair;
The frail greenness of apples in a gloom
Of chalk wall; round her head the watery boom
Of stool logs, crags and waves of hessian sea
Where driftwood pencils and books floated. She
Considered vaguely that the arching plume
Of her white cat's tail, too, was oceanic.
The sofa creaked. Cups smashed to smithereens.
The cat mewed like a gull, bounced off in panic.
Her feet still sprawling on the hall's wax tiles,
She cried. The sea-bed carpet stretched for miles
Where she lay drowning in the blues and greens.

White queen

Who has a feeling she will come one day,
No pretty, silly girl, nor beautiful
Like Marlowe's Spirit, unapproachable,
But grey, grey, grey from being shut away?

For this is what the poets will not say:
'Helen grew paler and was old, I fear,
(Sixty at Troy's loud fall) and for a year
Was seen by no one, wandering fat and grey.'

In her appearance all will have their say.
Movements of flesh about eternal needs
Promote the spectacle of Helen's deeds
In the mind's eye at least, but in what way?

What figure scampers as this verse begins,
Ashen and wailing, scattering veils and pins?

Sleeping

The princess was baptised inside a shell,
Nude, adult, rich and handsome, but a bitch.
Small wonder she refused to ask that witch
Who scuttled lecherous tars, dried up a well
That poisoned villagers, silenced the bell
Of the smug church and moved fat squashy cows
Whole fields away to give a poor man's house
Milk for a week! really, one just can't tell
This story after all the palace lies.
There was no curse. The princess sighed, and rust
Crumbled the pantry lock. The king yawned. Flies
Settled on footmen turned to snoring dust.
Churls grinned. Till through them, too, there
                                  flowed the deep
And uncontrollable desire to sleep.

Edwardian Christmas

Father's opinion of savages
And dogs, a gay Bloomsbury epigram:
'The brutes may possibly have souls,' he says,
'But reason, no. Nevertheless, I am
Prepared not to extend this to my spouse
And children.' This demands a careful pity:
Poor Father! Whooping and romping in their house,
A holiday from ruin in the City.
His wit falls flat, his tie just will not tie.
The dog's in chains, the reasonable books

Grazed by his children as they learn to fly.
He takes his dear wife's arm (his hands grow hooks).
Pirates and pudding! Come, such cruelty!

His beard is branching like a burning tree.

Band music

Cows! Cows! With ears like mouths of telephones!
They creak towards him with their heads thrust out,
So baby wauls among the cabbages
Till Betty runs to kiss his quivering pout
And lumping Ernest takes a stick and stones
To drive them off, cursing their ravages.

'Hush, child,' she whispers, rocking. 'There, there then!
Watch Ernest. Clever Ernest. Nasty cows.'
Inside the cottage from a dusty box
Thumps martial music. Flowers on Betty's blouse
Grow out in lines like cabbages while men
In gold braid blow among the hollyhocks.

In a railway compartment

Oxford to London, 1884:
Against the crimson arm-rest leaned a girl
Of ten, holding a muff, twisting a curl,
Drumming her heels in boredom on the floor
Until a white-haired gentleman who saw
She hated travelling produced a case
Of puzzles: 'Seven Germans run a race . . .
Unwind this maze, escape the lion's paw . . .
The princess must be lowered by her hair . . .'
The train entered a tunnel, shrieking, all
The lights went out and when he took her hand
She was the princess in the tower and
A lion faced her on the moonlit wall
Who roared and reached and caught and held her there.

5

Alex's game

He sets the table with sponge firs in tubs –
Lung sculpture trees – and turkeys' iron fans,
A palace-garage-castle, fleets of vans
In stalls flecked yellow-red, indian clubs
Mountains, and so on. When a lorry's hubs
Swerve and blurt off their midget tyres, a lead
Farm girl with plasticene and matchstick head
Stretches the baby quoits again and rubs
The axles with a margey thumb. He reaches
For a squat cowboy in red plastic breeches
Stretched round a missing horse, sets him to guard
The girl. But look what she does: up she swings
Her one stiff arm and belts the cowboy hard.
Now that was not in his imaginings.

Alex at the barber's

He is having his hair cut. Towels are tucked
About his chin, his mop scalped jokingly.
The face in the mirror is his own face.

The barber moves and chats among the green
And methylated violet, snipper-snips,
Puts scissors down, plugs in a plaited flex,

And like a surgeon with his perfumed hands
Presses the waiting skull and shapes the base.
He likes having his hair cut, and the man

Likes cutting it. The radio drones on.
The eyes in the mirror are his own eyes.
While the next chair receives the Demon Blade,

A dog-leg razor nicks a sideburn here;
As from a sofa there a sheet is whisked
And silver pocketed. The doorbell pings.

The barber, frowning, grips the ragged fringe
And slowly cuts. Upon the speckled sheet
The bits fall down and now his hair is cut.

The neighing trams outside splash through the rain.
The barber tests the spray for heat and rubs
Lemon shampoo into his spiky hair.

Bent with his head above the running bowl,
Eyes squeezed shut, he does not see the water
Gurgle and sway like twisted sweetpaper

Above the waste, but, for a moment, tows
A sleigh of polished silver parrots through
Acres of snow, exclaiming soundlessly.

Then towel round head. Head swung gently up.
Eyes padded. As the barber briskly rubs,
The smile in the mirror is his own smile.

Mercury

Scraping from the bench
Silver till it becomes
A quivering kidney, black
Under his thin thumbs,

The young apprentice thinks:
'How hot the sun will get!
When earth and rocks like this
Are liquid but not wet,

What will have happened to me,
Who am the only one?'
He weeps, and a dumb wind
Blows in from Asia, un-

-kempt as a messenger;
It slams the door and moans,
And the fingers work faster
At the end of his long bones.

Snapshot

A girl is twirling a parasol.
A dog is worrying a doll.

Postcards and lace shawls
Are sold by garden waterfalls.

Chopin spins from wax and horn.
The terrier bounds across the lawn,

Aching for rivers, while the doll
Gets prodded by the parasol.

Roger, fresh from soap and razor,
Approaches in his candy blazer

And strokes his Maupassant moustache:
'This July sun is really *harsh*!'

Soft and quiet as a panda,
She follows him to the verandah

Where the cool pebble lemonade
Burns and burns in a green shade.

Upon a chair of mother-of-pearl
He pulls his smiling panda girl

Into the crook of his striped arm,
His thumb upon her closing palm.

The girl puts down her parasol.
The dog swallows the doll.

Owls

The murderous owls off Malo bay
Can lure a sleepless watchman to the sea,
For their deep singing may be heard
Throughout a night of thunder and their red
Eyes take him dancing silently
Down to the choking sea-bed. Far away
His heavy wife sleeps like the dead
Upon the feathers of a bird.

In the Keswick Museum

O Lakeland Musical Stones! Played by
Negroes in faultless evening dress circa 1900!

Listen to the chopping clinks as felt
Hammers bounce on the slabs!

Like Debussy at the Odeon . . .

The Three Days' Riding

With his casque strapped under his chin,
The young captain from Japan
Won the jumping at Los Angeles.

With a furious determination
And his casque strapped under his chin,
The young captain from Japan

Splashed through the water-jump
At the Berlin Olympic Games 1936,
Watched by the giggling cameramen.

Waiting for a wind

Save us, we cannot see. Our eyes fail us,
But through the wrong end of a telescope,
Curled up in heat with salty hair and brows

The ragged mermaids perch on sloping rocks
Beside the waves' black glitter. The sun is white
And sheets of dazzling air hang all about

Their island, tightening and thick as steam,
Scorching and bright beneath descending sky.
A mermaid dives with arms held at her side

Down to wet depths of green and sunken blue,
To spiky fish, fabulous as explosions.
Can we imagine this, not hope for vision?

Slowly, with small and round exclaiming mouth,
She bursts up glistening from the broken sea.
Colour is the liquor of her eyes.

The scene grows taller in their sweet wet flood
Of swirls and washes. Light clears with bangs.
Yes, our hands shake. Our dream boat rocks.

Her sodden globes focus the dancing air,
Pinpoint to blackness, a tiny inky dot
Held for a second till it boils and splashes

Outwards into forms of hues and flames.
Waves gulp ultramarine on mustard rocks
Trailing a lemon lichen, while sea-flowers,

9

(Pale lipstick colours on deep brown or sage),
Cluster in sucking clefts of rock or drift
In fronds from humps of dead-eye mussels.

Some weed is khaki-ribbon, trailing arms
Water-plunged rouge-veined with colder blue,
Finger-nails pinched crab flakes, sticky hair

Of mermaids bleached like straw, the dryer strands
Whiter, whiter, dry as an empty ship.
The light burns. Only the sea can restore.

The world was formed within a mermaid's eyes.

Essay on Spenser

Clownish without his armour, he
Clamped down his umbriere. His sword
Knocking against the trees, men fell
About him, headless, twitching. His
Thick heart jumping, he plunged through
The steaming wood until against
His Lady's Tower, sword down, he gasped
The rune to move the man-high stone
That blocked her keeping, up again
He raced the spiral shaft and beat
In rage the spellbound oak. And died.
For a splintered mirror spoilt her plan
To save him from the littered plain,
And all that night fell frogs and rain.

Primary source

The Duchess complains her children die too young,
A pastoral counterpoint to infant labour.
The Tutor sympathises, holds his tongue,
Himself an offspring of the factory neighbour.
Blood wrestles with blood, and class with class.
Those threads of black against the hill's green throat
Which prompted her conceit, like a forged note

If, after one illuminating phrase,
I smash a pane, admitting the night air,
Shall I arise to stormy deeds of nothing
Or in a mirror see *your* glowing hair?

You thrill with your suggestions like a child:
Prompting my arm, you ruin the gathered page.
You are the startling conscience of us all,
The poking finger to a nervous age.

The ballad of Lord Timbal

Beside a flashing gramophone
And the latest magazines
Lord Timbal watched the chequered sea,
Its curling whites and greens.

Stretched round him on the silver sand
On turquoise towels lay
The last guests at his villa
Spending their last day.

Lord Timbal was a gentleman
And of the richest kind:
He bought his life with little cheques
And every cheque was signed.

And every cheque was handsome
And every cheque was met,
And each of his acquaintances
Was in Lord Timbal's debt.

Beneath a cup-shaped rock he sat,
His wristwatch lattice gold.
He did not buy love with his cheques
For love could not be sold.

He watched each pair of faces
That touched each other there,
And he sat unknown among them,
Among the bronzed and fair.

He slipped on his dark glasses,
Mirrors in precious stone:
He saw their puzzled faces,
But they only saw their own.

And in these one-way glasses
He heard their whispered words
As they huddled on his private beach
Like migrating birds:

'Why does he live alone here
At the age of twenty-three,
With his face as pale as a ceiling
And his hair as wild as the sea?'

'Who *is* he, our host, with his empty chair
And the presents on our plate?'
'Will he wave to us at the station?'
'Hurry or we'll be late.'

His servant drove ten hampers down,
Bursting with carp and hock,
And the train was out and the party gone
Like a glimpse of a summer frock.

Lord Timbal stayed behind alone,
And, like a gay reproof,
He saw the puffs of train smoke drift
Beyond the villa's roof.

He went from hut to bathing hut,
Frowning at what he saw,
And at a trace of woman's scent
He turned and slammed the door.

He entered all the bedrooms
And opened all the drawers,
And the sea's roar in his head became
Ironical applause:

'O honest player, play your hand,
Harden your honest face.
The ace is low in the game of life,
And you've drawn the ace.'

His man came back from the station
And stood at the foot of the stair.
The young lord went to the stairhead
And saw him standing there.

Lord Timbal looked down strangely
With his fingers at his cheek,
Parting his cold romantic lips
As if he meant to speak.

Amused, the servant turned away,
Began to pick his nails,
And Lord Timbal came down the staircase
Grasping both the rails.

He looked into his servant's eye
As if it held some clue.
And there he read the deepest scorn,
But a little pity, too:

'You've never really loved, nor will.
You love yourself, your past.
You are unhappy. You will die.
Need you ask?'

The cool stare sinking in his heart
As the sea receives a stone,
He opened the french windows
And strolled out on his own.

The bay was clearing its green throat,
The sea sniffed at the rocks,
A sudden wind rose up and blew
Lord Timbal's thinning locks.

He looked up to the terrace
And saw his servant there,
Wrapping away the cutlery
With a fatal, final air.

Lord Timbal now was fearless.
Grimly he clambered on
His cream and brass expensive yacht
And sailed off like a swan.

He sailed into a mid-sea storm
And there without a sound
The swollen sails exploded
And Lord Timbal was drowned.

'Lord Timbal is dead, Lord Timbal is dead,'
A wind to the people roared.

15

But they turned and sadly whispered:
'Lucky for that poor lord.

'Idle he died as idle lived,
Empty the life he led.
He spent his pounds like bullets
And his love like lead.'

A few crept from their dwellings
And then came more, and more.
With faces lined and heavy,
They waited on the shore.

They watched the ocean rise and fall
With the glow of the fishing floats
And their eyes stared long at the water
As the men dragged down their boats.

His body was slowly borne along
On the stretchers of the sea,
And all the drums of the Spanish coast
Beat in sympathy.

West Coast style

1

The young men howl to the moon with horns
As couples tread the purple lawns
And beaches under bobbing lights,
Drink black coffee. Music for nights
By surf, music to make you cry.
Cleaning its wrists, the fly
Frowns into the evening's core
And the warm winds blow over the shore.
The black stick and the golden swan,
Intruding, dip and grunt, go on
To banter. Hair falls over their faces.
Ladies in evening gowns by places
White beneath the hanging stars
Step laughing from their open cars.

2

At the most tender part, a song
Of immortal passion, a long
Aria of love, it will occur:
The lights and quivering voices blur,
The vision crackle, as a pond
Crackles when skaters waltz beyond
The safer ice, and once again
Cease or stagger off the plane
Of simple music. So one fears.
The noises get too savage, tears
Start, notes falter and the sound
Sobs, refuses to go round:
The slender record has unwound.

Fairground music

Dispirited, the Sun of Persia
And his hordes return
To distance and to longing.
Haggard painted horses
Glossy with angry curls
Express his orbit;
Paper axles spin and burn
With proper fury.
But flowered Babylon
Amid the smiling pipes,
Amid the gentle drum,
Is troubled still
By whirring scythes and music,
Sleeping, is oppressed
By alien beards and tents.
Rough Cyrus roars
For talismans and charts;
The whole collision
Is of smarting red and green
Thick with the smoking blood.
The fall of Babylon!
A mercenary there
Rummaged in slub and carcase
For some prize or toy

And found a thing that troubled
Cyrus so, he wept, and saw
Within the tinkling of
A turning box,
Shore-fighters, crabs,
Girl-scorpions,
Splashing in weightless
Liquid gold about the rocks.

A dialogue between Caliban & Ariel

Ar. Now you have been taught words and I am free,
My pine struck open, your thick tongue untied,
And bells call out the music of the sea.

From this advantage I can clearly see
You will abuse me in your grovelling pride
Now you have been taught words: and I am free

To pinch and bully you eternally,
Swish round the island while the mermaids hide
And bells call out the music of the sea.

I watched you closely from within my tree:
Explicit fish, implicit homicide,
Now you have been taught words, and I am free

To hear, who has the real victory?
For you may drown as I draw in the tide
And bells call out the music of the sea.

You lust for Her and bare your teeth at me.
Your roarings only mock the ache inside
Now you have been taught words. And I am free
While bells call out the music of the sea.

Cal. Have *you* no feelings that you cannot tame?

Ar. My target's everything, and in my aim,
        Achievement, while another,
            Lesser lusts may drive:
        Legs hate their lazy brother
            Who saps your precious Five
            To keep alive.

Cal. Have you no visions that you cannot name?

Ar. A picture should extend beyond its frame,
    There being no limitation
        To bright reality:
    For all their declaration
        And complexity,
        Words cannot see.

Cal. Are not the object and the word the same?

Ar. Words are but counters in a childish game;
    Each move you make is token
        Only of the rules:
    Any rule may be broken
        By the boy from a clever school
        Or a bored fool.

Cal. How is it, then, that words can hurt and maim?

Ar. If words do that, you are already lame,
    Bowed down by words like firewood,
        Clenched with words like ice:
    Language is for the coward
        Who thinks a rule is nice
        At any price.

Cal. O then unteach me language, let the cool
    Sea sidle up and draw me to its deep
    Silence. Teach me how to break the rule.

Ar. Once in the game you cannot make that leap.
    The sea will cast you up again if you
    Pretend to break the rule you really keep.

Cal. But tell me, then, if what you say is true,
    What was your knowledge when you could not move?
    What instinct told what function what to do?

Ar. Words would not help the channelled sea to prove
    It was not ocean-free, nor pine no fuel:
    I just existed, wordless, in my groove.

        Nor do I use words now, though you
        In innocence may think I do:
        We've left the island and engage
        In conversation on a page
        Sand-white and, like it, bounded by

19

A vast of dull eternity.
And I (since I can understand)
Am master of this paper land.
Think I am quick? I am so too,
But when I'm bored with biffing you,
Eve's monkey, still that is not all,
Nor Milan's ghost, his beck and call
To all the fancies that I can.
You are too human, Caliban.
You lunge and ape the human dance.
Music and love are sustenance
Withheld from you like tinkling charms
Beyond your crying outstretched arms.
You think I did not want my tree?
Or tire of showing off? Being 'free'
All of the time is like your choice
Of endless fireworks of the voice:
You splutter, gasp and madly shout,
But dampness seeps up: you go out,
The silly words trail off your tongue.
So wings get tired, flapping among
The fussy spirits of the air.
You curse. I sulk. Always He's there.
The bullet's speed is not a feat.
Of time, but photograph of wheat,
A summer fly caught in a flash
Of speckled stillness. Hear a splash?
You think a glacier does not move?
Brilliance of struggling wings can prove
Treacle of amber, and a spark
The universe, my world my bark
I long for, longing for the dark.

Cal. A language learnt but nothing understood:
Now you at large, and all I owned before
Lost like my name within the magic wood.

No word for saying 'no' to fetching wood.
The marvellous Glove splits on the hairy claw:
A language learnt but nothing understood.

At first I framed what syllables I could:
She laughed at me and left me on the shore,
Lost, like my name within the magic wood.

Think of my rage then, Ariel, as I stood,
(A picture in my head I could not draw,
A language learnt but nothing understood),

Weeping into the sea, hoping She would
Turn back to lead me through that little door,
Lost like my name within the magic wood.

Our Master calls: I think it is not good
To be unhappy with your freedom or
My language (learnt, but nothing understood),
Lost like my name within the magic wood.

Flood box

Wheels grind on the shingle. Round
And round the drenched machinery
Propels its oily bulk. The sound
Screams. The train enters the sea.
Blanched fingers from the bath, cold teeth
In softened gums and floating hair:
Down the Landscape of Underneath
The paradigms of panic stare.

Imagined depth! Within its grip
White figures struggle to be free.
Above, the motorboats unzip
Their tinted wrinkled scenery
And breakers fall like piano lids,
Unloosing liquid horrors: black
Regency-hair crabs, snotty squids
And cherub penises of wrack.

Or think of water running clear
Over moss channel, dyke and bed;
The torches lit along the pier,
A liquid garden, pale and red:
The tempo slows, a pulse pretends
To measure out eternity,
But no formality extends
The haggard ebbing of the sea.

Cones of the city, smoke and rain.
A net of amber rivers breaks
The water into shapes, but pain
Is built against the narrowing lakes:
The fevered cemetery bell
Mocks at the surface of the deep.
The leaping shadows sharply smell,
Terraqueous shadows of your sleep.

You turn upon your matchbox bed,
Your knees against the door, the lamp
A glare of violence at your head.
The walls bend outward with the damp.
Some flood inlays the solid floor
And chairs achieve the sense of stilts.
The slow meniscus at the door
Soon shoulders rats and sodden quilts!

Too soon, too soon, and yet you choose
To break the skin, and once the skin
Is broken nothing's left to lose.
You shiver in a dream of fin,
The blood leaked out, the mirrors free
Of your still figure, grinning, torn:
While you enact a scenery
Of silent quanting down the lawn.

You need a pause to recollect,
But speed denies what's lost amid
A sobbing urgency now checked
By closing inches of the lid.
The lungs are stretching to be free,
Down past the dimly burning light.
Open the window to the sea,
Push from the ceiling to the night!

Hands fluttering, you fade away
With an imaginary flute
Like a wood ghost, and what you say
Is lost among the final hoot
As you explode the busy robe
Of bones. Ours is a futile chase:
The limits of your endless globe
Magnify the dismal face.

Turn to the back. No one is right.
The dream contains us from the start.
The brain rehearses out of sight
The tender habit of the heart.
The room remains, embalmed and still
Like a sunk ship, and what we find
Impossible is the firm will
In the drowned shape you leave behind.

Landscapes of Western New York

1 *Lake Chautauqua*
Behind the sheeted lake the deer
Pose, whose forests pencilled-in
Contain quiet ambuscades of snow,
The tracks and berries they defend.

Skiers drop above the town
Where bubble elevators rise
And demerara tyre-treads squeeze
Their perfect diamonds, parked for lunch.

The hotel clinks its empty beer
And clocks eject the curls and slacks
To buckle juddering steel and crouch
At speed by telescoping barns.

Night sees the hotel desolated.
Smoking at a corner table
The waiters eat what no one ordered:
Soft cheese, expensive quarto steaks.

While from sedans a mile away
The skiers serenade the deer,
And in the dark the hard white lake
Stands still among delighted trees.

2 *Niagara Falls*
Fierce aquatic carelessness!
Your great arenas celebrate
The sensible decision of river
To undergo a sudden fate.

What struggle there has been is done.
The rapids gather for the ledge.

From ragged foam and rocks we see
How huge the force, how bulked the edge,

How ropes of crystal braided over
Quiver, continuously thick,
Spilling to thinness in the depth,
A change as skilful as a trick.

The conjuring light falls through the spray
And ghosts of equilibrists quail.
The graded colours curve down where
Imaginary barrels sail.

We look and gasp, and are deceived.
This stagey routine fails at length
To signify what it had meant:
The waters' wilful, sickening strength.

3 *Buffalo*
The metered tarmac elevates
Its clean technologies, distils
The whiff of chemicals, a mile
Of steel. And Erie shrugs the stains.

Far from the shore a city collapses
Into its suburbs: four-garage
Colonial, and shops for tartan.
Executives flop into pools.

Industry and avenue:
The civic idea pacifies
The furies. Winking boulevards
Offer a dangerous escape.

For tourists, curios and wreckers
Assert a kind of grammar, cars
Smooth past hotels coloured as cake,
A wilderness of lowered shades.

Warmed by the sobbing of the lights
We reach the core, a cut-price noon,
The taste of our solicitude,
The negro store, the golden dome.

4 *Letchworth Park*
Car horns on the scenic whorls
Puncture the coloured woods. Behind,
A weeping smoke of water spills
Through photographic crevices.

A vegetable empire drifts
Against pathetic monuments
To local rape and torturing.
The air is warm and fine with rain.

Like someone else's shoes the strange
Utensils of the pioneers:
The women come in Steinberg hats
To view the maps and dusty churns

And creep with ten-cent postcards on
The car park's sodden botany
While unfamiliar feral sounds
Disturb the undergrowth beyond.

The land is governed. The rain falls.
This love of history preserves
The sewn eyes of the Indian,
Fearless in their bright false glass!

In Kentucky

White wooden paling, the tremolo organ:
Marlins and family glassily stare
From the panelled walls of a Kentucky room
Furiously shuttered against the glare.

Beneath the racing Dufy clouds
A portico invokes the past.
Daughter and children visit the mansion.
Bourbon settles in a silver glass.

We love you, we love you still, Miss Lucy,
The phantoms of the house declare.
Though pretty farms turn real estate
And you have grown, we need you where

Plucked acres measured to the post
Extend beyond your hammock's lull
And horses' names like battleships'
Fade red upon the barn's flaked hull.

Though there is shouting in the lane
The painted summer is not dead,
For look! your iron negro grins,
The jockey cap upon his head!

Pictures from a '48 De Soto

1

Humped in this swart sedan, paper half-lowered,
The automatic at my side snug as a cancer,
I watch the house. Or in the house myself

Look at my wrist, insane with jealousy:
Her furs and veils lie on the front seat,
The tongue inside its curious second home.

Even banked high in snow, the engine dead,
The woven greenish braids and tassels swing.
A razored head lurches, lolls back, headlights

Shattered in the pursued and silent mirror.
The windows are shut: palms thud wildly on
The glass. Black opening mouth, the sound switched off.

2

The last owner lugged gravel, the wings
Rusted and bolted back. We drive it
Three thousand miles to the Pacific

Where the blind nude hulk, down to its canvas,
Like a slow fist hisses into the dump.
Now the yellow plates illegally decorate

The bathroom, and these, too, fetch improbable ghosts:
After days on the anvil, tanking through the dust,
We arrive at the coloured river. Our eyes hurt.

Dwarfs wrestle behind glass. Dresses
Are cut to the buttocks' cleft. Half-shaved men
Are running sheeted through the empty square.

Revolution

Celestial jig and orphic toot:
Elizabethans meant to please.
The vocal round and fingered lute
Reflected godly harmonies.

When oratorios of brass
Later erupted with the plague,
Like the expansive Middle Class
Their provenance seemed bright and vague.

But music of the baroque type
Evolved from cruel instruments:
The hangman's drum, the bosun's pipe,
The horn – curled for convenience.

Thus purged into its trilling were
Emotions of the rope and chase,
As wigs replaced the natural hair
And formalised each pitted face.

Lost was the music of the spheres:
The heavens now extended far
Beyond these little human fears,
Beyond the frantic orchestra.

Out of the wood

1

The music sent him stumbling through. One turn,
The dead skin lay. A century's use had not
Prepared for this refinement. Strings were hot
From fighting with the stroke that made them burn
And like the whole sea in a simple shell
They offered up their sound. The sudden wire
Snapped in the orchard. No use that the cell
In its conspiracy against entire
Death puts on fantastic masquerade,
The Chinese Box of gender, for as he
Broke from the silence of his family
So broke this music from the mind he played,
And mute within lurked this essential tone,
And he discovered it and was alone.

2

There were some things he did not understand,
Suggestive versions of some former text
Like colours in burnt paper or a land
Of circled wheat, and what might happen next
Was never plain. Ideas ran out like sand,
A dummy as his target oddly placed.

He bought no apparatus for desire,
Fired no invention in his mental waste.
In time, even his intimations ceased;
The wailing of the temples he dismissed.
Deceptive. Trivial. Yet the immense
Universe about his blindness spun:
The creaking beasts stared through the glacial fence,
And symbols flickered darkly from the sun.

3

His hand slipped back. There was a wilderness.
And moved it forward and the marvels grew.
The fountains and diseases could not guess
Which kind of gesture was not really true,
And all the frightened servants from the farms
Gasped when one morning there was wine and flags
And willingly exhibited their charms:
The posture showed the rose beneath the rags.
There is another project for defeat
Belonging to inheritance. The line
Expires in time, empty and incomplete
Within a habit-forming anodyne
And builds upon foundations of excess
A palace of intense mistrustfulness.

4

He's coaxed a hint, but if he should connect
He'd find mere fingering of the thing effete:
Rather complete, where wish and action meet.
Crouched, tunnelling to the source, abject
But delirious, sometimes we reject
Simple desire, sufficient but imagined,
And assume the thing ourselves, impossibly engined;
Steer for the possible and still unwrecked
Dazzle the watchers, dashing off a quick
Philosophy in flags. This is his need,
But spoils it for the secret. It's a trick:
How can he dare this method to succeed
When it will break unsatisfied unless
He risks all at the moment of success?

5

He dreams at night of epic bonne fortune
In castles where (no need to importune)
The daughters of his host, in casual dress,

Beg to enjoy his brand of wantonness
And he, forgetting sin and courtesy,
Outrages even their cool modesty.
Waking, he sees the mind, though well-disposed
To self-creation, never is quite closed
To that disastrous matter which surrounds
Invention: a quick spirit hedged by hounds.
It fears those punctuating jaws in flight
And even in their absence, through a night
Of warmth and safety, makes this same relation
Of its short freedom, their cruel limitation.

6

Come into this wood. The ground is cool
Under a dropping shade. Regain your breath.
Here you can gather all the strength that you'll
Require. The hunt pursues its certain death
Through glade and thicket. Sit. Unpack your fear.
The running stream tells us of trouble. Will
There be more savagery than we can bear?
And one of us must be there at the kill!
Muttering darkly, he walked onward fast,
Planting his stick a pace ahead each time.
If anyone had seen him as he passed
They had not guessed what lay behind such mime,
What source of gesture, rigmarole of pain,
Or what false puzzled landscape of the brain.

7

The hook is baited and the fishes sleep
With eyes half-lidded in the pencilled stream,
Their fawn and violet haunches moving deep
Among the deep green of the angler's dream.
But if they spring to snap with cartoon jaws
The angler tumbles in the woodcut reeds,
Hamper and worms behind him: he implores
Each watery god to wink at his misdeeds.
So we relax, suspending resolution,
Brood on opacity in a clear world
Till the events we gambled with are hurled
Behind us. We achieve our dissolution
In that cool time before the wheel spins faster
Between the reverie and the disaster.

8

He knew the signs: the birds croaked heavily
Into the garden elms from far away,
His horses coughed, his chimneys smoked all day.
There was a change in visibility
And subtle difference in things to see,
Certain contortions of the landscape where
It seemed that hills moved under trees of hair,
Certain submissions, as of sand to sea
That turns it over like a desired thing.
He felt commanded to some cruelty
As if this were a place he should not be,
A certain bone, a certain shadowing:
But, stirred to this, and moving back the curtain,
These certain promises seemed less than certain.

9

And there within the landscape was the answer
The cardboard hills and soft Gainsborough trees,
Like scenery about the single dancer,
Pronounced all was a game: immensities
Of matter, false and fragile as a room,
Trivialised his actions till they wept,
And when the furniture conveyed its doom
He ground the carpet with a toe or crept
Beneath a tasselled table to escape
Accusing objects. There imagination
Created pleasure in a private dream;
The actual was seized in contemplation
As mirrors yield not only what they seem
To be, but their superior, mimic shape.

10

All alive. The age will recognise
Variety. It is the central fashion
They say no one cannot believe his eyes
Or fail to live among these things with passion.
There are elaborate tensions on the side
Of law: familiar pieces, precise squares.
Yes, we want everything. But cannot hide.
This so, how may we order our affairs?
Slowly we learn that quality is free
To choose, that no move ever is the best

We could have made without its history,
And wishing merely puts some plan to test.
So many answers, and the questions few:
The tree that walked had nowhere to walk to.

II
1958–1971

Song

You don't listen to what I say.
When I lean towards you in the car
You simply smile and turn away.

It's been like this most of the day,
Sitting and sipping, bar after bar:
You don't listen to what I say.

You squeeze a lemon from a tray,
And if you guess how dear you are
You simply smile and turn away.

Beyond the hairline of the bay
The steamers call that shore is far.
You don't listen to what I say:

Surely there's another way?
The waiter brings a small guitar.
You simply smile and turn away.

Sometimes I think you are too gay,
Smiling and smiling, hour after hour.
You don't listen to what I say.
You simply smile and turn away.

On the stair

With a wave of the wrist
Seek to assist
Your dumb departure,
Prove the prettier
By unconcern,
Trying to turn
With ready dimple
The serious, simple.

But if I dare
Once hold your hair
To stay your stirring,
Perhaps preferring
Anger should grip
Your level lip,

Might you remain?
Could you complain?

A kiss in Galloway

Sea, buttoned snails and catapulted gulls,
Small world turned over and over on itself:
China and crystal on the cottage shelf,
The fire-reflecting brass and stranded hulls
In pale landscapes, steaming articles
For walking in the waves draped round the hearth
Like priestly robes. Coming back up the path
With beer, you make that gesture which annuls
Once more what gracelessness our history has,
And in the twilight where the butterfly
Unfolds her carpet beauty, slowly, as slow
As too-rich dew creeps on dead summer's grasses,
We seal our fatal promise to defy
That we may be delivered into woe.

Leontes, solus

I almost long for you to be as old
As longing for you will preserve you fair,
For love let loose in summer of your hair
Buzzes with anger, only after cold
Is still and beautiful, in the dull gold
Of amber. O that I might sing you there,
Moving my lips against the frosty air!
I do not think that tale can yet be told,
For as you toss your hair my heart must bow
To that sick organ which it would not own,
Questioning fancy why it should have grown
So independent of the body's good,
Why so ungrateful and immense, and how
It can continually cry for food.

Florizel's complaint

Gold hanging braziers, moss under pools,
The music vertical in silver strings,
And kings have now put off their masks of Fools,
And fools again are beaten by their Kings.
Our love, instead of getting warmer, cools.
She turns away to what the morning brings.

Where is my hold on her whom I find dear
And innocent? How may I keep her fair?
I hear the magic sea she will not hear
Simply because she knows it's always there.
I hear her hidden heartbeats and I hear
Wind in the tree of her unbraided hair.

The moon appears as snow smudged on a glass
Of blue. Together we embrace and say
What we are bound to say. It is a farce
That must be played day after endless day.
Her father claps our dances on the grass.
The whopping bed remains uncreased. How may

Our breaths pass ever freely and together
Under a father's eye we can't ignore?
Cold as a statue, breath a curling feather,
How may the lover not appear a bore?
For she needs flowers against her father's weather,
And flowers grow only on Bohemia's shore.

Hedge tutor

Consulting the calendar of hedges
Banked up higher than your head,
We seem to share the surprise of walking
On a riverbed.

Our hands touch the flowers, shocked:
A clutch of folded fern, a brief
Violet, crumpled like a girl's
Handkerchief.

And we lean to ourselves, and to
These rituals that love condemns

Us to, gathering until the hand
Is hot with stems.

Somewhere a long way back it began.
It spun and clustered, divided and broke.
The woods made way, your eyes softened
And the hedges spoke:

'We do not suffer. Roots are lodged.
We prophesy the past and free
The future from its curious bond
As history.

This is what we are and were.
You, like us, powerless to change,
Walk in the given garden. The rest
Time will arrange.'

Thick light and wet, a gradient's pull
Past the invisible coughing cows,
Shoes plastered with grass,
Back to the house:

Shall we be ashamed? You are scared
By the gassed turnip heads beneath a stile,
Take my arm tighter, hurry through the rain
With a homeward smile

To the timed clock and the caged flower,
The raincoats hung, the table laid,
The different books half-lit beneath
A single shade.

No one believes more than a tiny tract.
In the delirium of silence the vast extenses
Wheel inwards to you, the presumable
Spiral's axis.

The Aegean

Chickens on board, eyes blinking, trussed alive,
The siren's tongue of steam, a restless night,
White columns in the moon's decaying light,
Travellers humped in bags, awake; at five
The sailors uncoil ropes and we arrive
At yet another island. People cough.

The sleeping harbour sends its small boats off.
The anchor does a belly-flopping dive.

O night! O moon! Staring and staring, we
Might lie for ever on this parting wake:
Call up the waves and wind, stir us and make
Us crumble like these cities, stunned, until,
Another ruin on the endless sea
Our ship steams through, our love stands ever still.

The statue

Your buttonholes for eyes, your solemn face,
The golden hair against your sleeping back:
This is no other time, no other place,
A moment certain as the almanac,
Vivid as weather, quiet as the deep,
As innocent as hands that curl in sleep.

For dreams disguise our wish to be awake
With bells, lagoons and squalls of tinsel trees.
In dreams you have no will to undertake
Ruthless analysis of mysteries.
Later, we're on the road: our object is
To judge a dead art's possibilities.

The radiator choked with butterflies,
We reach the city in a thumbed-down car
And I discover that the staring eyes
And cool lips of the promised statue are,
Though recognised, immortalised in stone,
Less rare and calm and perfect than your own.

For, in the camera's illusion, he
Preserved a moment from a laughing past,
A consolation for inconstancy,
Carefree, amorous, dynamic, vast,
Making a message on a mantelpiece,
A famous face sent by a friend from Greece.

But when we view the postcard subject fresh,
Gazing from curls to reconstructed toes,
Gone is the gentle and the human flesh,
Slyly dramatic in a talking pose:
Instead I see, and think I understand
The broken smile, whips in the missing hand.

Peasant woman: Rhodes

These are my scarves and veils and boots of sweat.
My hands are horny with the donkey's straps.
I have not borne a living baby yet:
The one inside me may be strong perhaps.
In all this heat I wear thick wool. Beneath,
At least one slip I do not often change.
And if I smile I show my metal teeth,
But I must smile because you are so strange!
You smile back too. You came to have a look
And show your photos when you end your trip.
You seem to live by writing in a book.
We live off what we get from this dry land.
You understand, and leave a decent tip,
But here, you see, we do not understand.

Manzu

A girl is seated, nude and placid, lost
In quietness. The pig-tail thick and full
On flashlit shoulder-blades. The ankles crossed.
Lifesize, exact, supremely animal.

This lean and virginal formality,
A poised ragazza on a rush-seat chair,
Finds cloistral echoes. From a trinket tree
Chickens and saints puncture the thumbed-out air

And dolphins on the slow cathedral doors
Plunge like a drowning scalp. Within their globe,
Bemitred dancers tip-toe and then pause.
The cardinal is sensual in his robe:

One sees beneath embroidery bare toes
As long as fingers. Youthful age imparts
That faintly turnip shadow to his nose,
That silent smile, affinity of parts.

The buds are breaking. No one is annoyed.
It is a simple drama. Lavish, yes,
But white and delicate. And eyes avoid
The bland Italian ritual of flesh.

A footnote to Ovid

Arbor eris certe mea (*Metamorphoses*, I)
Run slowly now. And I won't follow faster.
Let me without pursuit catch up with you.
Or if my question fails, go on, go on,
But slower now. For see, it puzzles you,
You put down roots into my patient ground.
The tree stirs, seems to be saying yes:
Art is appeased. The slim girl running still.

Bronze Sardinian centaur

O sad large
Head and shrieking
Arms, like a dwarf
You are really serious:

As though the acute
Humour of your master
Found target in
The soldier's butt

For easy laughter
And yet returned
Your savagery upon
Their frozen smiles.

In his spare time
The temple craftsman,
Forced to spearheads,
Links, buckles, knives,

Produced grave you,
A votive centaur in
A shepherd's hat.
Perhaps I'm wrong, but

Do the shepherds
In the trampled
Hills entirely
Pray for victory?

41

The elms

Air darkens, air cools
And the first rain is heard in the great elms
A drop for each leaf, before it reaches the ground.
I am still alive.

Now and then

The year melts into rain. The months unstack.
Sliding into the chamber, April too
Is fired against years hurtling faster back
And the hunters of savage memory pursue
The shapes and griefs that they can never tame.
Time is a cocky bully that we fear,
Laughing at our future's middle name,
While the dead past, all mumbling, staggers near,
Feeling his pockets; temptingly allows
Our moments only through his door and tells
Them lies. One last quick look! and see those cows,
For instance, sitting in their drying smells,
And shadows of trees like long-legged children run
At evening down the field and please the sun.

The self-conscious lover

It looks like rain. Darkening of muffled drums,
Breathing of strings, depth of the spitting brass
Are signs of tempest when the tempest comes,
Yet sunny pipes shrill like the birds that pass
Above celesta's raindrops in the grass:
Fine or depressing, music depends on whether
The notes go up or down, like glass weather.

His indoor spirit, too, rises and falls
At gestures trivial as ink on score
Or graph, something for which he calls
As invalids delight to call for more
Attention: words, a touch. It is a flaw
Of expectation when he watches her,
Tapping the heart's sluggish barometer.

Needles can only tell us what will be.
Performance is a moment in the sound
Moving along in time. No note is free,
Or sorry to be sombre, but our ground
Is strong for thinking so. Alarm is found
In every tempo that foreshadows thunder.
She is the spell of music he is under.

Alive and dead

Dead rain breeding life. The acres heave.
Everywhere sap stiffens into bark
And I am sick for something to believe.
Kneading an untuned piano in the dark
Beneath the flooded window, I can grieve
Approximately to the printed mark.
I know my orders to the very breve.

And I pretend the piano keys are stones
On which emotion lying like a wreath
Gives order to the necessary bones.
Only in love and pain we show the teeth.
The human form is perfect. The lawn moans,
Alive with its malignant roots. Beneath
My fingers sprout the leafy quarter-tones.

Green fingers

1

Last year's sticks are holding out
For more. Away with them.

The soil aches, tilting over,
Worms waving from windows.

Then seeds: fine as gunpowder,
Horny as toe-nails. A palaver.

You could say that these shoots
Have done it before: frauds.

But at five my daughter is called
To bed. I am not exactly myself.

The garden is creased with buds.
The scent inhabits the glass.

Hands are finished with the
Amazing things they recognise.

2

The pond is hideous, a mug of teeth.
Snouts and flex of lilies rot.

Mud moves with halfpenny frogs
The colour of aniseed.

We tilt the buckets out
To catch the snot of newts

And barrows heave the life away
So that the children will not drown.

Man shudders from ungovernable nature,
His greatest deceit.

After a night of unsettled dreams,
The mirror merciless in horror:

Nose. Vulnerable eyes. Growth
Of hair. The whole stirring.

Goodbye to the garden

Pad-pad in the dark, the lawn's in tears
Where we somnambulate, fearful of worms,
In Andy Pandy nightclothes, needing love.

Before our hands we had what now we hedge,
And it confronts us like a crime: long after,
Seeming dull, it makes us desperate.

It must house much disaster. Something beats
Inside. It is a roof for multitudes.
Water is a fallen window in it.

And now the punctual stars converge upon it,
And the Creamola moon is seen to drown
Inside it. Well, it is time for the television

Brooding in the still room like ectoplasm.
Our present knowledge is our long disease,
Or something. Goodbye, garden. The night admires us.

The pit

From the beginning, the egg cradled in pebbles,
The drive thick with fledglings, to the known last
Riot of the senses, is only a short pass.
Earth to be forked over is more patient,
Bird hungers more, flower dies sooner.

But if not grasped grows quickly, silently.
We are restless, not remembering much.
The pain is slow, original as laughter,
Reaching for all of it, hardly aware,
Beginning again and feeling for its terrain.

We were often told and still we would not listen,
And closing fingers, those accomplices,
Took comfort from a lie. From lap to grass
Whining, motionless on the lowest branch
Above the pine needles, climbing the heather:

We did not listen. It hid there still to find.
Much since was hard to get, later displeased,
Nursing an ordinary complaint or waiting
For a reiterated brilliance,
Growing in ignorance, too near to see.

Now in the suburbs windows are on fire,
Pale globes quiver on their dusty strings
And afternoons disperse with mirth of gnome,
The rigid stabbed flamingo pink in the trees,
Split to the touch and walking by the pool.

Now life jerking in its sustained coda
Constricts its furniture and its events.
The frowning bus disappears down the hill
Or slides before the window with its bored
Passengers staring unashamedly in.

Now above the trees the ice-cream's bare
Electric tongue stammers its recitation.
Children run out in the dumb-bell cul-de-sac
To their cold delight, skipping between the turds
Of long-dead dogs, coiled thickly on the stone.

The children learn so quickly. The house stirs.
Swallows leave earlier, apples to be pressed.
Half the sky burns: the other half is dark.
Hair pushing slowly out, generations
Surrounding us with wonder, theirs and ours.

Nothing to give, nothing has been learnt.
The past simply denies the urge for a truce,
Creeping into the egg. When it is time
We can appoint a committee for the feasts,
And for next year's feasts, and the year after.

Locks stick, glass metamorphosed
In leafy caryatids of summer where
Heat packs the panes and fingers tremble in
Tobacco pockets, a tomato sniffed,
Its greenish acid bloom and tiny hairs.

The pain stirs again like a new life
To be unravelled. It had to come to this.
The body is nothing, the body thinks nothing,
The short senses grubbing on their sticks
Feel nothing, the forgotten carioca.

A line moves to the finger end, and curls,
Head fallen in helplessness. The wails
Of children break behind the woven fences,
Those minted faces far beyond our sight.
The gates shut: a parade of Japanese flags.

And alive on the porch the councillor lowers his pipe,
Comes down from the dunes a bathroom Arab
Firing off caps, or crouched over shells
Gathered in sodden pumps, the soprano waitress
Bringing hot tea across the evening sand.

The nights come in slowly. Behind a half-curtain
The impossible is completed. A single lamp
Weighs down its ornaments in pools of light.
Shadows crawl over the crater, roped
To the terrain's recoil, roped to the pit.

An exchange between the fingers and the toes

Fingers:
Cramped, you are hardly anything but fidgets.
We, active, differentiate the digits:
Whilst you are merely *little toe* and *big*
(Or, in the nursery, some futile pig)
Through vital use as pincers there has come
Distinction of the *finger* and the *thumb*;
Lacking a knuckle you have sadly missed
Our meaningful translation to a *fist*;
And only by the curling of that joint
Could the firm *index* come to have a point.
You cannot punch or demonstrate or hold
And therefore cannot write or pluck or mould:
Indeed, it seems deficiency in art
Alone would prove you the inferior part.

Toes:
Not so, my friends. Our clumsy innocence
And your deft sin is the main difference
Between the body's near extremities.
Please do not think that we intend to please:
Shut in the dark, we once were free like you.
Though you enslaved us, are you not slaves, too?
Our early balance caused your later guilt,
Erect, of finding out how we were built.
Your murders and discoveries compile
A history of the crime of being agile,
And we it is who save you when you fight
Against the odds: you cannot take to flight.
Despite your fabrications and your cunning,
The deepest instinct is expressed in running.

The safety-valve

Examples of our self-regard:
The bloated sow of Mandeville
Gobbling a child, a beggar's tray.
Relief must satisfy the will.

For see! the frauds insert their crutches
Where it hurts most. The farthings bounce.
In drawing-rooms the tales of rescue
Politely urge the pig to pounce.

Young ladies, surely you agree
No altruist is quite convincing?
The bristling jaws of charity
Provide the safety-valve of wincing.

Helen and Saul's Atlantic Pindaric

The horny secret shells of kneecaps float
With equilibrium of tortoises
Who, pressed on one slow side, like Citroëns
Allow the weight. See how like tortoises
His knees support the Hindu world he eats:
Breakfast in bed. Thunder inside the bed,
The grinning bacon and short-sighted egg.

Think, if you like of Fastitocalon,
That emblematic snare of idleness,
Whose stony colour and unyielding skin
Lure voyagers to moor their swan-necked ships
With grateful ropes to the imagined land:
Tired, they encamp, whet blades, take off their boots
And kindle fires on the enormous fish.
All night they sing, with whirling banjos, thumbs
Spring-snapping to the clack of wooden heels.
Till morning shows the water pink and calm,
Empty of men, and Fastitocalon.

The shades are drawn. Fantasies exercise,
And chronic time snarls on a silver leash.
How to accomplish this horrific meal
Of frozen possibility? He eats!
Only the wet clutch of his working gullet
Can actually fulfil that octopus egg,
The embryo cereal. What's happening
Is simple fact. The chromosome marmalade
Spreads planets on the toast. He eats! He eats!
To the flat tray he's heretic Columbus,
Tasting the pared Bartholomew's Regional Orange
And the Polar Equidistant Grapefruit. Juice

Welcomes the tongue, smiles, and explains the spoon.
Something exact has been discovered here.

And yet, and yet. This is an innocent age.
The sea erodes but continuity
Of maps is comfortable. Winds are children
Puffing the voyagers down the liner's arrows
With bossa nova and the plaster gull.
To true globes the comic elephant atlas
Promises distinction like an art
But fails. In unperceived exactness spheres
Revolve, breeding the cold impartial future
While the excitable and curious
Imagination toys with what's to come.
Think of this. The grave cartographers
Ignore horizon, take no stock of chance.
Leaflets assure. The landing date is fixed
Yet you have paused, slide shaking down in bed.
What are these eyes? What are these eggs? These hands?
The waters bounce in the planet's cavities.
The route extends. The map becomes unsafe.

Mr and Mrs Bones

He thinks of ogre-statured Mrs Bones,
Watercolour lips, and hair in braided phones,
Chopping about with her dangerous hands,
Loading a tray with matutinal viands:
Delicate and wafer-slivered breakfast courses,
Toasted kidneys like new pigskin purses,
Folded ham, and chops with various sauces
Served with mushrumps black as hearses.
Meat sickness, it is the sickness of Greed
Who full to bursting still wants to feed,
Eating and eating with extraordinary vigour,
As though to become different we must get bigger.
O Mr Bones, growing in bed
With a pillow propped by your tea-cosy head,
Here at half-past-eight o'clock you lie
Wrapped in your breakfast like divinity.
Your knife flashes. The eiderdown groans.
O carneous Mrs, O ravenous Mr Bones.

The Cook's lesson

When the King at last could not manage an erection,
The tables were wiped down and a banquet prepared.
The Cook was a renegade, a master of innuendo,
And was later hanged for some imaginary subversion,
Found laughing in the quarter of the filthy poor.
This, had we known it, was to be his last banquet,
And as such was fittingly dissident and experimental.
Often he had confided to us the tenets of his craft,
How a true artist is obsessed with the nature of his material,
And must make evident the process of creation in preference
To the predictable appearance of the finished product.
The charcoal-burners were lit, the porcelain laid
And the simple broths prepared in which the meal was enacted,
For this was a living meal, a biological history of food.
I cannot remember much. We sweated and fainted and were revived
With fragrant towels. We ate furiously and were rewarded
With knowledge of a kind we did not even recognise.
Spawn in the luke gruel divided, gilled and finned,
Swam down flowered channels to the brink of oil
And fell to the plate. Before our eyes
The litter spurted into the fire, picked out by tongs,
Eggs hatched into the soup, embryos bled,
Seeds sprouted in the spoon. As I said, we ate fast,
Far back into life, eating fast into life.
Now I understand that food is never really dead:
Frilled and forked, towered, dusted, sliced,
In mimic aspic or dispersed in sauces,
Food is something that will not willingly lie down.
The bland liquids slid over our tongues as
Heartbeats under crusts, mouthfuls of feathers.

The Choir Master

Alkman, seventh century BC

Oh my sweet girls, dear girls, with your so clear round voices
Linked in the sounds I taught you, your eyes on the page
And all the air no Siren struck with such compulsion
Alive in my ear like the breath of our own Kalliope
Without whose favour dance is graceless, no song moving,

Whose name is always on my lips, and is your name
My dears, as I urge you on like horses to your goal.

Now my legs fail me, standing in the colonnade
Clutching my black heart. If only I could be a bird!
An unharmed gazed-at bird, the colour of distant water,
A bird not alone but flying in easy neighbourhood,
A noble cormorant or tilted migrant gull,
Each far wave bursting for a moment into flower,
Oh my singing pupils, flowers of the sea's same song!

I am old. Your hands slip into mine for friendship
And you sing of the new life, all that I cannot teach.
For there are three seasons: summer and winter, and autumn is three,
But in the new life when buds come there is no satisfaction,
Fruit and harvest, none, and no store. Spring is an ache,
In spring the mountains break down and weep, the snowdrop
Turns away, heavy with grief. And I clutch my heart,

My heart which is like spring lightning in the mountains when
A lantern is dashed to the ground and the gods roar with laughter.
In my dream I am rooted and a witness, amazed and curious:
They bring a simple dairy churn, though cast in gold,
And you, my dears, fill it yourselves with the milk of a lioness!
And proceed to turn out a monstrous cheese which Hermes himself
Might well have had appetite for after he'd murdered Argos!

Ah well, my own tastes are simple enough. Something like porridge
Suits me now. You I've groomed and coaxed, my dear sisters,
It's no wonder your skills and beauty astound me still,
As hooves, as wings. You think me an old owl chunnering
In an attic, perhaps, or dare I hope as a ship's pilot
As we steer with one voice like a swan on the streams of Xanthus,
Oh my dear girls, Kalliope's daughters, my daughters, my music.

Riddle

What can she be? Can you guess? You should do, it's really quite easy.
Seek her familiar taste with the soft machine in your bone box.
Most of your life's involved with the murderous name she's hiding,
Mockingly putting her nose beside an upright finger,
Secret and smug, and knowing you know her dark intentions,
Knowing you know her real and wilful desire to trap you.

51

Should you say: 'Look, I am trying to read. So please go away now.'
Do you imagine that, edgy with print, you've a chance of succeeding?
Into the house she drags her unused power like a satchel,
Carelessly breaking your minutes, laughing and sweeping the pieces
On to your spotless boredom: one glance is enough to undo you,
Sitting in failing light with your endless fear of the cold cook.

Think what the finest mind, his wild hair streaming with silver,
Think what the wistful mind in the end is bound to feel like:
Nobody comes all day. Nobody comes to see him.
Nothing to do but hum and play with his *arbor vitae*.
Opens his beans at five with a steel rhinoceros opener,
Aching for wakeful nights, the dragon upon St George.

Pillow talk

Wondered Knob-Cracker at Stout-Heart:
'Are you timed by your will, does your pulse
List credit, ready to slam like a till?
Can you keep it up?'

Growled Beard-Splitter to Smug:
'Your forces delay, bibbing at Northern walls
While snow drives rifts between, barring the way.
I am sufficient.'

Pleaded Knob-Cracker with Fail-Safe:
'You've boarded at last, your hands in your pockets,
Hat on the back of your head and flags up the mast.
Can't I come with you?'

Nodded Beard-Splitter to Sorrowful:
'The islands are prisons and no one returns,
No power or possessions where my rule is.
I will make you mine.'

Star bestiary

Lacerta
I finger the portals of some strange event,
Unseeing,
The watcher.

52

Cygnus
From beam to beam, extended and powerful,
My neck soft,
The weeper.

Lyra
No matter what escapes me,
At the centre, the recorder,
The dream.

Vulpecula and Anser
Meanwhile at the back gate
With stuffed grinning mouth and silent paws,
The crime.

The two sisters

He saw her fingers in the candlelight
Crooked with the needle, poised to break a thread,
Or at her temple pressed to ease the sight,
With one thin strand of hair loose from her head
Falling in its tiredness, cedar red,
Across the bent and pale half-humorous face,
Hair like a precious garment of the dead
Tucked now behind the ear into its place,
An automatic gesture yet with grace
To make a ceremony of her task
When fingers smoothing down the finished lace
Are answered by the question that they ask
Of labour's quiet satisfaction, such
As simply sanctifies the sight and touch.

That one he loved, the other in a dream
Possessed his spirit, though she never smiled;
One with rolled sleeves or lost in linen's steam,
Fruit in her apron for the orphaned child,
The other walking by herself, beguiled
By passing beggars and by horoscopes;
That home to him, this every day more wild;
One was his shelter, one played out his hopes,
A mind that grasps uncertainty and gropes
For wind-wide vistas from delirious rocks

While others go no further than the slopes
On which they tend the necessary flocks.
Both sisters were his world. From each he learned
What man must die from. And to both returned.

Her sister wasn't helpful, that was certain,
Lying with headaches on her bed all day,
The neighbours wondering at the fastened curtain,
At the strange girl who only knelt to pray
With steps to scrub and the day's fires to lay,
Who stared at breakfast, had no time to spend
In gutting fish and could not see her way
To lay the table for her brother's friend.
The world would take more than one life to mend,
The other thought: there simply wasn't time
To moon about the inevitable end,
For death remained as private as a crime
And as improbable, so long as life
Whitened her knuckles that enclosed the knife.

They told her not to think about the fish.
The fish was simply something they could eat.
It had to die to turn into a dish.
Once dead there was no memory in meat.
She bit her lip, muttered and left her seat,
Her plate untouched. Apologies were made,
A mention of her efforts and the heat:
No wonder nerves were just a little frayed.
But who foresaw as she did death's curved blade
Casting its shadow on the company
And their autumnal guest whose hands displayed
The future's frightening leap, his ruined tree?
Her brother lost to him, white as a sheet,
Her sister still, devoted, at his feet.

And now as if a promise were fulfilled,
Insistently, uncruel, even with joy,
As children tread the towers that they build
And love the crouching cat that they annoy,
Death with his conjuror's fingers took the boy
And left his body still, as one might leave
Forgotten in its box a broken toy.
Mourning has very little to achieve:
A neighbour wiped his eye upon his sleeve

54

And friends came to console them for their loss.
The sisters found that they could better grieve
If death were seen as swaddling pinned across
His face. They moved their fingers to the brooch
That held it there. Their hope was a reproach.

Death was the knowledge that eluded him,
The senses stunned to feel the body cease,
The spirit sobbing in the missing limb,
The sisters exiled from their brother's lease
And its reversion. In the perfumed peace
Of living's shadow nothing was revealed.
He realised the strangeness would increase
As time unwound its laps about the field,
Forever following the power that healed
Its stubborn strokes: those hands laid on his death
Were lent themselves to death and so unsealed
At once his own and every stifled breath
To speak, amazed, of what life was about.
And turned the everlasting inside out.

He was still alive. And the sisters passed
Silently and with great joy into
The landscape of his unbound eyes at last.
One in the wisdom of her insight knew
How life describes its need to be thought true
In terms of its illusions, and she made
Her happiness the air to which she grew.
The other was content to live in shade,
Grew downwards, desperately, undisplayed.
Both were his nature. That he understood.
Perhaps uncertain, even half-afraid
Which to embrace, he knew that both were good,
As on his heel, beneath his wrinkled skull,
Moved the creased sweating happy miracle.

So when the perfume filled the house she smiled
Inside herself. It was the good part. Both
Were good. She was excited as a child
Though busy with preparing food and loath
To leave it. Someone present swore an oath
It would have paid a labourer for a year,
But who could measure growing against growth,

Or time the seed against the waving ear?
And now one knew it, what was death to fear
But this extraordinary ritual where
Its moment was acknowledged to be near,
Its mystery by a sister's healing hair
Divulged? To smile was to betray her sense
Of love in perfume, tears, experience.

Scenario for a walk-on part

The borrowed walking-stick that makes me lame,
The single curiously worn-down tyre,
The hanging button and forgotten name,
The grinning of the vulnerable liar:
These are the gambits of a chosen game,
A well-cut personality on hire,
Mirrors too low, the eyebrows graze the frame,
Warming my hands before an unlit fire.

Dinner a skirmish, legs uncrossed and crossed,
An alp of linen and the sight of nylons,
Pudding arriving full of fruit and frost,
And, swimming in their syrup, smoking islands,
Lips at a silver spoon proclaim me lost,
My single joke counters a threat of violence.
The table cleared, I cannot count the cost
Of dinner or of nerves. The rest is silence.

Now in the sharpest lock at close of day,
Hands as if manacled, the gravel spurting,
My hosts with linked arms waving me away,
The gulf of what I didn't say still hurting
(Since you are only known by what you say),
Yawning beneath my silent murmur skirting
The dangerous excuse, the wish to stay,
Like the evasions of protracted flirting:

Alone I drive away with my awareness
That once again I've failed the magic word
Whose demon locks me up inside my bareness,
The charming openness unsaid, unheard.
Is love the better for its hurts and rareness?
I frown and think so. Falling into third

On a hill, I glimpse a face: the sheer unfairness
Fights with my sense of shame at being stirred.

The sexy minister reclaims his scarf,
A girl in denim runs to meet a train,
Mrs Jocasta bastes the fatted calf,
The guests have taken to their beds again:
I hold the floor but nobody will laugh,
No one is there to kiss if I complain,
I enter only in the second half,
Unwilling, underwritten, used to pain.

Her morning dreams

I trail in my sculpted sheets to the misty window
And rub a patch there like a liquid bruise.
Yes. Stooping in blue. Propped bicycle.

But absence is your only sort of news.
Over the toast and the slit boring letters
The damp end flares in ribbons like a fuse.

What do I think? Do I think it matters?
Do I think what matters? Do I think?
Oh yes, I think. Don't worry, you wouldn't notice.

The unmade bed. Finger on my pink.
Dead as he groaned upon a linen ocean,
Who would have thought he had such little ink?

Dreams for you. The head is cut in walking.
Sour puff balls. Silence. Clouds of dust.
It's a bad day for any sort of singing.

I thought that you were someone I could trust.
I can begin. Well, I can try beginning
If only somebody will say I must.

Are you my pal? Are you Ardent Ardvaark?
At first I took you for the kind who while
He sobs sinks fangs, while he sings does murder

In blue clothes, greets with insinuating smile
Across the gravel with his hands extended
In preacher or in nightclub singer style

Under a pained yet cheerful load of welcome.
Now you are someone in my morning dreams.
I was so bored that summer. Can you imagine

Life shrunk and wrinkled to its seams,
Its hopes on threads, its memories in pockets,
The sluggish mouth disowning all its streams?

Can you imagine the clean shock of naming,
And love acknowledging its paradigm?
With you misery had as little meaning

As backfriends to fingers galloping in time
With the Catalan pupil of the Neapolitan master,
Each note as true as an expected rhyme.

Perhaps you never meant that sort of magic,
Perhaps the fault was mine, grateful allure
Scoring a million in the cheated darkness,

Pretending the experience was pure.
God help us, darling, aren't we only human?
Kiss me again and let's be really sure.

I believe all disasters now, believe all pain.
As for your life, however much you hate it,
However bad it smells upon your bed,

You simply cannot go back and create it:
Something will tell you that you have to cry,
Something will tell you this was always fated.

So I have tried beginning. Or is it ending?
Things I remember cover me with shame,
They linger obstinately every morning.

Stupid. But every day it is the same.
And nothing felt like that is ever final.
Not you. Not me. Nobody is to blame.

Dreams. You walking down a dusty pavement.
Your head is always strangely turned away,
Carried as though bandaged, with little movement.

Now is the time to say it: nothing to say.
You came and went with carefully rolled forearms.
You held life in their empty space that day.

I pad from bed to stove to fill a pan.
Sometimes a step is just a step too far:
No time to think what it has got you into.

Even the job of knowing where you are
Becomes a full-time dangerous occupation.
It's honey at the bottom of the jar

But no one can be sure until it's eaten.
Not everything is right. What's possible?
I pull the whole drawer of my mind down on

My foot. Hell. The cat's beneath the bedspread
Like a blister, showing that you have gone.
I walk from room to room, trying the answer:

One from two is wrong, and one from one
Is neater. Morning dreams are calmer weeping.
All my indignities spill from the sun.

Listen to it now. All night like wedded chaos
The creeper's down, the storm makes such a fuss.
Trying to count the blows of rain is useless.

I shall sit it out, here by the misty glass,
Till I can face the morning's empty graces,
The window sill become an abacus.

London songs

1 *Missing*

Lonely in London is an endless story,
Tired in the sun on the District Line,
With Barons Court baked beans opened in Ealing,
Tossing in bed and staring at the ceiling,
And: 'Yes, Mr Holdsworth, I'll put you through.'
A lot of work and not much glory
And a letter to Mum that says you're fine.

You played me songs on your piana.
Its E was missing like a tooth.
It always rained when I came to see you,
Rained like the mint, the window creaked with rain.
You sat in the window and I told you the truth.

Lonely in London is an endless story.
Where did you go to? Who do you see?
I played at being with you, yes I'm sorry.
Now in this dog's soup I'm less than me,
Miss you, your piana, your piana and your cardigan,

Miss you on Friday, miss you on Monday,
Your cardigan, your tears and the baked-bean smells.
You're like a secret that nobody tells,
Lonely in London, somewhere, now.

2 *Dusk*

Rain on the river, and this hour of dusk
Settling slowly, imposingly, on London
As though its greatest shopwalker has died
Like a pianist about to play Busoni,
Hands resting in waxen contemplation
In white cuffs quietly upon his knees,
And women, weeping pearls, are gathered now
In Bond Street as the black discreet cortège
Rumbles slowly down to Piccadilly.

Rain on the river, and this hour of dusk
Settling on a city inventive of pleasure,
Secure in pleasure, in its terrible pleasure.

3 *Fruit machine*

In love I take my chances,
In love I eat my greens,
Too old for idle glances
I live beyond my means:
I've tried the dogs and dances,
And now it's fruit machines.
From New Cross Gate to Deptford
The fruit is spinning fast,
And as I range I save my change
And make the bitter last.
Oh it's cherries and bells on Friday,
On Sunday plums and pears,
But pounds and jars and sevens and bars
Means whoops up the Saturday stairs.

The girls hang on my shoulder
To watch the fruit go round,
I may be getting older
But I certainly hold my ground,
And if it makes them bolder
I stand another round.
From New Cross Gate to Deptford
The beer is brown and deep,
Just a veal-and-ham and a Babycham

Will make the dollies leap.
Oh it's cherries and bells on Friday,
On Sunday plums and pears,
But pounds and jars and sevens and bars
Means whoops up the Saturday stairs.

The spinning fruit has woken
That child of dangerous charm
Who lures me with a token
And keeps me in alarm:
My envelope is broken
To pull his magic arm.
From New Cross Gate to Deptford
Happily after dark,
When fruit falls thick I dance out quick
With a girl in Greenwich Park.
Oh it's cherries and bells on Friday,
On Sunday plums and pears,
But pounds and jars and sevens and bars
Means whoops up the Saturday stairs.

The father's song

Dear girl, your bud unfolded
And brought you to this peace,
But my drab heart is still patrolled
By its corrupt police.

The past is eyeing hungrily
The future it denies,
And I look jealously upon
The angel in your eyes.

My body's single, and my love
A melancholy roar.
The children hide their faces when
I stand outside the door.

In dreams of the advances
Of loud uprooted trees,
I stand in quiet terror
While you sleep at your ease.

When men give birth to nightmares,
Their precious oil is spilt,

Yet love's enlarging waters guide
The voyage of his guilt.

Bound to the mast and deaf with shame,
He has to suffer much:
Dear child, hold in your little hands
His conscious, fatal touch.

And ride upon that jumart
Out of the sinking pit.
Hold the instant in your hands,
Oh bless and admonish it.

Lullaby

Sleep little baby, clean as a nut,
Your fingers uncurl and your eyes are shut.
Your life was ours, which is with you.
Go on your journey. We go too.

The bat is flying round the house
Like an umbrella turned into a mouse.
The moon is astonished and so are the sheep:
Their bells have come to send you to sleep.

Oh be our rest, our hopeful start.
Turn your head to my beating heart.
Sleep little baby, clean as a nut,
Your fingers uncurl and your eyes are shut.

Blind man's buff

Round and round and round and round,
Shapes in the giggling dark revolve
His body three times like a charm.
It is a problem he must solve.
They dodge beneath his scarecrow arm.
The handkerchief is tightly bound.

Covering the deceptive ground
He's warmer as the blindfold eases.
The fun is that the catcher's free
To catch at random whom he pleases.

He knows they know that he can see
Round and round and round and round.

Round and round and round and round,
Twisting away from him girls flee
And taunt with shrieking and mock sneezes
Till, with a gay complicity,
In hushed delight the Chosen freezes
And the bright room has come unwound.

Now the next victim must be crowned,
Blind in her sacrifice and fear.
Where is there someone who will dare?
Love calls the willing circle near,
Under the windmill, over a chair,
Round and round and round and round.

Musical chairs

Ten says, we are important men,
Facing outwards, debonair,
Marching smartly in a square,
Keeping corners, back again.
But the music stops, and out one drops,
And all you know is that you know
There's nothing to hope for, nowhere to go.

Nine says, we think we're doing fine,
Nose to neck we follow round,
Listen to the tinkling sound,
Heel to toe and keep in line.
But the music stops, and out one drops,
And all you know is that you know
There's nothing to hope for, nowhere to go.

Eight says, we haven't time to wait,
The square is smaller, life is short,
Never give it another thought,
The one who lingers will be late.
But the music stops, and out one drops,
And all you know is that you know
There's nothing to hope for, nowhere to go.

Seven says, we think it's heaven,
Raggle taggle, stumbling on,
Grateful and dizzy, one by one,

63

Surely this will last for ever?
But the music stops, and out one drops,
And all you know is that you know
There's nothing to hope for, nowhere to go.

Six says, we've got to learn some tricks,
Her fingers coming from the keys
Eliminate the one they please,
You think it's you the stillness picks.
But the music stops, and out one drops,
And all you know is that you know
There's nothing to hope for, nowhere to go.

Five says, we're here and still alive,
Not too far and not too near,
Straining to hear before we hear
The sudden silences arrive.
But the music stops, and out one drops,
And all you know is that you know
There's nothing to hope for, nowhere to go.

Four says, we know there's not much more,
Back to back and tighter now,
What will the greater chance allow
Of biting closer to the core?
But the music stops, and out one drops,
And all you know is that you know
There's nothing to hope for, nowhere to go.

Three says, we hear but do not see,
For love is blind and fear alert,
Faster, faster, still unhurt,
Will it be me, will it be me?
But the music stops, and out one drops,
And all you know is that you know
There's nothing to hope for, nowhere to go.

Two says, we've got to see this through,
In front, behind, and man to man,
Play it calmly while we can,
Fifty-fifty it isn't true.
But the music stops, and out one drops,
And all you know is that you know
There's nothing to hope for, nowhere to go.

And One is alone, for one is one,
She blows a sigh for all you did,
Stack the chairs and close the lid,
Who can win when the game is done?
For the music stops, and out you drop,
And all you know is that you know
There's nothing to hope for, nowhere to go.

Charades

Out of the room, out of the room and back:
Look at me again and say the word again.
I hear it but I do not understand.
Something important you alluded to,
Smiling behind a hairy plastic hand.
Out of the room, out of the room and back.

Out of the room, out of the room and back:
I caught a syllable I thought you meant
And then another that went with the first,
But soon I realised I was quite at sea:
It was a fiction carefully rehearsed.
Out of the room, out of the room and back.

Out of the room, out of the room and back:
Look at me again and say the word again.
I know you'd tell me, but I dare not ask.
This is the last time and I must give up.
Wellington boots and vampire mask.
Out of the room, out of the room, out of the room.

Song for a condemned queen

Shall you revisit as ghost or shadow
This world of waters that you wept?
Shall you revisit, though it be narrow,
The bed of tears your weeping kept?
We smooth the creases in your pillow
    Where you have slept.

Silver glitters in the furrow
Where the lost coin records your name.
Winter fastens clod and harrow

65

And a cloistered queen the same.
Though ice describes the grassy meadow
  Your tears remain.

Shall you revisit as winter's fellow,
Shut in his coldness with your fame?
Shall you come startled to the window,
Finding frost-flowers upon the pane?
They will remind you of your sorrow
  And turn to rain.

Though the world sink again we follow
The pain and patience of your love.
Though waters spread they will be shallow.
Familiar hills will peep above.
You will return like the shot arrow,
  Like the first dove.

The wreck

Above the lake
The peaks in line,
Roped by the book
And measured rain,
Knuckle on arrow,
Welcome in stone
Our slippered hike
From hidden forms
Of barking farms
To open narrow
And tilted plain.

The space between
Our eyes is drunk,
Legs are in line
And the hands link
As clouds unslacken,
Changing the bank
All afternoon
Where bouncing shape
Of knitted sheep
Disturbs a bracken
Like old ink.

You last men
Who mind the map
Will shelter an
Uncertain hope:
Forgotten song
Can make you weep
And fail to win
The backward praise
Of future's prize,
Slither along
The gradient's slip.

We have your lack
And have it ever
As a thrown stick
Falls to the river,
An endless story,
Asking no favour
Wading to wreck
Nothing answered
All unsaid,
A promontory
To look over.

Dear bellied earth
Hangs at the edge
Of despair's path,
The bad cells lodge
In favourite valleys,
Raving the ridge
And curtained heath
Of withdrawn state,
With pain in sight,
Fearing its malice,
Its secret badge.

Our miniature's
Your memory,
Your end is ours
Going your way.
Heart is beating
At open view:
A mountain's laws
Impress the species
As being spacious,

A useful meeting,
A way to go.

And is much more,
Is love, its breath
That climbers share
In being both.
The landscape yawning
Hides a truth
We are quite near,
But trolls and pooks
On misty peaks
Whisper their warning
To find the path.

From distant ice
Fell finds its fall,
Water the peace
Of perfect will
And we the weather
Of being well,
Lifting the face
To the dangerous light
Of getting late,
Treading together,
The instep full.

The labours of Hercules

1

I did all that I had to do, for you
Exacted like a shadow every part
Of the compelling bargain. At the start,
With all the brashness of the strong and new,
I vowed to see the hateful business through.
I tried to learn my destiny by heart
And shape my future like a work of art
As though your pressing cries were real and true.

My deeds were natural at least. They kept
On being found out, though they always hid,
Like animals whose shelters that they make
Show the devourer where they lately slept.

I raged. I boasted. Undid what I did,
And what I did was nothing, some mistake.

2
And what I did was nothing, some mistake
On which there had to be a compromise
Since you were weak by virtue of my size
And only your demands could make me quake.
But you were not to spy nor I to fake.
I could not hesitate, retort, advise,
And you could never flatter or tell lies.
There was too much for both of us at stake.

Did the gods envy us this contract, then?
And did they visit on the hero, curled
Still inside his shell, the double snake?
Who killed them both? And O who sobbed out when
Their flat skins like a fable showed a world
Where time was drilled and matter kept awake?

3
Where time was drilled and matter kept awake,
Where danger crawled into a door and soon
Stood upright on its shadow, where the moon
Dropped lions which with an idle bite could take
A finger off, as little girls eat cake,
One pair of eyes watched through an afternoon
Across the stones and sand where bones were strewn
For the appointed lord they could unmake.

Squatting in silence I could almost hear
Bored laughter from the clouds. I seized a tree,
Uprooted it, and made my peace. I slew
That ordinary shape that was my fear
And found that I could walk upright and free
Beneath a careless and impartial blue.

4
Beneath a careless and impartial blue,
Beyond the friendly hills of childhood, lay
A second mystery, and in its way
The only mystery to which was due
The courtesy of genuine struggle. Few
Had ever come back from that squelching fray
Where the strange beast in bracken, mist and clay
Rose as it had to, did what it must do.

Again, again, again, again, again,
Again, again, again! I felt to hunt
Those lurching heads through their organic glue
Brought small relief, for you lay panting then,
And of the cost were blankly ignorant,
And only my achievement really knew.

5

And only my achievement really knew
What lay beyond their stink, and what the third
Pursuit and the most sacred was. I heard
A different voice in that subsiding brew,
Small voice of sighs. With horns of golden hue
It lifted nostrils of alarm and stirred
The cold air with its breath. I knew no word
To tell me where it was, or what, or who.

I think you understood, and we conspired
To lure that creature from the freedom that
Defined its beauty, flickering in the brake.
And there was nothing. And I was too tired
To cry it was not my fault all fell flat:
What it was for was only for your sake.

6

What it was for was only for your sake
And your desire. You wanted what was lost,
Thundered to greet it like the horns that tossed
A favourite. In ignorance we break
What we love most. That was the hollow ache
That haunted me unkindly as I crossed
To the fourth labour where through drift and frost
I tracked it like a thirst I had to slake.

How strange the impulse captured in the ice!
It carries many frozen loves. It steers
Them hairy still and gaping, half-opaque,
To my unwilling strength, the spoiling price
Of my perception, paid for with warm tears,
Dragged from my existence like a lake.

7

Dragged from my existence! Like a lake
Around which bathers test its clarity
With toes and leave it muddied, I was free
Of your bad dreams until you tried to shake

Me into them because you could not wake.
How deep they were! I shudder at your plea
To cleanse you of them: it was not for me.
And yet for you I took up brush and rake.

This was the fifth and foulest. And deformed.
It seemed the weakness of the endless giver
To do it just because you asked me to.
Yet strong in this as always, I performed
The idle deed like a diverted river
Brought senseless in to its admirer's view.

8

Brought senseless in to its admirer's view
The living brain seemed greenish and disused,
Pulsating slightly, shiny, apple-bruised:
This too was dreaming, for the silent queue
Of mourners shuffling to the ill-lit pew
Turned and showed us beaks, screamed and refused
To sing. I tried to catch them, but amused
They wet the floor and tried to fly. And flew.

This sixth was for the birds, but not to lose
Is only one prerequisite of winning.
The brazen fancies fall as they are hit,
But you are always there to make me choose,
And as you governed me from the beginning
So we shall never see the end of it.

9

So we shall never see the end of it:
Without your needs I've nothing to be bold
About: without my arm you're uncontrolled.
Together as that thread in fat we fit,
Dark, soft and clear, hot in its narrow pit.
But when we walk, my dear, we are unrolled,
A solid shape and hard, so white and cold
We burn our energy when we are lit.

After the seventh, something I had complained
About, colossan on the sands, you lied:
'The dual freedom of the three-legged pair.'
Chained to the path we tread and yet not chained,
We trust each other not to step aside
Since our continuing is what we share.

10

Since our continuing is what we share,
Come with me then! Our running daughters clean
The grains in air. The breakers gasp. We mean
Only what we mean. Skin strains. Birds scare
Above a chequered hill of shouting where
The happy ugly family, unseen
By gods and suchlike, feasts upon the green,
And they, and light, have everything to spare.

The eighth is easiest. Something to do
With death, implacable, yet of a kind
That seems to soothe: 'You do not have to die.'
As though one drunken meeting makes it true
That no one of authority will mind
When we contrive our parting by and by.

11

When we contrive our parting by and by,
My dear, the desert will be there to hand:
Not as you might imagine, a dead land
Where nothing's coloured, trees don't even try,
Where water is uninvited, where birds sigh,
Flapping like tents over impermanent sand.
Not dead, but without meaning; rich, unplanned.
Not dead but mad, mad to the single eye.

Nine times we have mewed our triumph: now
Something is really up. The scenery
Closes like an album and we sit
Knowing the why at last but not the how.
We shiver slightly now. When both are free
It will not matter which of us has quit.

12

It will not matter which of us has quit,
Though now I know (perhaps knew all along)
Which of us finally would prove the strong:
Not me. Into my vice-like grip your grit
Seeded opacity until I split.
My harmony foundered beneath your song
(Ten for the ten contentments; not for long)
With all the discipline of licensed wit.

Home, herds: you are a thin posterity,
The generations' pleasure. Like a stray

I stumbled righteously back to my lair,
And left pretending that I cannot see,
Caring immensely, no, I will give way
For no one, left pretending not to care.

13

For (no one left) pretending not to care
Becomes an academic exercise:
I could as easily hold up the skies
As sit here writing in a summer chair
Or find that voluntary garden where
I can assert my title to the prize
That's mine if I unravel the disguise,
That doubleness we live in as in air.

I do care. Even at the eleventh hour
One has to hope for a miraculous birth,
Though from the golden tree the dragons sigh
Who have the whole of life within their power,
Who will yield nothing. And the widowed earth
Will sit there bravely smiling and not cry.

14

Will sit there bravely smiling? And not cry?
Yes, even so, the heroes gone at last
Who were the only status of a past
That bored us all and lied compulsively
Though we all knew it really had to lie.
We honour it in memory, though fast
The memory goes, new words to learn, new cast:
New how, new when, new where, new what, new why.

And on the stroke of twelve, the twelfth deed done,
As I return now from the shapeless dead
And the final dog, let me with calm review
All my great failures, sum them up in one,
And above all, my dear, let it be said
I did all that I had to do for you.

15

I did all that I had to do for you,
And what I did was nothing, some mistake
Where time was drilled and matter kept awake
Beneath a careless and impartial blue,
And only my achievement really knew
What it was for, was only for your sake

Dragged from my existence like a lake,
Brought senseless in to its admirers' view.

So we shall never see the end of it
Since our continuing is what we share:
When we contrive our parting by and by
It will not matter which of us has quit,
For no one left pretending not to care
Will sit there, bravely smiling, and not cry.

Power cut: USA

Six months of ruined steak:
Plunged in the dark, bumper to bumper,
    Salivation is an
Exercise of marital restraint,
    The vermouth brought within
A length of prostration from the gin.
    And now the life floods back,
The eyes glaze, policy circulates
    At the touch of fingers
Expert in the running of the cage.

In the dark I dreamed I was burning.
    My two sons were watching
And all the villagers were on fire.
    Somewhere, a great eye shut.
The lesson ended, children chanting,
    The hand on the plectrum,
A child's hand on the pinball mortar.
    Cage-lover, see me climb
Shaking with rage to the chimney stack:
    They are marching to me!

God Bless America

When they confess that they have lost the penial bone and outer space
    is
Once again a numinous void, when they're kept out of Other Places,
And Dr Fieser falls asleep at last and dreams of unburnt faces,
When gold medals are won by the ton for forgetting about the
    different races,

                                            God Bless America.

When in the Latin shanties the scented priesthood suffers metempsy-
  chosis
And with an organ entry *tutti copula* the dollar uncrosses
Itself and abdicates, when the Pax Americana cuts its losses
And a Pinkville memorial's built in furious shame by Saigon's puppet
  bosses,
                                            God Bless America.

When they can be happy without noise, without knowing where on
  earth they've been,
When they cease to be intellectual tourists and stop wanting to be
  clean,
When they send their children to bed at the proper time and say just
  what they mean,
And no longer trust the Quarterly Symposium and the Vicarious
  Screen,
                                            God Bless America.

When they feel thoroughly desolated by the short-haired Christ they
  pray to,
When they weep over their plunder of Europe stone by stone,
  releasing Plato
And other Freshman Great Books, when they switch off their Hoover
  and unplug Nato,
Pulling the chain on the CIA and awarding *Time* a rotten potato,
                                            God Bless America.

When qua-birds, quickhatches and quinnets agree at last to admit the
  quail,
When Captain Queeg is seen descending from the bridge as small and
  pale
As everyone else, and is helped with sympathetic murmurs to the rail,
When the few true defenders of love and justice survive to tell the tale,
                               Then, perhaps then, God Bless America.

Lecture room: ten a.m.

Robed in black, like surgeons already in mourning
For a dramatic failure in our usual techniques,
Amputation of Wordsworth or extraction of impacted Keats,
We hold precious as the last candle carried in cupped hand
The notion that here, at this place and at this time,

The twin tyrants of passage and location with their goads,
The murderous rubato, the spiritual ampallang,
Might for once be cheated of their inevitable victory
And something simple and other, like a flickering flame,
Be held a moment for surprised contemplation.

They are not appeased. Their anchors weigh down hands and eyes
To abject homage before their disgusting achievements.
Amusement, idleness, study: all are irrelevant
Since the black conspiracy equally absorbs them all,
And the life that should be shocked and free is still tame.

The heroes are shown not to falter, or to falter superbly,
And voices from all the rooms rise gradually through the walls
In acknowledgement of the cult which binds us:
''Tis not contrary to reason to prefer the destruction
Of the whole world to the scratching of my finger.'

'The last passage is not yet sufficiently explicated.'
'No one has ever seen the female palingenia:
Fecundated before even getting rid of her nymph's corset,
She dies with her eyes still shut,
At once mother and infant, in swaddling clothes.'

Examination room: two p.m.

All the ingredients of interrogation, green baize,
Papers strewn with care, faces averted in unconcern,
Impossible questions: these establish and then relax
The identity-conditions. Thus, as colours are real
When we say 'red' and 'yellow', and yet are hard to find

Within such generalities, so the predication of interrogation
Locates the candidate only within those classes of candidate
To which he may with safety be admitted, and today
All the submissive accidentals, fainting, beauty, garrulity
And wrong clothes, are simply the material for anecdotes.

The old hate the young for believing them to be really old.
The young hate the old for knowing that they are in fact young.
Both are dangerously polite. Only these must for the moment suffer:
All aggression, all curiosity, all friendship is put aside.
They weep with gratitude, with laughter and with being hurt.

Upper reading room: six p.m.

In the guilty half-silence of this long
Waiting-room, allusions buzz for us
Like flies, chairs scrape back for topics leaving
From a different platform. Lugging each hero's baggage,
We lie: 'I am like you. You are alive in me.'

Kipper-tied quinquagenarians, tramps
With satchels, academic teeny-boppers
Their carrels piled with hats and avocados,
Knee-locked civil servants of apparatus,
Nuns: we are shades that have lasted one more day.

And our eyes meet over the low partitions
In tentative love, sharing our furtive sense
Of the insults of that antagonist with whom
We ever contrive grandmaster draws, who sets
The problems that we compromise, from whom

We all on some long morning learned the rules.
He stains the stones. The scaffold streams with him.
Leggy girls on their venerable monosyllables
Are led by him to a gagging dryness. Boys
Smooth their balding heads, invoking his praises.

He brings the wrinkled clean expatriates
To the dug-outs of a mad ambition, shading
Their narrowed eyes on the beaches of exegesis,
Saying: 'We will return.' He likes to see
A gulping of tesseracts and Gondals in

Our crazed search across sands of the impossible
For the undying, and he annotates
Pistacia terebinthus to a sacrament,
Its sweet stench long evaporated
In the pages of a demythologised

Indexed kerygma. But we refuse to be bullied,
Even as hammers slog the walls crumbling
Around us. Books are about life, and life
Is somewhere here. On paper. In eyes. Somewhere.
So now we stack our cards. We reserve our defence.

All the members of my tribe are liars

Think of a self-effacing missionary
Tending the vices of a problem tribe.
He knows the quickest cure for beri-beri
And how to take a bribe.

And so the mind will never say it's beaten
By primitive disturbance of the liver;
Its logic will prevent its being eaten,
Get it across the river.

But faced with this assured inconsequence
That damns the very method that is used,
It leaves the heart unproselytised and hence
Admits that it's confused.

I know I'm acting, but I still must act.
I melt to foolishness, and want it ended.
Why it continues is this simple fact:
I'd hate to end it.

For now the jungle moods assert their terms
And there's no way to check them if they lie:
The mind attempts to solve the thing, but squirms
And knows exactly why.

The world is everything that is the case.
You cannot see it if you are inside it.
That's why the tortoise always wins the race:
The very terms decide it.

I cannot help it if I am contented
With being discontented that I falter:
That's why psychology was first invented
So that we needn't alter.

It is a strange position to be in.
It would be different if I didn't know
Why the unlikely animal should win,
Which cannibal should row.

You'd think there'd be a way of cutting out
Those self-destructive layers of introspection.
To reach the truth at last without a doubt
Of making the connection.

That's why the missionary, on his guard,
Is wondering why the cannibal's so merry,
And why it is so very very hard
To be a missionary.

Aberporth

Sky is performing feats of weather over
Hills wooded to the top, humped private hills
Whose birds look down not up. Briar's between
The fields: he keeps the eating sheep from knowing
What's on the other side. Beneath the path
A culvert runs, hidden for fifty years:
Some work will dig it up again.

Yes, nature is incurious, we know.
The butterflies as big as prayerbooks draw
No lesson from the india wings they thumb through,
While chapel slate aches with its uglification
Of primrose and violet, and the gold-black graves
Make even death elaborate and absurd
Like a bad conjuror.

The sea is much visited here, whose colours are cooler
And life uncertain as well it might be in
The earth's tears. Gulls on the sand look sharp.
Without anxiety the jellyfish is hideously still,
And the same could be said of the cliffs where wind carries
The loves of freewheeling crickets across a haze
Of sun-baked blackberries.

But we so easy are still not at our ease:
Such closeness open to us as though to a
Laconic Christ, hands flat to the ears with pity!
How we wish not to judge, wish for the starlight
And its emblems, the foliage globose and witchy,
With sounds coming nearer (Frrr! Frrr!) speaking
Of something that might content us.

Ghost village

Something takes me away, even from the spotlit
Indian clubs of our small happy government,
The gasp of hope and memory's applause,
In brown rooms, in yellow rooms, in red rooms by the sea,
To the colourless and soundless world we half-remember.

Presaged and annotated by our paltry sobs,
Older than all the lives we know or ever knew,
So sharply critical of the success of matter,
Keeping its own activities a deadly secret,
It is blind and alert as the black eyes of negatives.

Something said somewhere at some time is not enough
To appease its absorbing interest in what we did not mean
To old friends suddenly noticed as they glance up from books
With the sort of look which asks nothing because it is not worth it,
By the curled sea in rooms we shall half-forget.

Old friends in new rooms, new friends in old rooms:
It sees them come and go, because it is not worth it,
But a path down the valley cracked with grass
Brings us to the ghosts who must be faced,
Who questioned the blind world and would not let it lie.

Ghosts have hunters, but hunters lose the track,
For the craned neck does not suspect a reply
And the star or the heron is never asked if it requires
To be looked at, by those who glance up from books
When the curtains are drawn back from the evening sky.

Friendless, rootless by choice, they made a home for this bay
Where pairs of stone windows were set to frown at the sea
With all the gloomy unconcern of self-absorbed exiles
Whose delineation of the jealousies and dribbled ghylls
Only betrayed their real longing and peculiar laughter.

Did neighbours wonder at the striding, the leaping of gates?
Did Squire Tribute, coming from beyond the ridge
Where the harnessed pismire superb in its plumes of dust
Pretended to be a horse on a careless errand,
Judge? Or was it changed, the outside world?

When Mistress Tidings courted Sinful the Silent
And whispers sent sidling three sides of the square
Returned across the gap, shocked and delighted,

Was it too much like what had always been known
To make much sense, the inside world?

For we have known that difference as well,
Hands drumming impatiently on green baize
As we listen to the next to last report,
The tank brimming, the wipers running freely,
Set for the coast and the foul pinks of love.

They took the mountain for its broken counterpart.
Steamers visited the creaking pier and the washed gravel
Lay heaped like wheat on the shore of their closed lives.
In front rooms hands were folded on knees. A ticking clock
Enlarged the stone silences, defining a central gravity.

They saw the cow turn her tail into a handle,
Replenishing three or four fields beside a cliff,
And resolved as they walked alone at evening in watchchains
To make their lives acceptable to others, their deaths
Only to themselves. And the fields steamed with joy.

Their children were the first to make shy advances,
Wove with fingers, were pinioned, wept, touched,
Cruelly accused the unhappy of being only unhappy,
Talked incessantly of the marriage of headland and valley
And thought of nothing much to say, but learned to read.

Until one day these became themselves the brooding exiles,
The best cap square set or the downed pick at noon,
The mountain unshaped with interjections of dynamite,
Tired of responsibility, dreaming, easily wounded,
Crying out to be, and being, successfully lured by cities.

Nothing is changed, and most of the dancing is still glum
In neighbouring villages where they watch and wait
For the silver band to assemble in the Sunday dusk.
Nothing is changed, when wishes are fulfilled
And again we stare into the boiling centre.

Nothing is changed, but everything will alter
And the blind world exults as we expect it should
Over the first and last, the inside and the outside,
The forms and secrets, friends and generations,
Pacts made by ghosts that some of us have tried to love.

So thinking, a tiny swivelling figure in the bay,
Hands in pockets, turning over stones with a holiday foot,

Posed between the unravelling tides and the abandoned houses,
Made an uncertain gesture, ceased watching the sea,
And plodded up the hill for company.

Annotations of Giant's Town

1

Living in the air
Sleeping anywhere
Sheep are known to fall
But safe behind the wall
Cutting a fine edge
On outcrop or ledge
Gone if I look twice
Stones black with ice
Groan beneath my feet
Or make a cold seat
Storms come like love
Are level not above
Far is down not high
Tiny to the eye
Shining to the west
Wrinkled fishes nest
Blinking in the sun
Living is begun.

2

Height dizzies me
And what I see
Standing in his palm
At the end of his arm
That is our fort
Is beneath thought
Miserable track
Trees folded back
Sea's lazy licking
Thin picking
Fin and feather
Out of the weather
Shouting defiance
Loud nonsense
Cloud stuff
From having enough

Come out of stone
Height is alone

    3
Summer was his table
Eating what we were able
Sweet berry and grass
Cattle run in the pass
That will not meet their owner
Fool that is their donor
Who let them run away
Now we can eat all day
Cow-milk that we squeeze
Dripping into cheese
Ripping her fat sire
Out of the turning fire
Doubtful of our luck
Having bones to suck
Saving something for
The greed we can't ignore
Hugging us to death
Summer is his breath

    4
Once by work of frost
Rocks split and were lost
Fox hid in their boulders
Fur-smells on shoulders
Stirred memory of fear
When alone and fox near
Then fox-fear and fox-coat
Settled at the throat
Met on the hill one night
Faces not in sight
Spaces behind the ears
Cold with fox-fears
Older without thought
Rambled beyond the fort
Scrambling down the scree
Knowing what to see
No more seeing what
Once seen and is not

5

Something happens there
Thunder in the air
Under a trickling stone
Where sheep have gone
Staring at his face
Or its liquid trace
For all above the hill
His expressions spill
This way and that
Careful as a cat
Hairs out on the neck
Ribbed like a wreck
Gibbering in the rain
Lightning like pain
Night closing in
Fur round the chin
Stirring of ember
Something to remember

6

Fear is no longer
When we grow stronger
Then the clean stranger
Is known danger
Visible and small
No longer tall
Whole bands at the border
Keep in order
Leaping from trees
Hear metal knees
Gear snatched away
Only the weak stay
Grown attached to death
Short of breath
Brought to some harm
By the timid arm
Die in his cage
Fear's hostage

7

Winter in the wood
Trees where they stood
Pleased to be seen
Though no longer green

Rowan and oak
Cut for smoke
Hut-warmth for songs
Fur and gongs
Stirring his tribute
With bared cubit
Pith and sour berry
To make us merry
Brew for love and him
For his unseen whim
Or for his pain
The cold come again
Luck running thin
Winter closing in

III

Epistles to Several Persons

(1973)

To James Fenton

The poet's duties: no need to stress
The subject's dullness, nonetheless
Here's an incestuous address
    In *Robert Burns'* style
To one whom all the Muses bless
    At *Great Turnstile*.

I've no excuses for this theme.
Prescription is less popular than dream
And little rhymes, God knows, can seem
    Much too laconic,
Bollinger's visionary gleam
    Turned gin-and-tonic.

But ssch! you know and understand
The way these verses have been planned:
Gritty like little bits of sand
    Not shining quartz;
No pulsing from a higher gland
    Just random thoughts.

Let's start by thinking of objectives.
Poets hate to have directives:
They're on their own, not on collectives,
    Share and share about,
And what inspires their best invectives
    Is what *they* care about.

You, *James*, collapsed upon our sofa
As though being driven by a chauffeur,
Won't fail to tell us what you go for:
    Managerial boobs
And answers that you won't take no for
    From *Fine Tubes*.

Reporters never throw in towels.
Their prose is written from the bowels.
Ottava rima about owls
    Printed by *Sycamore*
Is worlds away from *Enoch Powell's*
    Plans for the blackamoor.

But are you *James Cameron* or *Flecker*?
Are you a maker or a trekker?

What is the nature of your *Mecca*,
　　Your *verum pulchrum?*
I'm glad, of course, that you're with *Secker*
　　And not with *Fulcrum.*

Poet and traveller have quarrelled
And now you canter where you carolled.
We're waiting still for your *Childe Harold*,
　　Though quests in *Poland*
Find you fixated and apparelled
　　More like *Childe Roland.*

It *is* impressive, I agree,
Although I know it's not for me.
I take the windfalls from the tree,
　　I'm much too lazy,
The prisons that *I* want to see
　　By *Piranesi.*

You say that *Oxford* has no marrow,
Sucked dry by *Trevor-Roper*, *Sparrow*,
And others of reaction's farrow
　　In their fat cloister,
Though if my eye is just as narrow
　　It may be moister.

We never see our feelings through,
And weeping only makes us blue.
It may be beautiful and true
　　But it's not action,
And nothing the bourgeoisie can do
　　Gives satisfaction.

How can we alter our behaviour?
Should we deny our gravy's gravier?
Leave *Cleopatra* for *Octavia?*
　　My life is inner,
And someone I don't think a saviour
　　Is *B. F. Skinner.*

Avoid that fashionable flock:
To be refitted in their dock
Your common-sense must take a knock
　　As it took a course on
The reflexes of frogs, and *Locke*,
　　And *P. F. Strawson.*

Much of the Left we can ignore
(Sheer anarchy I don't adore).
The trendy educate the poor
    In greed and fear,
While *Labour's* entered on the war
    Of *Jenkins'* ear.

No. Righteous more than He who Hath,
More reasonable than New Math,
Momier than the *Mome Rath*
    In their outgrabing,
Glossing the *Variorum Plath*
    From *Krafft-Ebing*,

Apostles of determinism
Whose hero's *Mao* or *Virgil Grissom*
Won't interest your mind one rissom:
    You're too empirical.
What about *Neo-Imagism*?
    Impossibly lyrical.

Such knowing brevity needs patience:
As unfastidious *Croatians*
Upon quite intimate occasions
    Shun body-talc,
So leave your interpersonal relations
    To *Colin Falck*.

For poetry to have some merit he
Requires it to display sincerity,
Each pronoun to convince posterity
    With deep emotion
And an invigorating verity
    Like hair-lotion.

Well, that's unfair. I'm glad he lives.
Just think of the alternatives!
Those whose verse resembles sieves
    Or a diagram,
And foul-mouthed transatlantic spivs
    Wooing *Trigram*.

For they are all still with us, *James*,
Fiddling among the flames,
Brandishing the brittle fames
    They soon arrive at.

It's better not to mention names:
    They'll wince in private.

Orating offspring of *Urania*
(No fault of yours that they're not brainier)
Have an immodest dogged mania
    For autobiography
Disguised in concrete or the zanier
    Forms of typography.

The wide-eyed audience they're rooking
Would secretly prefer a booking
From a quartet like the backward-looking
    Rank Ailanthus.
They'd jump to hear what's really cooking
    With the *Black Panthers*.

Whatever props the poet uses,
Whether he accepts, accuses
Or gives up, he must know his Muse is
    A sensible girl.
Even some antics of *Ted Hughes's*
    Make her hair curl.

And so you need a form to play
About in but which will convey
Something of what you want to say
    Without evasion,
Adjusting like the *Vicar of Bray*
    To each occasion.

The size you haven't found as yet.
What *Nabokov* calls the 'triolet'
Is much too trim a maisonette
    To dawdle in,
Unlike your shabby Cloisters set
    In *Magdalen*,

Which made your poetry much dandier,
Much like *ottava rima*, handier.
You needed in its chilly grandeur
    To turn the fire on
For times when you felt even randier
    Than *Lord Byron*.

Still, you found sonnets quite inspiring
Although some rhymes like ancient wiring

Showed the circuits could prove tiring
 (Though not unduly,
And no one could be more admiring
 Than Yours Truly).

So carry on: your talents hum.
No one will ever find you dumb
While you avoid the slightly rum
 Like the *White Goddess*
Or *Black Mountain* (and *don't* become
 Roger Woddis).

I'll send a sub to the *IS*
(Please let me know the right address)
I shan't turn up, but I confess
 I'm not a traitor.
I just don't want to think the less
 Of *Teresa Hayter*.

Some day I'll join you in the street
Where suffering and truth must meet:
It isn't easy not to feel effete
 This side of anguish,
When those who can't choose what to eat
 Don't speak our language.

Meanwhile we have to try to bring
Some order to that circus ring
Where people think and feel and sing,
 For at its centre
There's no escape from anything,
 And we must enter.

To Bryan Kelly

Decorum of the VHF
(We breakfast to *Balakirev*)
Brings in its plan to make us deaf
 The usual melée:
Tallis, Brahms, Prokofiev
 And *Bryan Kelly*.

A jolly piece. You'd earned your oats.
There were the right amount of notes
And most of those composed in quotes:

It isn't easy
To make half sound like *Eric Coates*
And half like *Bizet*.

In fact just what the *Corporation*
Finds suitable to the occasion:
Your score becomes an invitation
    To cake and tea.
She does her duty to the nation,
    The *BBC*.

But not to you. From all the data
It's the composer who's the martyr.
His major work is a non-starter
    To programme planners:
To fill-in with your *Stabat Mater*
    Would be bad manners.

Still, where one igneous arm of *Wales*
Throws off accumulating veils
Of cloud to where cruel *Ireland* sails
    Beyond her bounds
We hoard in chimney-lifting gales
    Its human sounds.

It's true the valley's creatures bring
All the sweet noises of the spring:
We hear the idiot *cwcw* sing
    And rather grand
Yet distant strains of practising
    From the prize band.

But nature's music's far from jolly.
Two ravens and a yapping collie
(Even rehearsed by *Barbirolli*)
    Would make you weep.
The mountain whines with melancholy
    Wind and sheep.

Wrapped in real music from the cold,
Inventive, urgent, manifold,
One gets quite careless of what's gold
        And what is phoney:
It's all so beautifully controlled.
        God bless *Marconi*!

And yet the other evening we
Tuned in (with certain difficulty)
To . . . mumbling. No tonality,
        Rhythm or pitch,
Like someone trying to catch a bee,
        Or a technical hitch.

One doesn't want to feel inferior
(We hear our fill of *opera seria*).
It clearly wouldn't get much cheerier
        And we swapped glances:
With what inducement to hysteria
        Art's guard advances!

Apollo, live? A foreign station
Emitting coded information?
No. An audience's elation
        (We were ruder)
Greeted a serious creation
        By *David Tudor*.

The electronic Emperor stalks
Naked through the popping corks
And music played with knives and forks
        That makes one poorly,
Accompanied by broadcast talks
        From *Roger Smalley*.

The ultimate is the blank page,
Narrowest of narrow gauge,
Yet curiously it's all the rage,
        This deathly silence.
Four minutes 33 from *Cage*
        Could lead to violence.

Or just a *very* hard-boiled egg
So bad you'd see the curate beg
To be let off the social peg.
        What can it mean?

Tell him to pull the other leg.
    It's not my scene.

When Governments reach in their purses
For sounds fit only for our curses
This is the worse than which no worse is
    (See *Father Gerard*).
It prompted me to write these verses –
    Far cry from *Herod*!

And yet I'm sure you will agree
With a relieved complicity
This is one point on which we see
    Eye to eye.
You can't bear such solemnity.
    Neither can I.

Take *Stockhausen*. I have some qualms
About his being 'heir to *Brahms*
And *Mozart*'. I'd not take up arms
    For his *Kontakte*.
Lack of true gravity and charm's
    The main factor.

It's the whole *Schoenberg* thing I dread:
Romantic pangs brought to a head
And dignified by sums instead
    Of being ethereal.
I find it hard to keep the thread
    When music's serial.

The theory's bolted stable door
Is something that we can't ignore.
It's unassailable as law
    And in full force.
But one thing's missing – that's the poor
    Musical horse.

A revolution safely weathered
And captive *Pegasus* untethered?
I rather think the beast's unfeathered
    And limps in anguish.
The point is that the twelve-tone method
    Yields no real language.

The meal's bizarre with misplaced sauces.
The palate mourns what greed enforces.

Wondering what the next strange course is?
 You needn't try.
To music's eloquent resources
 You've said goodbye.

A sense of timing gets our votes:
I see why space between the notes
Is buoyant, why the music floats,
 Why we don't sink.
But random noises burn the boats –
 We're in the drink.

Webern shot and *Orff* applauded?
Agreed, the facts have been recorded
As sure as anything the war did
 In spheres political.
The implication's pretty sordid
 And quite uncritical.

Such digs at *Orff* I find unnerving.
Berlin (the capital, not *Irving*)
Maintained a love that was unswerving
 For *Mickey Mouse*:
Was this poor rodent, then, time-serving
 Like *Russell's Strauss*?

The other (victim of some sentry
Taking pot-shots at Jews and gentry)
Made tunes seem crude and elementary,
 Though I don't mind
His music, a frail diary-entry,
 Being so refined.

God knows, I'm not an aesthete but
Though music gets you in the gut
It's no good if your ears are shut:
 You miss its grammar.
The tone-deaf Zhdanovite's 'tut-tut'
 Sounds like a stammer.

Mistrust of *Shostakovich* grew
Out of his *Lady Macbeth*: not through
Its being politically untrue
 To what was Russian,
Simply that *Stalin* sat next to
 Deafening percussion.

It served the smugness of the West
To praise him for his love of jest,
Find his Fifth Symphony a test
        Of ideology
And claim to be not much impressed
        By its apology.

His work supposedly survives
In the same way you chop down chives
For thicker growth, and fame arrives
        When he's 'correct'.
(Blame for the oddities of *Ives*
        Years of neglect.)

The porcelain culture of the French
Was founded on an Empire's stench:
Dien Bien Phu was quite a wrench
        Since fifty coolies
Go to make up one übermensch
        Like *Pierre Boulez*.

From *Couperin* to *Erik Satie*
Was one delightful cocktail party.
It made each lover, sly or hearty,
        Go all goosey
To hear a trill from *Sarasate*
        Or *Claude Debussy*.

Les Six will always play a part
In the strict audit of the heart.
A circus troupe, a minor art,
        Familiar ground?
But shapely, sceptical and tart,
        My kind of sound.

Despite a taste for fourths and slosh,
Theirs was a *musique de la poche*,
Not sentimental like *les Boches*
        But wry instead.
Il faut la faire bien, mais moche
        As someone said.

Shostakovich and *Poulenc*.
The tall one tinkled (to be frank);
The frail one hammered like a tank:
        Confounding us

In concert, honoured with the rank
    Of *Oxford's* D Mus.

A nice *New College* tale which shows
How music keeps you on your toes:
It's human, though you blow your nose
    And a bassoon
In a completely different pose
    (One makes a tune).

I mean the composer launches out
In seas he hardly knows about
Where phobias float and passions spout
    Like the white whale,
Where he will find he has to shout
    Against the gale.

He may sit by the metronome
Secure in his maternal home.
A symphony for paper and comb
    May bring him fame,
With themes upon a palindrome
    Of his own name.

Yet somewhere in this dry farrago,
Like the spark that makes a car go
Or like a gangster in *Chicago*,
    A lurking numen
Links it with *Hair* or *Handel's Largo*
    As something human.

Is this to say I am not far
From *homo sum*, etcetera,
And kindly middle age, blah blah?
    That's not quite right,
Since anything not up to par
    I'd burn on sight.

My love for tuneful music dates
From *Figaro* on 78s
At four or five. When I'm in straits
    With *Cage* or *Nono*
I'm glad to know that somewhere waits
    The *dove sono*.

Or the cool clarinet *con brio*
In his incomparable Trio.
Later I liked *Ravel* and *Milhaud*
    Or the sensation
Of singing *Rolling down to Rio*
    Or *The Creation*.

My piano made the prefects deaf
Both with the bass and treble clef,
I downed the oeuvres of each chef
    At a single gulp,
I battered poor *Prokofiev*
    Into a pulp.

A thousand schoolboys can't be wrong
To murder *Chopin* and to long
To be *John Ogdon* or *Fou Ts'ong*.
    You fail them by
The score from *Yorkshire* to *Hong Kong*,
    But let them try.

At least an appetite that's vast
For all the music of the past
Played wretchedly and much too fast
    Gives one an inkling
Why some is tough enough to last
    Without crinkling.

One's private landscape's thus created
Out of the way the works are rated,
A scene you feel you've long awaited
    To feast your eyes on,
Where untried sounds are relegated
    To the horizon.

Mine, like the panorama here,
Moving, familiar and dear,
Contains both gentle grass and sheer
    Exacting rock,
Where, though the light is bright and clear,
    Loud winds can shock.

Igor, *Dmitri* and *Sergei*,
Gigantic mountain peaks at play,

Firmly command the landscape; they
    Need no discussion:
What's grandest since the *Rite*, I say,
    Is mostly Russian.

Those grassy slopes provide a focal
Point with sheep and the odd yokel:
Vigorous, pastoral and vocal
    And sometimes skittish,
Nearest is dearest, well-known, local
    And wholly British.

At times a plaintive cow is heard
Standing sadly in a turd
Wishing it sounded like a bird.
    I can't determine
Just how many of this herd
    I'd claim were German.

And then, at dusk, the hidden streams
Bubbling madly like our dreams.
A charming sound: doll-like it seems
    And ithyphallic,
Eloquent, if short on themes,
    What if not Gallic?

A varied scene. Perhaps you can
Compare it with the one you'll scan
In *Gozo* with superb élan
    On a short lease.
Which brings me back where I began,
    Hearing your piece.

Forgive my buttonholing you.
Nice of you to hear me through
A ramble that's become far too
    Elaborate.
There's something better that I do:
    Collaborate.

The poet's the composer's feed:
You must be thinking as you read
That stuff like this just goes to seed,
    That I'm forgetting

101

All about those words you need
      For your next setting.

OK, I'll stop. But I'm no meany.
I'd like to end with just a teeny
Tribute to those we love: *Bellini*
      And *Diabelli,*
Donizetti, Verdi and *Puccini*
      And *Bryankelli.*

To Angus Macintyre

From windy *Llanaelhaiarn* to
Far *Achaglachgach* just a few
Nocturnal stanzas penned for you.
      The form is Scottish
And pocket-sized to suit those who
      Live in a cottage.

Achaglachgach – is that right?
Too many achs? Too few? You might
Get headed paper. In this light
      I'm going blind
Wondering how many achs to write.
      Ach, never mind.

As dons grow stout from small successes
Put out by academic presses
To catch the textbook boom, my guess is
      They'll all buy places
With unpronounceable addresses
      In open spaces.

By disused pits, on bogs and moors,
Are shacks for sale with earthen floors.
It hardly matters that the doors
      Are off their hinges
As long as they're within, of course,
      The Celtic fringes.

Nature is all around and *so* near,
For us from *Brecon* to *Snowdonia,*
For you from *Skye* to *Caledonia.*
      We often go,
And the exertion makes us bonier,
      Nicer to know.

102

Although the landscape's much enjoyed,
Still a few fields are unemployed:
Campers are not now much annoyed
        By concrete Gents
And where there isn't one, avoid
        Pitching their tents.

They bring air-beds and doilies, pink
Paraffin, the kitchen sink . . .
And these are just the sort who think
        It would be deathly
To usher *Rio Tinto Zinc*
        Into *Dolgellau.*

Expecting *Wales* to be like *Borrow*
Has filled the tourist with deep sorrow
(It will be twice as bad tomorrow).
        An unspoilt view's
Unlikely as an uncleaned *Corot,*
        A falcon's news.

There once were eagles here, don't worry.
They must have left in quite a hurry.
Now only buzzards wheel and scurry
        Over *Gurn Ddu.*
Trig points on every peak? *Eryri,*
        How we mourn thee!

Are we much better? Aren't we fakers
Pacing about our fenced-off acres?
Aren't we the economic *Quakers*
        In a cold war
Between the strikers and strike-breakers?
        What are we for?

A rustic view in *Coed-y-Brenin?*
A waste to keep a cow or hen in?
What about all the jobless men in
        The National Parks?
(I make no reference to *Lenin*
        Or *Karl Marx.*)

The unemployed are twelve per cent
In *Blaenau* where the rain squalls dent
A century's slag, a broken tent
        Of splintered slate.

103

I wonder where the profits went,
       And who to hate.

Too late for accusations. While
Someone somewhere made a pile,
It's part of an extinct life-style.
       The simple proof?
Compare the outlay on a tile
       And a slate roof.

It's no one's quickie in the *City*,
It can't be saved by a Committee,
And yet because of this unpretty
       Straggling town
Most of *England's* dry. Pity
       To let it drown.

I think of you in wilder greenery,
Indulging in gentlemanly venery
In miles and miles of private scenery
       With gun and rod.
You'd think old workings and machinery
       Completely odd.

How was your reading party? Tough?
Did you decide once was enough
Or will your pupils call your bluff
       And come next year?
Was it like something out of *Clough*,
       But not so queer?

Plunging clean limbs into the burn,
Steering superbly from the stern
Or watching in the reeds for tern
       While you complain
They haven't got the wits to learn
       Your line on *Paine*?

Poor dears, just now we're dipping lambs
While they in *Oxford* on their hams
Are sweating through sub-fusc exams:
       Though quite reviving,
Sabbaticals are really shams,
       A form of skiving.

A chance to swim and look less pale
Or hit the *US* lecture trail,
Modestly – from *Smith* to *Yale* –
    Or quirkily –
Risking co-eds at *Texas*, gaol
    At *Berkeley*.

I'm glad we didn't cross the pond
For though the Dollar waves its wand
I feel somehow we've gone beyond
    That second salary,
And if of greens I'm fairly fond,
    Not greenery-yallery.

Those close-kept manuscripts we need,
Acquired through academic greed
For home-grown PhDs to read:
    Well, let them lie.
They'll wait – while *Texas* barons bleed
    Our history dry.

Sweating in seminars is not
The nicest way of being hot.
The company of one is what
    I hold most dear:
The summer's rotten, but we've got
    A hammock here.

Our estivation with our books
In our respective rural nooks
Like nearly all our actions looks
    Like compromise.
We have our alibis, like crooks
    When someone dies.

And do we like the life we chose?
Might as well ask the blowsy rose
If it approves the way it grows
    When autumn's near.
At least I don't suppose it shows
    When we're up here.

Or does it? We're as incognito
As is the *CIA* in *SEATO*,

A worker Jesuit in *Quito*
    Selling pardons
Or trilbied *Emperor Hirohito*
    In *Kew Gardens.*

With luck we can avoid being hated.
Perhaps our kind are merely fated
Smilingly to be tolerated
    Like lunatics –
Not dangerous but dissipated,
    Not keen to mix.

– Except our worlds like cocktails: loath
To give up either we live both,
One for yield and one for growth.
    Contemptae domin-
us splendidior rei quoth
    The happy Roman.

Let's keep them well apart. Too late
Unwittingly you'll recreate
The one world in the other. Wait
    Until those craven
Oxford rituals infiltrate
    Your Scottish haven.

You'll be Vice-Chancellor, fit station
To rule your woolly congregation
Where you'll be welcome like an Asian
    In liberal *Kenya*
And baa'ed through your inauguration
    At *Creag's* encaenia.

Prelims in shearing. Every lamb
Must pass. Lectures for ewe and ram
On weaving skills, plus diagram
    Of warp and weft.
At breakfast circulate the jam
    From right to left.

There will be several printed rules
On what the cows may wear in Schools,
And only three-legged milking stools
    Will be allowed.

For ignorance of farming tools,
      Fields will be ploughed.

I won't go on. It isn't true.
Nor is its opposite, where you
Take sandwiches to Hall and do
      What you are able
To climb up to a decent view
      From High Table.

Or poke your pupils with a straw
To see if they're alive, and bore
Them with all kinds of country lore
      Not known in books
And imitations of the caw
      Of various rooks.

The academic's one excuse is
He knows about the gastric juices,
Suppression of the anacrusis
      And *Ararat*.
Such subjects no doubt have their uses:
      Leave it at that.

If these impinge on *haute cuisine*,
A deathless verse or the Unseen,
If there's a soul in the machine
      To prove me wrong,
Well, that's OK, but we've both been
      Around too long.

For it's not only earth that's cooling,
Something commands us to quit fooling,
Not facts but truth we should be pooling
      In the global village
(Though I'm not one for the de-schooling
      Of *Father Illich*).

Where has the living starlight gone?
The owls are loud where once it shone.
We see the archetypal don
      Pen in his cloister
A footnote to a footnote on
      Ralph Roister Doister.

We need some vision to achieve,
A heart to wear upon our sleeve,
We need a holy spell to weave,
    Some sacred wood
Where we can teach what we believe
    Will do us good.

I see you smile. All right, it's late.
But, Angus: though it lies in wait
With terrible reproaches, fate
    May yet forgive
Our scared retreats, both small and great,
    And let us live.

To Ian Hamilton

So the *Review* is ten years old,
Five times as many thousands sold
And all you've touched has turned to gold!
    At least in theory:
There's still the printer's bill, I'm told.
    How very dreary.

I'd like to see its name in neon
But I'm afraid this humble paean
Will have to do. It seems an aeon
    Since we last met.
I promised you a letter, *Ian*,
    So one you'll get.

If *Ian Hamiltons* galore
(Offhand, I can distinguish four
Or five. I hope there are no more)
    Think it's addressed
To them, too bad. You're tooth and claw
    Above the rest.

The ignorant must think you cater
For every cultural taste, creator
Of symphonies, an adumbrator
    Of army tricks, a

Late Editor of the *Spectator*,
      A concrete mixer.

But anyone who really cares
Will know just who you are. He shares
An interest in your affairs
      That goes much deeper
Than literary bulls and bears
      With you zoo-keeper.

I'm glad you let me in on what
Has proved to be, like it or not,
A property that's very hot.
      What magazines
Of verse require, this one has got:
      It beats as it cleans.

Ten years! Your longest venture yet!
I well recall when we first met
You'd got your latest, like a pet
      On a short run.
But soon you left it with the vet:
      You'd had your fun.

Time passes: in its mirrored gloom
Stacks of *Tomorrows* richly loom,
Three quid a copy now – for whom?
      We were too feeble
To fetch them from a cleaner's room
      In watchful *Keble*

Where you were not *persona grata*,
Your credit balance a non-starter.
The magazine had made you martyr
      To unpaid batells
(I hope they're not averse to barter
      And kept the chattels).

You found it wise, promptly and gaily as
One might go out and buy azaleas
Or like a crook adopt an alias,
      To start another,
Proving the happy rule that Failure's
      An elder brother.

White-shield *Worthington* was still
Around and we'd got time to kill
(Pages were harder than beer-mugs to fill).
    We broke the tape
Playing bar-billiards until
      The thing took shape.

We chose a fairly flat name, though
We didn't then think of *Defoe*,
That literary one-man-show
    Of bourgeois letters,
Whose honest prodding, as you know,
      Put him in fetters.

Remember him when you are belted
By puffs whose icing you have melted:
In that rough age you'd think he felt it
    More than in ours,
But in the pillory he was pelted
      Only with flowers.

Bouquets to you too, *Ian*, then,
Most incorruptible of men.
Ten years seems very little when
    The job's done well.
We may yet see another ten:
      Who can tell?

Lively, irreverent and human,
Harpo to poetry's *Sig Rumen*,
You lit a memorable *lumen*
    And held it steady,
Heroic like your favourite *Newman*
      As *Fast Eddie*.

The Fat Men quivered at your glance,
Careers destroyed by your advance.
Still you are wooed at every chance
    Like an heiress,
And lead the dunces quite a dance
      From *Westbourne Terrace*.

At least ten years ago there were no
Worse than those who, sipping *Pernod*,

In Lallans ruined the *Inferno*
    With tips from *Pound*.
Now we've (*facilis descensus Averno*)
    The *Underground*.

Ten years have witnessed a gigantic
Increase in the transatlantic
Subterranean mode, each antic
    Sillier than the last,
Most a mere throwback to a frantic
    Dadaist past.

Sexual boasting, prayer mats,
Ampersands, athletic chats
On breathing or the evil that's
    Instinct in iambs,
Tall stories, empty as the flats
    Of *Harry Hyams*.

Oh those Primitivist Panzers
Steamrolling *Newcastle* or *Kansas*
With misspelt lower-case bonanzas
    Of pot and *Zen*
In which mistrust of things like stanzas
    Shows they are men

And fit to blast an epic trail
Though with a certain mannered, frail
Excess that rises to a wail
    When they're ignored,
Ripe as the scrawlings in a gaol
    Or a locked ward

Where mania's nurtured by the nurses
Eager with poultices and curses:
For unread poets get free purses
    From an *Arts Council*
As interested in their verse as
    In kinds of groundsel.

You haven't stopped all this, but still
You've drawn attention to the ill.
Though to the Bank of Time he will
    Remain a debtor,

The patient's choking on your pill
    And may get better.

I hope so, and I'd like to see
The *Review* out with the frequency,
The brightness and authority
    Of a new penny,
So wish that all returns will be
    Happy and many.

To David Caute

John, as I take my pen to write,
The world is spinning through the night
While, blindingly upon the sight,
    With dreadful starkness
Random flares of evil light
    The massive darkness:

A sniper wiping off a debt,
Still-smouldering crops, a swooping jet,
Guerrillas caught in their own net,
    A blown-up *Boeing*,
An interrogator's cigarette
    Quietly glowing.

The shooting flashes like marsh-fire,
Illuminating wall and wire
Where nervous governments retire
    (History has shown
That Greed and Terror both require
    To be alone).

But history's your pitch, dear friend.
You understand the things that send
The rest of us around the bend.
    We find them eerier.
Forgive me if I seem to tend
    To mild hysteria

For life gets madder every day,
Achieving the status of a play
Where everybody has their way
    And people mean
The opposite of what they say
    To steal a scene.

112

The nations' urges are still liable
To be racialist or even tribal:
Al Fatah, prompted by the *Bible*
    (See *Deuteronomy*)
Kidnap *Dayan's* other eyeball
    With fine economy.

Marauding pop-stars strum their anguish
Over the loss of the Welsh language.
I can't say it's the sort of pang which
    Moves me to anger.
I bet there's no Celtic for 'ham sandwich'
    Even in *Bangor*.

In drunken *Ireland* half the nation
Welcomes the English Occupation
As just the sort of situation
    They revel in,
Halfway to the Finland Station
    With *Miss Devlin*.

(Sometimes when the smoke clears, hazily
We glimpse the girth of *Ian Paisley*
Running about and shouting nasally
    To small armed bands
While throttling Roman Catholics lazily
    With his own hands.)

Even sectarian unease
At terror turns into a wheeze.
When good *Lord Longford* on his knees
    With *Myra Hindley*
Raises a doubt, forgive him please.
    He means it kindly.

When *Dr Ramsey* mildly prays
That wicked men may change their ways,
Happily viewers fix their gaze
    Upon his vestments,
Proving to the *Church* it pays
    To have *in*vestments.

The mishaps of our legislation,
The bores of our administration,
Can be, if it's our inclination,
    Turned down or off

Or over to the real elation
   Of *Coleman* and *Bough*.

Sport is the thing. We watch it gaily.
We get it, like our murders, daily:
Another gold, a dead Israeli,
   A fire in orbit,
A gift of jelly at a ceilidh,
   Or *Olga Korbut*.

The toughs are measuring their phalluses
And most of them upon analysis
Prove to have general paralysis
   Of the insane.
Wallace (I don't want to be callous) is
   Upright again.

Howard Hughes has lost his, *Nixon*
Proves to have one that only sticks on,
Agnew's is as real as *Dixon*
   Of *Dock Green*,
General Westmoreland's glows and clicks on
   Like a machine.

Mailer's is penalised for fouls,
Cassius Clay's is wrapped in towels,
Andy Warhol's raises howls,
   Hefner's is past it.
Fischer shows his to *Spassky*, growls:
   'Beat that, you bastard!'

Autumn was in the air today
As well-worn leaves began to fray
And ruffled swallows on a spray
   Sat side by side
Looking ready to fly away
   Or thumb a ride.

What message will they take abroad
Where winter sees cool drinks being poured
And planters sitting slumped and bored
   On the verandah,
As mad *Amin* fills camp and ward
   Throughout *Uganda*?

What image do we put across
Now that we're no longer boss,

114

Relieved of the parental cross
    Of a mother country,
Finding it hard to bear the loss
    Without effrontery,

The kind that offers *Heath* the myth
Of being polite to *Ian Smith*
While groaning at 'Cymru am byth'
    Or at *Kaunda*,
Of being pally with our kith
    Down Under?

England is small and very cold
And parts of it are growing mould.
The people do what they are told
    With little protest.
The young are happy, though the old
    Are not much noticed.

Some of the women live with cats,
Some wear bare feet and some wear hats,
Some call their children stinking brats
    And yet have lots,
Some simply like to show their twats
    (Or is it twats?).

The men are silent and suspicious,
Witty, bald and superstitious,
Sometimes maudlin, sometimes vicious,
    Yet always ready
To yield a point, to do the dishes
    Or be called *Freddie.*

For only one thing really vexes,
And that's the muscles that he flexes
In intercourse between the sexes,
    A subject which
Sees little praxis but much lexis,
    A seven-league itch.

The topic even haunts the Left
Who show that they are quite bereft
Of staying power (at least, though deft,
    They haven't shown it),
Who know that property is theft,
    But like to own it.

And those who see through the charade
Find that the going's rather hard,
As though they held a trumping card
    But (silly fools)
Allowed themselves to be debarred
    Because of rules

That none of the players has admitted
Save those whose winning has best fitted
Them to win. Who's to be pitied
    In this argy-bargy?
Your novels are at least committed
    To be enragé.

You show what forces pull the triggers
While still creating living figures.
Decline of the West is quite as big as
    It sets out to be,
Though that earlier one about the *Diggers*
    Seems best to me.

Fiction will naturally tend
To do its best not to offend.
A start, a middle and an end
    Do come in handy,
Though some books try a curious blend
    Like *Tristram Shandy.*

(Happily, though. Poor *Aristotle*!)
Into the straight with open throttle,
Each modern writer, like *Dave Wottle*,
    Will surge in front
Baying for blood, and the poor plot'll
    Fall in the hunt.

Still, you don't want the Tower of *Babel*,
Simply a self-conscious fable
That lets the contents clinch the label
    Not merely *be*,
With all your ideas on the table,
    E & OE.

Should Art's House therefore lose its roof?
And can the writer stay aloof?
I like my fiction on the hoof
    Not on the slab.

But still, your pudding is the proof.
    Your hand is dab.

You like to see life as it is
(And risked a cosy niche to quiz
Rich *All Souls'* secret entrances:
    Although well wined,
You found it all a dirty swizz
    And you resigned).

You are the man we want to read,
The kind of writer that we need.
I'd like to see you take the lead
    In those *Foyle's* lists
Where sales flirt with the thwarted greed
    Of novelists.

After your brilliant *Confrontation*
You ought to get an invitation
To take a Chair of Alienation
    Where you would clear
Five grand, have total dispensation
    And live near here.

You'd turn it down. Good: I admire
Your firm decision to retire.
Oxford must seem the perfect pyre
    To one who's seen
A few burnt children shun the fire.
    You know what I mean.

Inter silvas Academi
Runs a seam that's very seamy.
You'd think the life was soft and dreamy
    But not at all.
Much of it's grovelling and schemy
    And full of gall.

It must make novelists feel neuter
To be a subject for a tutor,
For even *Naipaul, Caute* or *Butor*
    (Without a cheque)
Are on the syllabus at *Utah*
    Or *Clapham Tech.*

It would have cramped the style of *Homer*
To see himself as a Diploma,

117

Put *Poe* and *Godwin* in a coma
    To be bits and pieces
In *Antecedents of Sax Rohmer*,
    A Master's Thesis.

But though you think we're so much dead wood,
Come for a week-end soon with *Edward*
And *Daniel*. While the kids trek bedward
    We downstairs
Will push those bits of white and red wood
    Across their squares.

There's our friends' futures to decide,
And Queen's Side openings to be tried.
There's claret lying on its side
    With other wines.
I've got a desk sixteen feet wide
    For narrow lines.

It would be nice to see you and
To know what writing you had planned.
I find such meetings rather grand
    And stimulating.
It helps me to keep in my hand
    And stop stagnating.

I envy you the scope of prose.
I like the way your oeuvre grows,
Reflecting what its author knows
    And how he feels.
It never simply seems a pose,
    Never short-deals.

While the State's wrists are being cut,
The poet squirms and says Tut-tut,
Unless he is some kind of nut
    Or of the far Right.
Both ways there's lots of *Dichtung* but
    Too little *Wahrheit*.

We do things in a 'God I'm bored' way
Or on-the-back-seat-of-the-Ford way
That need a touch of that 'Oh Lord!' way
    Which would create a
Riot in an off-off-*Broadway*
    Free theatre.

Something imagined and intended,
Put into action and defended,
Something that's serious and splendid,
        Not just a token.
But now least said is soonest mended,
        So nothing's broken.

And yet *die Kunst ist nicht das Brot*
Aber der Wein des Lebens (wrote
Richter, I think: forgive the quote)
        And even when
We're being stirred by reading *Caute*
        We're only men

Who have to suffer and to act
However much our brains are packed
With characters and doubtful fact,
        Bringing confusion
Unless we recognise with tact
        Its small illusion.

The swallows have already flown,
The summer's babies are full-grown
And launched into the world alone.
        The leaves will fall
And all our futures are unknown,
        Our chances small.

From the closed rooms we wander through
We'll get an ever-changing view,
And some perspectives may be new.
        And then again
There will be little things to do
        To keep us sane.

While all about us atoms take
Infinite trouble for our sake
To look as though their antics make
        Some kind of sense,
And all our brave equations ache
        At the pretence.

So I propose the toast of art,
The wine of life and of the heart,
To greet my friends before we start
        The long contentious

Unhopeful consequential part
>Of our adventures.

Friends are what much of life's about,
Though some of us are getting stout.
I think of mine a lot, without
>Our often meeting.
Until we do, then, *John*, don't doubt
>I mean this greeting.

IV

The Mountain in the Sea

(1975)

Up and down

1

This is where it begins:
A cairn marks the place
Where sky negotiated
A hasty truce.

Thrown up like apophthegms
Of a phlegmatic culture
During some geological
Tedious prologue

They shoulder for position
While offering their profiles
Like notables at a spa
Grouped for the lens.

They have settled into age
With a fear of being alone.
Such gaunt tranquillity,
A herded peace!

You stand at its foot
A mere nanunculus,
Or whisper at its brow
An imprecation

Which the wind removes,
Whisked into the air
With all your vanity,
A minor annoyance

Not to be compared
With trigonometry,
Telescopes, masts, picnics
Or the puncture of flags.

Or that old enemy
Who at his leisure reduces
Outcrop to random rocking
Impedimenta.

For as you slither down
The mossed escalation
Of shifting lichen-wrapped
Smashed crocks

A vertical wall to your right
Unbelievably still
And staunch to its terrain,
A ruinous piping

You see what brings you down
Fear stroking the scalp:
Not mere height or exposure
Or being alone

But the dawning role of invader
Animated, flushed, hostile,
Conspirator and wrecker,
Almost indecent.

Up there are old mysteries
Much better left alone,
Safer with our structures
Of docile stone.

2

They own everything,
Saddled with foot-thick wool
And a family resemblance
Like the first Marlboroughs.

Inquisitive and alarmed,
Their slit eyes blank
As undone buttonholes,
They circle the cottage.

To them it memorialises
Worlds of purpose and concept
Unhabitable, like
A stone footprint.

How we come in and out
Is certainly a puzzle
For there they are, puzzled,
Whenever we do it.

Grouped on frosty nights
When with a cautious beam
We tread into the black
Their eyes are green.

And on misty mornings
Moving like ancient sofas

On castors over the gravel
They keep their watch.

For the mountain is edible.
Its small geography
Is their prerogative:
Their paths are meals.

They might even admit
To being its parasites,
As they have parasites
Nuzzling richly.

But what of a creature
Who lives not by the grass
But by the hidden stone,
Its skeleton?

Not as the tasteless crag
Or scrambling sideways scree
Whose dangers are well-known
But a shut cave

In which unspeakable acts
Of gregariousness and greed
Or of sheer stupidity
Are hidden from them?

They may, though bewildered,
Secretly guess our kinship,
Nomads to them and less
Aristocratic.

This would certainly account
For their intermittent patience,
Explain why we feel just
A little sheepish.

3
She makes a quick escape
As from a cold cauldron,
Seeping frugally but
In slight panic

Moistening sheer outcrop
With tears of brave joy,
Long legs down the rock.
A flicker of lace.

125

Just a slip of a girl
But something to be proud of
Elbowing thorns and stones
And growing stronger

Talking at roadsides where
A small declivity
A tumble of clod and pebble
Whitens her falling.

Rushing on in excitement
Through a fledgy wood,
Dropping helter-skelter
Flirting with fish

Lingering in pools
Where hardly visible flies
Have just time enough to cast
A static shadow

And moving down the hillside
Through half-flooded meadows
Where thirsty herds make for
The tell-tale hummocks.

Soon her progress is statelier
On the reed-crowded route
Under footpath and bridge
To her dissolution.

We admire this quality
Of drawing out as on
A thread an argument
Of pure persistence

Until diversity
Sinks with delicious freight
The empty tanker of
Our finite voyage.

For see: the ravine holds her
Where sun-worshippers trudge
With all their full baskets
To the earth's lap.

Whereupon she promptly
Disappears, spilled
Out to random skeins
Across the beach

126

Rejoining, without complaint,
The globe's great cycle
As who would not wish to do
Did we not stop here?

4

For this is what it comes down to:
After repose, erosion.
From grandeur, detonations
And heartless breakdown.

But if this were the way
We died into the earth
Think of the discretion,
Such privacy!

Privacy of worlds
Not wasted but perpetual,
Tons and tons of indifference,
Lightness of heart.

Grain by grain it offers
Little resistance, only
Corporate mass and that
Agreeably wayward.

Wet, it preserves the wraith
Of toes. Dry, it dissolves
The tread to dredged craters
Lodged with beer-cans.

The loose configurations
Of this sterile humus
Are without finitude:
Frankly, a mess.

Its yellowness is false,
A lie to anger the blue
Which hammers arms and fists
In tears against it.

For down there the chiselled specks
Are proud of their lineage:
Crystal, tan, charcoal,
Their colours are sober.

Flushed by the watery beast
They assert their freedom
In voluntary association,
A righteous rebuttal.

Good reason to admire, then,
The ultimate in stone
Neither to be climbed nor hewn,
The body's haven.

For here we face our star
With least speculation,
Here we are revolved
In certainty.

Here warmth is transmitted.
Your idle hand reaches
And grasps a myriad boulders
Of impossible size.

As they bounce off the palm
Like sparks from a welder
Your hand seems invulnerable.
Colossal. Painless.

Cairn

Stairs leading nowhere, roof
To no accommodation, monument
To itself, half-scattered.

An old badge of belonging
To the available heights,
A shrug and a smile, as though

Having climbed two thousand feet
You could climb a few feet more
And the view might be different.

Silhouette

Men, who when we look keep still,
Or images made by men: such would be
Dangerous, would have designs upon us.

From here the stones are shape only,
Blocking their small outline of sky,
Too far to move, or seem to move.

Hat in hand, a wave from the shoulder,
A shift of plane, colour catching the light,
Fanning of sheep or delay of shot:

There are no signs like these to tell us
What it might be, high up on the mountain.
And we shall not be climbing there just now.

Grasshopper Mountain

Down we go, hand in hand,
Jolted at each step, laughing
And stumbling. It's impossible
To place each foot in haste
Squarely on tussock or stone
For spraying out beneath us
In fountains like little delayed springs
Are all the golden grasshoppers of Penllechog!

We seem to descend like gods
With news that there are no gods:
'The lids are rattling! Heather
Has the secret: his cups
Are full of sun!' Down
We go, while at our feet
Patient of our absurd clumsiness
Are all the golden grasshoppers of Penllechog!

Wild raspberries

Wild raspberries gathered in a silent valley
The distance of a casual whistle from
A roofless ruin, luminous under sprays
Like faery casques or the dulled red of lanterns

129

When the flame is low and the wax runs into the paper,
Little lanterns in the silence of crushed grasses
Or waiting chaises with a footman's lights,
Curtains hooked aside from the surprising
Plump facets padded like dusty cushions
On which we ride with fingers intertwined
Through green spiky tunnels, the coach swaying
As it plunges down and the tongues slip together,
The jewels fall to the floor to be lost forever,
The glass shatters and the heart suddenly leaps
To hear one long last sigh from an old blind house
That settles further into its prickly fronds,
Speaking of nothing, of love nor of reproaches,
Remembering nothing, harbouring no ghosts,
Saving us nothing at all but raspberries.

Hut groups

On these small eminences above the valley
So hugged by excited bracken from which the wind
Enforces obedience that their very insignficance
Seems a quiet triumph, their demise an unfortunate
Accident reversible through incantations or simple good will,
On these stand the hidden foundations of the Dark Age farms,
Their slight turfy bulk squaring a hillside or a field.

An eight-figure map reference will find them
Though they are less visible than an overnight
Encampment of moles. Where even their simple doors were
Can't be rumbled through the attentions of the illegible grass.
You may stand in them as the sheep do and not feel at home,
And yet delight in the mere persistence of a habitable shape,
A ground-plan of biographies which might yet be relived.

We have stood in our own foundations, haven't we,
And marvelled at the exiguous dimensions? Later,
Closed from the elements and their whining questions
By the courtesy of a roof and walls that seem solid enough,
We may cheerfully forget our portion of earth and its location.
While we are alive we may hold each other in three dimensions,
Safe from the wind and, miles down underfoot, the turbulent weed.

130

What shadows we cast, what infirmities and endurance,
What ghosts we send stumbling up ivory keys in deserted rooms
Or sobbing from scenes of defeat too shameful to be remembered,
What touch implanted carelessly or with fondness on skin and stem
Which hold their parley with oblivion and the encircling air
Can so establish the certainty of our distinctiveness
As these can time's hunger? None, I think.

Dug buttons and plates

The hill is on the move, grass to be scraped
Again from cobbles, bridles where they lay
Now dug from inches under, shirts leaving
Their skeletons of buttons, hostages
To contours only perceptibly the same.

Crouching with trowels we are moved by these
And by the swallows and blue bridges of
A commonplace mosaic, lost fragments
On which again the leaves and shoots might steam
Did not the blackened edges interrupt.

All the dead meals dwindle to their seeds,
Cuffs unfastened and rolled back for the heat,
The spade working not at random but in rows,
Sweat wiped on forearms and the soil lying
Choiceless, uneager, for what it will receive.

These buttons will not grow. The shape-echo
Lives only backwards, to hands unbuttoning,
The act forgotten, pearl and bone sucked thin.
But come, let us gather them for this reminder:
The drill of seeds, the hill coming down.

Evening signs at Gallt-y-Ceiliog

Why here? Have we stopped pretending not to notice?
Glance up to the window: something has just disappeared.
Try to read, and find it clamouring for attention.

The house is establishing its relations with the hill,
Its corners not its sides at compass points,
The hill edging it out into the sun.

The evening chaffinch scours for basking grubs.
The long-shadowed flock squeeze their tattoos of dung
Like dropped jewels pattering on the gravel.

What does the house know, patient of all its creatures?
Patient of bird and sheep and the small movements
Of uncollected insects and the first bat?

It must be the hill's secret, older than the stones
Which make the spaces we furnish with our laughter
And chill the natural warmth of turf and spray.

The chairs are angled for conversation like
A stage set. A hand writes, detached and horrible.
One more bottle and the mountain will be level!

Why here? Is it something about to come or to go?
The house knows nothing, neither does the hill.
The creatures walk in their created shadows

Noiseless as the burning tread to the west of the sun
Returning from its career as a minor god,
Parting the sea, coming at last to land.

Why here? The meeting-place of all the made
And unmade, is it, a point of old discomfort?
The signs are upon us, friends. We've no roots here.

In the room

A leg walked into a room.
A grubby plaster assisted
The bending of the knee.

A hand was seen closing a door
Or bunched over an eggcup,
Wild grasses and a smudge of harebell.

A foot offered itself for inspection
Beside an empty sandal. The long nail
Curled slowly away from the scissors.

For a moment the mirror contained a face
And the face looked back at itself,
Incurious but content, as at the first chapter
Of a book read for the second time.

Boundaries

Trees have come up as far as they can
And stand about uncertainly.
Beyond the thistles of the last field
A stream rises, and a lane links
The few farms.

Maps show the contours of the clays
And fields the justice done to heirs.
Down in the village the stream is boastful
Though it does nothing much up here.
You can walk across it.

Boundaries are what link us, surely,
When neighbours turn together from barren
Pasture, when new walls remember
The passing of patriarchs, the drying
Of shared waters.

As trees send saplings to the valley
And all the lanes wind down again,
As the sun rises and sets, creating
New shadows from the same stone,
We are all one.

Within the exact boundaries of
Our skins, of which one inch beyond
Is Nomad's Lodge, the shivering crevice,
We create friend, daughter, lover.
The map converges.

Falling

Signs of the apportioned
Unburdening earth:
Air's negative
Of slow stalk
Massed above it,
Collapse of blossom,
Drift of clocks.

So we go down,
Agreeable to the earth
Or sprawled on its skin,

133

Restless and fertile
As these spores and dust,
Though weight keeps us
Jogging and smiling.

An enemy plays
With all our secrets,
Sneezing clouds
And fruit spillage,
Precarious traffic
Of the atmosphere
Aching to be still.

Your hand in mine
Loosened on the gradient
As the valley rises
Moves to the dance
Of the leaf's spin
And the seed's arc
And my hand knows it.

Fingers part
As the path winds down.
Careless and obstinate
The grasses lodge
In long-lived trees,
In old roofs,
Wherever they fall.

And I am happy
If you are happy:
The slow-paced
Heavy on his heels
And the clown windmill
Taking a tumble.
Both of us falling.

Sleeping out at Gallt-y-Ceiliog

Something, perhaps an idea, is again eluding me.
It belongs nowhere in particular but might
At any moment appear and surprise me.

It's not part of the usual epiphanies.
It has no colour, or even night-colour, since

134

Lying awake half the night will not fix it.

The trees are alive, the candle flame gusty
And flattened. We lie in our quilted chrysalises
With still heads, like ancient funeral masks.

The moon at our backs rises over the mountains:
An understudy, practising with silent lips,
Sharing the sky with one star above the holly tree.

Nothing is spoken. The precise text of leaf
And crag is not known, or has been quite forgotten.
We're happy with what is offered, like visitors.

Perhaps after all there is nothing to remember
But this simplicity. The grass is grey
At dawn. It is the earth awakes, not I.

Morning

Again the curlew rehearses
His rising liripoop
And the shepherd walks up there
In the shadow of the early sun.

Here is the gate which still
Is icy-cold to the touch
With memories of all mornings
In a short share of time.

These long low whistles
Stroking the humped hills
Are like old spells for waking
The unbroken light.

Now a celebrant cock
With fantasies for news
Locates a distant farm
With a strangled dignity.

A hand on a gate is enough
To thrill through to the bone
With love for such strange sounds
And for a still sleeping house.

Ear, eye and hand
At once precise and blurred.

Dew handprints on iron.
The valley filled with mist.

Walking below Carn Guwch

It's going fast. Old roads
Are green again and gates
Tied up. The little church
Shares its field with a blind
Congregation of straggling
Mushrooms. Below, the river
Bends as we expect it
To, attended by curlews
That no map needs to show.

It's going fast and we
Will never find it once
It's gone. Not in stone
Or surprising photographs,
Not in handwriting
Or careful recipes.
Far from our sealed diseases
We sense it in the river
And the sadness of the curlews.

It's going fast. Somehow
It rises on the wind,
A metamorphosis
Of an idea pursued
Until it took quick fright.
The bodies of the children
Are budding, an old response
Which says: It's our world now
And going on forever.

Mushrooms

Elusive to our spells, these chambers
Tented in grass: we stoop and plod
About the church insanely, like penitents.

White and soft as conjurors' gloves,
Edging like eggs or ears out

Of the field's moist green table.

Wedded with fine hairs to a mystery
They part from when tugged like a plaster,
The thumb stump delicately clogged with soil.

Frightening, the exuded tips and domes!
But still we search and pick, our baskets
Smelling fragrantly of underground caverns.

It's as though if we left them they would bud
Into faces and not, as we know, grow skirts
Which drop to a black lace as the air melts them.

Nant Gwrtheyrn

Clouds accumulate, darkening
The worn face of the mountain. The striped
Cry of the oyster-catcher cuts
The sky. Impossible to join the spaces.

One mass against another. Frail
Sounds falling like ribbons or wounds.
Bits creeping, vegetation,
Distraction under the small rain.

The sisters clump up the Nant in boots,
Damp hair close to the forehead, sorrel
In warm folds of the palm, feathers
And granite sugar, so far ahead.

One lingers on the path, smooth grass
Where sheep have nibbled. The blue husk
Of a tiger beetle cradled there
Is spiritless, an Egyptian relic.

It is borne up the valley, joining
One thing with another. The day
Lightens. Clouds break up the sky.
Jerseys are tied around the waist.

The spaces grow between them, dislinked
On the gradient, frowning and looking
Back. The battered sky opens.
The treasures slip from opening fingers.

Voice and eyes

Pleased at an unknown bird,
A custom or a trade,
As for a moment the voice
Falters and the hands
Are masterful, or eyes
Move upwards to the mountain
And conversation stops.

Quiet when listening,
Or at a familiar task,
As in a wood a voice
Calls, a shape among
The leaves, or eyes
Stray over the bushes
Sprung with the weight of bees.

Alone and conscious of it,
Or waiting to be met,
As from the cliff a voice
Returns upon itself
In laughter, or eyes
Look down the lane at nightfall
For the eyes coming up.

Sea and mountain

Up and down confounds
The globe's hydraulic hunger
Whose brimming tide would run
From pole to wrinkled pole
And find no crawling margins
Where the pendulum breeds
Our ancestors to whom
A gradient is a challenge,
The developing eye relieved
From horror of horizons
Endlessly the same,
A liquid plain
Windless, unspiriting,
Unblinking solitude
And a blank weight of sky.

Up and down confirms
The three dimensions of
The map's hypothesis
As, strap loosened at nape,
The eyes sweep out through tubes
From fresh heights that delight
Them with hills plucked up
And tumbling farms that dare
To cling to the deep folds
Of a surface that might subside
But for the attentions of
Our god who charts small routes
Of time and fruit for the bee,
For the noisy bee and for us
Spinning in his palm.

Fire on the beach

The wrinkled web between
The thumb and finger
Is where hands meet,
Lizard hinge that makes
A magnet of the skull
And the heart race.

Such diplomacy
Can scarcely guard us
From greater intimacy,
Palm containing palm
Lifted slightly like
A letter guessed for weight.

Beacon to no ships
Its purpose is to burn
All that will burn,
Consuming every plank
And furred splinter,
Raising tar to a froth.

We stagger round it
In a comfortable stupor,
Raking the tideline
For the unlikeliest offerings:

Nets, dolls, feathers,
Great wigs of weed.

Now it cracks pebbles like eggs
Where once with cautious hand
We held out only what
The flame could bear to touch,
Thin stuff, stripped by the sea
But dry enough to catch.

Caer Arianrhod

A village in the sea! The map says that
Tradition says so, barely casting doubt
On the gaze and gossip of those generations
For whom a map could never end at the shore
Where livelihood begins, that salt harvest
To be shared with busts of seals who come to dine
Alone, like emperors, in the black waves.
Or with ghosts that the sea claimed from time to time
As at low tide upon a summer's night
A homeward boy tugging his skiff across
The calmed surface saw lights and shapes down there
Like faces of strangers in doorways looking out
Through unremembered evenings, and not a cry
To break the silence of the flood but the small
Pirate clink of the rowlocks at the pull of the oars
And the boat's terrified speed over the roof of the sea.

Tides

It's time to go, but still we sit
Lingering in our summer
Like idle fingers,
Like fingers in the sand.

Or like a tiny snail that moves
Beneath a gravelly pool,
Taking its life to travel,
Taking between the tides.

Down and up

1

More roots bared this year,
Turf-iced wedges of cliff
And caravaneering fox-gloves
In ugly slumps

Sheared off by the beast,
Struck down by arched gallons
No machine could weigh,
Too slight for maps.

The coast will never alter
While we watch it, though
Tides creep up like grannies
Silent and grinning.

Each day we stand defiant
By our reduced worlds.
The prints and slithering castles
Alike blur.

The moat is filled, the bridge
And ramparts undermined,
Loose and lapped again
The seaweed dado.

Shells although vacated
Regain their absolute form,
Little dentated genitals,
Ceramic trumpets.

Creatures so suspended
That their third dimension
Brings no laboured breathing,
No fifth-floor stomach.

A depth of placid matter,
Of anonymous straggling motes,
A drifting perpetual stock
Of cold grey.

Inquisitive as we are
We somehow fear these salt
Acres our tears and blood
Call cater-cousin

141

For though its skin shrinks
At motions of the air,
Slopping and turning about
With a useful precision

And though it finds a constant
Level which is the zero
Of all our measurement
Of earth's heights

It is mindless non-memory,
A trap for vain actors
Who have never finished rehearsing
Disobedient dreams.

It is a private roar of applause
For their stupefied silences.
It is shapelessness, the world
Beginning to dissolve.

2

What can climb walls as we do,
Send messages from chimneys,
Ragged like the trumpet's sound
Heard in half-light?

We shoo it from its sown brothers,
Running with hoes and shouts
Along the straight rows
Like pole-vaulters

As though it would die of shame,
Wither away or creep
With little lurches like
The copper frogs

Who visit the damp shade
Of a half-neglected plot
That is trying hard to remember
It was once a meadow.

Whether clustering to broad spears
Or curling blanched under stones,
Neighbour of the sleeping worm
Or ruffling wind

Whether free to colour a field
With its frail stubble, or falling

In swatches to the metal moons
Of tea-time mowers

It tells us that something will last
For a while at least, admitted
Slowly in the course of time,
Crowding the doorways

Where it has long wilted
Or whispered, springing to attention
With an air of faithful service,
Disciplined to the tread.

The graves will come alive
And pavements sprout, mallets
And hoops will disappear
In fright-wig lawns:

A pardonable licence,
Its single form of art,
A far-off future event
We may not book for.

Don't think it grows only here,
Where the long local skulls
Bare their fluted teeth
At nothing much.

It is waiting for you too.
It is down there waiting,
And will not care whether
You notice or not.

Walk proudly, guardedly.
Much climbing will not
Particularly leave it behind.
The flags are furled.

   3
Like dear surfaces in the
Dismayed third quarter of
Our lives, or like smiles
In crowded rooms.

Flapping ghosts struggling
From quotidian prisons,
From treacherous dead branches
Or hotel linen.

Shapes that made us wary
When habit drew the curtains
Or threw one leg across
Another leg.

We wake to trees of fire
That cracking windows frame
But do not isolate,
Bringing them nearer.

Walking on wet timbers
With attuned nostrils later,
Something moves in the shell,
A smouldering horror.

A night sound sailing
From leaf to leaf to leaf
The whole length of a wood
Has something of it.

In legend it was trapped
And yet released by flame,
The burning boughs it takes
A lifetime to find.

Halfway up a mountain
Where trees of any kind
Are notably infrequent,
We give up the search.

For the squabblers in the oaks
Are too like people we know
Accusing each other of being
The immovious one.

From splotched feathers or
Nude spilled children
We turn away with a mental
Grimaldi grimace.

Worms delivered in walls
And frequent messages
In Viennese cadences
Merely delight us.

There must be some good reason
For this ascription of spirit
To such a woundable form,
Such creaturely noises.

Perhaps it is the rising above
The topmost bulk of leaves
Effortlessly. As we
So wish to do.

4

We trust nothing now,
As if living against
The hour of an awakening
When bonds embarrass.

And there is nothing to say
That may not prove a burden
Equal to undying vows
Or last instructions.

By one effort of will
Like our first steps across
The million stitches of Persia,
Its pink and green,

Like our first arch
And calculating salute
To his suffering servants,
Trapped like us

Though with a lurking power
To thrust in our unsuspecting
Hands the simple secret
That will undo him

We may still placate a host
Who is otherwise bored with us,
May still arrest the hand
Reaching for the blade.

How unlucky to have fallen
Into his clutches and not
Remained at large, composed
Of what defeats him!

The old desire, though, to be rid
Of his hydraulics, seizures
And yards of inching sludge
Gives us these joys

Compounded of large illusion
And sheer absentmindedness, when
The astonishing zoetrope gull
Alights on a furrow

As if to bless the filthy
And prolonged enactment
Of our contract with the world.
To the last clause,

Turns a perfect head
Half in suspicion, half
In peaceful acknowledgement
Of our mutual plight

And then takes off again,
Lifting in the pure element,
Large, fragile as china,
But purposeful

Till it is beyond sight.
And with it for a moment
We too climb up and up.
And up. And up.

V

The Most Difficult Position

(1974)

The most difficult position

– Wer mit dem Leben spielt,
Kommt nie zurecht;
Wer sich nicht selbst befiehlt,
Bleibt immer ein Knecht.

(If life for you is just a role,
You'll not succeed, no never;
But once you lose your self-control,
You'll be a slave for ever.)

Goethe

1 *Staunton prologises*

(Spring, 1858)

Now mind those papers with your pretty foot!
They may not seem in order, but they are:
The order of the mind at least, the mind
That stacks the evidence with faultless art.
Dead king. Wicked uncle. Mad prince. Queen
Unusually weak, ambiguous.
I speak now of the Bard. The trick's the same:
To link the salient facts organically.
You see my labours at their deepest here,
With analogues from Scandinavian myth
And penny fables. I'm too proud to tread
The pitons of the frozen commentators?
Fair charge, not true. They're harbingers, not rivals.
I map what they surmised and at a stroke
I free the ice-bound glacier of their text
Till all is moving river, warm and full.
That's Theobald you tread on, Whiter you clutch
As though to dub me silent to your service!
My dear, I'm sorry. Something in your look
Speaks of a small offence, and yet you smile
Despite yourself. I like to talk to you,
Rare visitor, as Gertrude will not talk,
Nor talked to Theobald or Whiter neither,
Whom you may now put down. He cost me much
To find. What is it, dear? Is that the time?
Well, well, I see. Is dinner cold? I'm sorry.
A fruitful morning swollen to a day
And like to drop untasted. I've worked well

149

But work's a tyrant. My edition grows
An ogre's task, eating up time and life;
Truth's straws for spinning into gold,
An ogre's task without the lucky ring,
Though you, dear, are my ring, and golden too
To help me shift the straws, defeat the ogre.
   I saw you in the garden through the window
Reaching for roses. You sustain my labours
As the bright stream an oak that arches over.
Thought in your presence is a growing silence
That feeds invisibly upon my love.
(Pass me my cigars: you will not mind?
Thank you. It helps me to unwind my thoughts.)
I have been thinking for an hour on end
About the guilt (or innocence) of Gertrude,
Who had no time for roses, and was weak.
Strange that the ivory there, the red and white,
How strange that in her realm of four and sixty
Small distinct dominions the queen
Is most powerful! Did Shakespeare play the game?
Undoubtedly. And missed his dinner too,
Writing his high and witty heroines
Whose power lay in their tongues. (Another match:
The leaf is unwilling to admit the fire.
Sit down, too, and be patient. I will come
To sift the prandial leavings soon enough.)
   Time tells all, backwards as well as forwards,
Turns stage to altar and the luscious hybrid,
Static in crystal vases, to a nomad;
Chequered applewood and trailing hems
To our nude parents; and the ivory *vierge*
There by your elbow to a Persian *firz*,
Proud Amazon to greybeard counsellor.
When my edition's done, I may find time
To write a paper on the piece's role,
Its history and curious change of sex.
Yes, it would please me to explore the case,
But time's my tyrant, as you know, my dear.
If I could queen my hours into years!
I have my public and my publishers
Hot on my neck; the endless correspondence,
Friendly analysis of my past games
With Anderssen (the gross presumption of it!),

150

Offers to play, requests for information,
The search for books; the endless annotation,
Feeding the *Illustrated London News*,
My all-devouring column; queries from Routledge,
Hints of the advance and long delay.
It never stops. Look at this letter here.
It came this morning. No, you didn't see it.
You had that letter from your Indian cousin
If you remember. The New Orleans Chess Club,
I quote: 'The undersigned committee has
The honour to invite you to our city
And there meet Mr Morphy in a chess match.'
(Do they think that I could take the boat tomorrow?)
'We see no valid reason why an exercise
So intellectual and ennobling is
Excluded from the generous rivalry
Found between the Old World and the New
In every branch of human industry.'
(Pompous asses!) 'It unfortunately happens
That serious family affairs prevent
Mr Morphy from entertaining, for the present,
The thought of visiting Europe.' (Mummy won't let him!)
'The amount of the stakes, on either side, to be
Five thousand dollars.' Five thousand dollars?
Really, my dear, it is intolerable.
Does the boy think that life all over Europe
Can grind to a halt merely to give him the pleasure
Of sitting and facing his elders and betters over
A lilliputian army of carved ivory?
　　You smile, do you? Am I unreasonable?
You think I should be gracious and consent?
That I am world champion and can afford to?
Am I world champion, then? Am I indeed?
Don't you imagine that Mrs Anderssen
Is saying just the same today to him
And over the very same letter? Oh yes, I know
That I was out of practice when he beat me,
The grinning schoolmaster from frozen Breslau!
'Poor Staunton was out of practice.' It was a mistake
And I shall not repeat it. I am a scholar
And my work comes first. Five thousand dollars!
Someone somewhere hopes to make some money!
Morphy's games are very pretty but

They will not bear the test of analysing.
(My cigar is out again.) He's just a child!
A child beginning a career of conquest!
More like Barnum and Bailey's three-ringed circus
With General Tom Thumb and other wonders.
What does the drum beat and the billboard say?
That Morphy played in the cradle; scorned his books,
Guessing the gambits as Newton knew his Euclid,
By intuition; beat Löwenthal at thirteen
And Paulsen in New York last year; recites
Unfalteringly from his memory
The entire Civil Code of Louisiana,
And what not else? With such politeness too,
The newsmen marvelling: 'Mr Paulsen never
Makes an oversight; I sometimes do.'
A circus! Am I to put on greasepaint then
And tumble for the eager multitude?
Would you like me to? You think it important?
You see me as your valiant Perceval?
    Important? My dear, consider. Please don't mistake me.
The game of chess is supremely unimportant:
As, shall we say, a trellis of climbing roses
Watered and cut by a sweet and gloveless lady
(Now, now! Don't hide it! Give me your tender scratches
So I may make a handy sandwich of them.
There, hidden in mine and healed by love!
I thrive upon such spiritual dining).
The game of chess is unimportant as
The exercise of dogs or whisker-wax,
Hot meat brought level in with steady wrists,
A letter from a cousin in Jodhpur
With talk of franchise and a sale-of-work.
You see? It neither does nor does not matter.
A rose is beautiful, the meat gets cold
Or eaten, the cousin relieves her loneliness,
The dogs are healthy. So is my moustache.
Thus the queen moves this way or that way, thus
She is sacrificed, no more or less a queen
Than that in stone and sepia, two removes
From the banality, work of the box
And chemicals and ineffable loyalty
Of the Jodhpur cousin. Don't take away your hand!
I'm not teasing. It's true. Don't you see?

152

I love it. It's delightful and it's moral.
Its mimic battles are engaged upon
For neither prize nor honour. It's a game
For Aristotle not for Perceval
So how should it be used for a career?
   I'll show you what I mean. We'll play together,
You and I, as lovers used to do
In Europe's maytime. Push the board between us.
It's white and red, a contest like the roses.
I'll give you knight and rook, and you begin.
Every little lathing sings of the stage
Now, doesn't it? You see the fascination.
The happy warrior pops out like a sparrow
Quick under the blossoming may and steady,
His head small and alert upon its ruff.
There on the lawn, you see one? He's pretending
The philopluvial bisexuals can
Escape him, one eye out for the dangerous rival.
A page or two, attendant on the king?
Slight and foppish? Yes, but watch that worm!
The throat moves. A glove or fan's adjusted.
Some grand theme is broached. Do you hear the words?
No matter. The scene changes. Sir Something's bold
To make a broil, raise an old quarrel or
Concoct an accusation of a sort.
Familiar story. Anything will do.
Sir Other's at him, and the pages freeze,
Locked face to face. The Sirs are at a distance
But engaged. Is it the Quiet Game?
You have me waiting. Thorns' stigmata hover
Above the board. I'm in my heaven now.
It's an age-old theatre that nature knows
And mounts each year not thinking of expense.
Infinite shapes! Tautologies of flowers!
Is it the Quiet Game? You like the Scotch.
I'd wager for the Scotch, a safe good game.
Your eye is sparkling, though. You know how custom
Stales. In moves your bishop like a cruet!
Down to Knight Five: that gives it flavour, just
A taste of risk. But can you see it through?
I never like to play this opening
Named for the sage advice of Ruy Lopez
In his *Libro del Arte del Juego del Axedres.*

153

Too much decisiveness too early here
And larger birds, their beaks festooned with worms,
May fly to freedom from their ravening.
But still, you see the life of the thing. My point
Is that it *is* like life, supremely so,
And all the world's a stage. The entrances
And exits finely done. Above all, exits!
Bishops arraign the weak Plantagenet,
The queen has vigorous notions of her own,
The old knight blusters, humoured by a boy
Who is not ignorant of the eighth square.
Plantagenet retires into his castle,
The queen has executions to arrange,
The knight must go. Yes, going out is all.
So many ways of going, many deaths.
The beak stabs suddenly like this, my dear,
And look: I have your pawn here in my hand,
Bald as a baby and as helpless, too.
As helpless as a worm. So many ways:
The boast, the whimper and the silent prayer,
The brute resistance and the daring feint,
The outraged protest and the resignation,
Self-slaughter, sui-mate, the noble gesture.
So many ways, and Shakespeare knew them all.
I understand it, or at least I try to.
I've mastered what I can. I am respected.
It is the game I love and not success.
Five years ago I challenged any comer
And no one came, not even Anderssen.
Now comes this boy, this Morphy. Shall I wait
On him? I think not. Shall I jump to the challenge
Of a boy with the face of a young girl in her teens?
I decline. I have a significant position.
I am Howard Staunton. I believe that I am happy.
The sun is low and strikes across the lawn
As the birds begin to sing. One crimson petal
Falls from your excellent roses. Your move, my dear.

2 *Morphy persists*

(Summer and Autumn, 1858)

Mother, you'll think I've not written before because I forgot to
Or maybe because in the end I only too well remember

154

Your tears at the quayside, your tears and your casual hurt
   exhortations,
Your tears at my firm uncancelled intention, your tears at my silence.
Yes, I remember it all and it seemed a fitting departure
For one who had vowed to defy such an elusive opponent.
Tears cover many regrets and emotion's a difficult subject,
Likely, I think, to defeat all but the most assiduous,
Likely to daunt any student with its impossible answers
To all the unknown questions. Ascribe a motive to weeping!
Might as well go to the Mississippi for a true confession
Or rifle the desert for clues to long-lost extravagant feelings.
Moisture flies up the offered cheek and the ducts receive it,
Kisses stagger back through the no-man's-land of volition
Quite unhurt, though dazed and shocked and totally useless.
The *Arabia* hoots for the very last time and the hawsers are slackened.
There in the mind the dubious orders, checked and rechecked,
Yield not the slightest clue towards their interpretation.
Mother, I ask you: just what do you think you are losing?
Is it a dutiful son, or is it the wealthy attorney
You hoped perhaps I'd become if I persevered with my studies?
Have you examined the terms of that familiar equation?
Where is the unknown factor, the one that you've cancelled out?
Wouldn't success in itself give a more satisfactory answer?
Isn't it just the factor that all the terms contrive to
Shape to some kind of formulation, however clumsy?
Wouldn't success in this way be a relative sort of objective?
Not as a matter of pride, and certainly not of money,
But simply all by itself, being the common factor?
Well, neither is wholly true nor wholly false: I assert
Over the black and the white the exact ascendance of greyness.
That is something I fear they don't understand in New Orleans
Where questions of fact with the guns hang silently over the fireplace
And motive is whispered in fields or assassinated in ballrooms,
And pride is assigned to success, and weakness of course to failure
(Try telling Uncle Ernest to take a pride in failure!).
Can you honestly say that this disturbs and dismays you?
Mother, I ask you again: what do you think you are losing?
Is it my loss you fear, or might it be *my* losing?
If it were *that* I should smile, for it seems a fitting emotion
For one who has vowed to defy such a majestic opponent.
But, as I say, I find emotion a difficult subject.
That is of course my weakness, but weakness may lead to success,
For only a firm resolve and a singleness of purpose

Keep us applied to the matter in hand where feeling is stranger
And the mind runs even and smooth, oiled in a beautiful silence.
Here in England, chess takes its proper place as a pastime.
It is not such a solemn affair, and yet, to be sure, it is serious.
Mother, I fear you could not understand the way it is taken,
Though sometimes when you sit at the piano I think you must know,
But if you know, you are silent, and silent most in talking:
There are some desperate silences when you're engaged in talking!
Hell. This looks like being another one of those letters
In which I say too much, – which I never get round to sending.
It's not so much a case of distance lending enchantment,
Licence to speak one's mind while the magic spell's unbroken;
Simply that such a perspective inclines one to see things clearly.
So must all travellers feel getting down at their end of their journey.
   For me, as you know, the event had a strange and significant
   meaning,
Liverpool sighted in patchy fog, June the twenty-first,
The *Arabia* docking at noon on the eve of my coming-of-age.
Newspapermen were not slow, I'm afraid, to remark on the date:
Did my parents object before, and was that the only reason
Why previously I had seemed unwilling to make the journey?
Facts, facts. What could I say? *Did* you give your consent?
I have to admit to myself that I really can't remember.
To the newspapermen I admitted the name of my hotel only,
Tired as I was and endlessly probed by their fatuous questions:
How many shirts did I have? Would I visit the opera?
That seventeenth move in my game in November with Paulsen,
Did I remember? Of course. The sacrifice of the queen.
I offered a clear and simple exchange of my queen for his bishop.
Paulsen was sure at the outset that it was a trap, cunning but
Obvious in a way, not one to easily fall for.
'Paulsen had worked out the combinations for six moves ahead, sir,
Six moves ahead! Taking an hour, and all the spectators
Excited and restless. An hour of thinking, and still couldn't see it.
Did he think you were mad, sir? He sat and he sat and he wondered
And took your queen. And the crowd gasped! And you said nothing.
Paulsen retired from the game at the end of eleven moves,
Eleven incredible moves ahead. Can you say, Mr Morphy,
What went on in your mind? Did you know? Had you worked it all
   out?
Or was it simply a stroke of luck, a leap in the darkness?'
   Silly to say that there's nothing to say, but it's true, there isn't.
All of us live in the dark, and many decline to leap

156

And so I knew that Paulsen would find it a deal of trouble.
Would it make news? I'd no idea, but I hoped it wouldn't.
News isn't really news but a long continuing process,
Daily refinement of what the readers have learned to expect.
Mine I have kept to the last, though you won't be thrilled to hear it.
Perhaps it won't absolutely displease you. It fills the paper,
And what is there else to do but to come to the end of the page,
The period which our pen proposes, or else turn over
To find that the sick white blank of the other side awaits us?
For pride is assigned to success, and weakness of course to failure,
And silence (how can we doubt it?) has nothing to do with feeling.
No, mother, I sign off here, and say: I have written to Staunton,
Written again to Staunton in the friendliest possible terms.
Can you in honesty say that this disturbs and dismays you?
How can it do that? No, I think you must wish me success,
But don't imagine it's pride that leads me on to the conquest.
No one who saw me now could ever think that it was.

*   *   *

No letters from home as yet, from you, or Helen, or Ernest,
But then there's nothing from Charles, and he would certainly write,
So I don't say this to rebuke but to damn the Atlantic packet
And to show how sick I am of the praise and the pearls and the parties.
Last night I heard Miss Louisa Pyne at the Philharmonic
In a pretty duet from the *Freischütz* before the Queen and Prince
   Consort:
Such idleness, such automatic applause before such beauty!
The English are superb, superb in their lack of thinking.
Quite early in the evening the gas went low and nearly
Disturbed the spectators' sleep with a fear of being left in the darkness,
Small drama, I know, but a real one, this fear of being left in the
   darkness.
Real like the fear of silence, the fear of the empty page.
To date I have written two, no three, plain letters to Staunton,
Three plain letters of challenge and always the same:
I will play you, he says, in September, in September or else in October.
I need just a few more weeks to brush up my openings and endings.
I will play you, he says, in October, in October or else in November.
   The curtain is rising for ever and the stage is always empty,
The rooms are impeccably dusted, the rooms with the lilies and roses,
The rooms that look out on the front, the rooms above Piccadilly,
The rooms in the feminine capital, the rooms of the Second Empire
(All good Americans when they die end up in Paris!),

157

The rooms all over Europe whose doors are incessantly opening,
Inviting the guest to flip open the well-filled silver inkwell,
To dip and relate with unaccustomed pen his travels.
All over Europe from room to room and always the same:
The doors are opening freely and the curtain is rising,
The sofas and chairs are placed just so, and the roses and lilies,
All the forwarded messages, cables and invitations,
And the little escritoire – there, in the right-hand corner!
Inviting the guest to record a transient name on the blotter,
Faint and reversed as the dreams he will dream on the single pillow.
Where is the action? Where is the speech and magnificent lighting?
Knuckles are still in repose at the end of my cuffs like tree-roots,
Springs of expensive clocks dilate in their glittering coils,
Visitors come and go on matters of no importance
And the curtain is rising for ever and the stage is always empty.

*   *   *

That was a month ago already, and the letter's still with me.
Letters not sent assume a life of their own like monsters:
A sudden slow stare right into the gilt frame of the spirit
When only the eyes are seen but you know they belong to a stranger
And the memory can't be dispelled; it horribly lingers for ever.
The mouth is gaping open, the sickening flap unsealed.
You can't escape that singular moment of recognition:
Turn on the polished heel, fold back the unfolded paper,
But ever the haunting vision hovers over your shoulder,
Something that you created and will not let you ignore it,
A poor disfigured creature full of immortal longings,
A sort of ideal maimed by the uncontrolling hand,
A life that only endures as a vestige of what was intended.
Are we the same as we were, and will that be always the same?
My letter begins with rebukes, but that was a month ago,
A sloughed-off self in a limbo of lonely introspection.
That was already a month ago, and the letter's still with me.
I found it just now in the drawer with my socks in the hotel bedroom
And thought about what you had said of the praise and the girls and
    the parties,
And all my anger was gone when I came to the matter in hand.
At a distance all quarrels diminish and tend to resolve themselves into
A hard plain conglomeration of fact like a lawsuit.
But what is the law to say of the distance of space and time?
The law has nothing to do with time, as not of its making.
The law has nothing to do with space, for that it may break.

158

I felt today the first futility of the challenge
And all the sad impurities of life rose up together
As if to seize for themselves a prize that was not awarded,
And whiskered faces cheered, and no one was any the wiser.
   Can you imagine an afternoon in the north of England
In a flat damp August, sticky enough, but more dirty than sticky,
Walking across the Queen's College, Birmingham's, brown narrow
      lawns?
On one side your true representative of modern American manners,
On the other the large *doyen* of large British Chess, Mr Staunton,
And as umpire Lord Lyttelton trotting, perspiring a little,
Blotting his face with a large chequered kerchief covered with pawns?
No one would try to keep the peace between two such as
Staunton and I seemed to be on that gloomy and brief occasion,
Only a man who had nothing to offer, and he had nothing.
'Howard?' he kept on saying, in a tone of interrogation
As close as it could get to an undemanding statement:
'Howard?' But Staunton, in the blandest possible manner,
Pausing only to lift a fading rose with one finger,
Talked without saying a thing, talked without making an answer,
Talked in a general way, smiled and was utterly charming.
'I will play you,' he said, 'in September, in September or else in
      October:
I need just a few more weeks to be clear of my other affairs,
Affairs of the greatest importance, I'm sure you understand.
What a delightful game! Delightful and scientific!
Scientific and moral, too, most moral of hobbies!'
   So it went on, and he forced me to feel the shame of persistence,
The squirming abject shame of inflicting myself upon him,
Taking his time and trying to hold him down to a promise;
Forced upon me the role of callow importuner
Seizing my chance to exploit a gentleman's casual interest,
Working with careful words and casual professional phrases
To lure him to some intense and somehow dangerous tourney;
Forced upon me the role of the eager smooth-talking gambler,
Cheeky at roadside inn or on Mississippi steamer;
Forced me to nod insanely at his procrastination:
'I will play you,' he said, 'in October, in October or else in November.'
What could I say? I felt I had somehow yielded a move for
Though in England chess takes its proper place as a pastime,
Though it is not such a solemn affair, it has its own logic,

And none in its deadly motions more practised than Howard
    Staunton,
Motions of serpentine skill and brazen prevarication,
Motions that know how they can afford to be lazily charming.
Lyttelton did his best, but his best was quite sadly useless:
November is merely a dream. The summer will fly like a winner,
Turf be untrodden, the crowds dispersed to their occupations.
Nothing can season the shocking taste of his blank refusal,
Nothing awaken him from his dream of victorious inaction,
Nothing disturb the unruffled surface of condescension,
The idle furloughs and barracks of a giant reputation,
The imperious posture of one who's unwilling to risk defeat.
I know it. And yet I hope. Hope against hope that sometime
The proud façade will crack, and light flood into the building.
But the curtain is rising for ever and the stage is always empty.

*   *   *

To have no desires; worse, to have a desire for desires,
Is the death of the soul in its terrible grip of desiring to please.
Not the ideal, the burning ambition or even a hunger
For the trivial flush of content, the certain fact of fulfilment,
Simply the struggle to act one's part with the secret knowledge
That *this* is how it must be and nobody else may gainsay you.
How can I keep some sense of faith in my own objectives?
No one to trust, no one, and least of all the dragon
Roaring slightly again with his still-smouldering breath,
Saying at first he would only play in consultation,
Prowling about the tournament hall like a proud head-waiter,
Ready to offer advice to anyone he could rally,
Bland as a fighting bishop blessing the last battalion,
Lyttelton in despair, the Birmingham hotels full.
Now he announces his entry as quietly as he is able!
Staunton's decided to enter now that the lists are complete!
What's the idea? Does he want to storm his way through the talent,
Blaming a lucky accident if I manage to stop him,
Hoping I'll fall by chance to the Reverend Henry Salmon,
Hoping one way or another we'll never actually meet?
Credit will have to be given for such an adroit reversal
Coolly and casually made when nobody seemed to be looking!
    One thing is wrong with his plan, though: I shan't be there in
    person.
I wanted a private match, and the tournament doesn't amuse me.
Tomorrow I have proposed eight games without sight of the pieces,

160

Eight games together on Wednesday, sitting away from the tables.
Avery, Kipping and Wills, Rhodes, Carr and Dr Freeman
All have agreed with indecent haste to the blind encounter.
Lyttelton too will play, and the Reverend Henry Salmon.
Then I shall leave for Paris to see what *they* have to offer.
Anderssen will be there and others, perhaps, with manners.
Nothing is left for me here, at least until Birmingham's over.

* * *

The curtain is rising still and the stage is always empty.
Why must we have a will when we don't know how to direct it?
Why must we have above all this dreadful desire for desires?
Where does the impulse come from? Do we acquire it, I wonder?
Or is it a secret alloy in the chain of bleeding that binds us
Fast to our foul perpetual history? Unwilling victims!
That I suppose was what in the first place moved me to study
How men have so arranged their affairs to make some kind of sense:
Power to do what the law allows is the only freedom.
Wriggling cells succumb to these ordered inventions of man, but
What is the law to say of the struggle of space and time?
The law has nothing to do with time, as not of its making.
The law has nothing to do with space, for that it may break.
Only the rules it energises, the rules and the fictions,
And I feel your heart across the sea making do with fictions,
For I sacrificed your strength for the sake of a wretched stalemate.
Some sort of brilliant sacrifice lies behind every challenge,
But to offer Andromeda up as a tasty bait for the dragon
And the dragon to turn up his nose: I can hardly bear to think it.
At Birmingham, Staunton was out in the second round. Retiring
To Richmond to lick his wounds, he used his column to bait me.
It's clear we shall never play, and I will be home by Christmas.
And the *Illustrated London News* and the *New Orleans Delta*,
Even the *Birmingham Post*, will have to make do with fictions,
The fictions of law, the fictions of rules, the fictions of papers,
And the fictions of red and white, the thirty-two little fictions
Which have nothing to do with the heart, for that they may break
And what they break stands apart and watches in space and time
And I have failed you, mother, and cannot bear your look.
I have failed to kill the dragon, though Europe bows down before me.
I have failed to fulfil your strength, though Anderssen smiled in defeat
And deafened Paris suspected another revolution!
I have failed in the field of success, and my pride must give place to my
     weakness,

161

The weakness of wishing too much to engage in the pure world of
  mind,
Flickering light beyond the frowning behind the blindfold,
World where the thought rides on blood, instinctive in the darkness.
And what has the law to say of this fear of being left in the darkness?
What has the law to say of a son and his broken heart?

  3 Staunton epilogises

  (Spring, 1865)

  The desk is piled. Untired and regular
As mercury the level in trunk and stem
Rises, the old engagement, the old trumpets.
No question of anything different ever happening!
Those ducks on the lawn: every May they come
From their slowly moving home to a green slumber,
Heads tucked, dozing obliquely in marital content
Too far for snappishness or love's mirror-tricks
But close enough to have the air of posing
Like frugal boulders in that Kyoto garden
Perry reported, or perhaps a cannon at billiards.
All Nature mating with a *pion coiffe*!
Wasteful, prolific of rejected seeds
So one, the most unlikely, should win through.
And early roses just the same: trustful!
  There will be frost, and you are far from here.
There will be frost, and nothing is the same.
Nothing can last, and everything is different.
I miss you! There's no one else to gather roses
And float them in silver dishes on the table.
Shutters are flapping. The hall is like a ballroom
Polka'd with dust. Strange: you learned your freedom
From your dependence, and that long beautiful boredom
Rose armed from the gradual wreck of a girlhood frolic.
Much too young to be shut up in a tower!
You said I kept too long away from you
And so men do, I think, but it's not right:
The shoots burst from the fragile trellis, all
The buds in wild profusion lean in the air,
Crossed, straggling, heavy, burdened down.
All of us bear our load, but the free spirit
Never forgives the bondage of its peers.
We have no time, alas, for heroes now:
Beneath snug tailoring its fiery hair

162

And plated muscles of a Fuseli angel
Strain to express a quiddity. And you,
Your head full of such antique pictures. My fault.
I should have seen your meaning better, dear.
I should have taken greater care of you.
You and your perfect body were my text
And all its cruces hidden. Now it's too late.
   A life of caring for the insights of
Another man! I sometimes felt, with Pope
And the finest of the early editors,
That the real task lay not in tidying-up
Errors and riddles of the leaden case
But in the niceties of taste and skill,
The signposts to the choicest passages,
Reader to reader. Likewise the pleasure lay
In the approval not the scorn of moves,
And I could well have wished a silent mark
Of exclamation to adorn the Swan
Many and many a time. What can one say?
When I approved, you glowed, or seemed to glow.
Perhaps unspoken pleasure in your graces
Seemed like a deafness where in truth it was
A simple echo of your quietness.
I was there. I heard. And in the end I lost.
   At least I have preserved ascendancy
In the science. Anderssen is broken and
They tell me Morphy's mad now: shouts in the street
And follows no profession. Sues his brother
For the father's fortune. Certainly won't play chess.
Well, well. One might have guessed it, but the cause
Is none too clear. What was the truth of the matter?
Did some kind tutelary spirit lean
From the rococo clouds with ready crown,
Strike Harrwitz down and give him Anderssen,
Whose play afforded shocking evidence
Of being no longer the victor's of '51?
Did we resent his luck and nerve? For my part
I had no particular feelings, retired as I was
From practical chess. How could I risk the stakes
So rashly offered by my generous friends?
I might have played a game or two, *sans façon.*
I even steeled myself to Birmingham
And entered with a show of chivalry:

Morphy refused to play! There one has it.
The tender bloom, forced under glass, must wilt
On contact with the ordinary air.
That *you* would understand, I think, my dear!
Who gave me at the time one long cool stare.
Yet those who would perform *kotoo* before the boy
(And rush to do the same before whoever's
The times' top-sawyer) can't be satisfied
To give him endless *kudos* among themselves
Without the blowing of a penny-trumpet
To call to homage all the sentient world!
Grant the achievement, and the wish to play
David to Europe's grave Goliaths, yet
It was not such a salient episode.
There was a basic failure of the will,
A trust to risk, exploiting combinations.
Eight blindfold games, remembering all the moves?
A piece of rhetoric, the science served
To better purpose by my little handbook,
Bilguer and der Laza much improved,
And read in clubs and cafés everywhere.
    I still have that, and much besides. Or do I?
At night, after some bruxist escapade,
Waking in sweat, I pad down to this study
And stare at the piled desk and all these papers
To which the attached ink is a history
Of a long hunger and fatal miscalculation.
I could be Claudius at prayer! But no,
That's silly. Even a villain has some presence.
Once proud of my pride in what I had achieved,
Now I have only the abject achievement.
Once in love with the harmony of our orbits,
Now I feel only the fierce lack at the centre.
I've risked nothing and everything is lost!
Ah, well. The deadly promptness of the spring
Becomes a kind of welcome remedy.
Its scenery is sufficient. It obeys
The rules. Those ducks, the ostentatious roses,
Even the diligent editor of Shakespeare,
All move in free compulsion to one end
Which though unknown is wholly necessary
And has some joys, I think. Or sometimes does.

VI

The Illusionists

(1980)

Chapter One

The beginning

1

Experience is an easy master,
Easy to stall – though not to fool:
However fast you go, he's faster.
He's there in front of you. Each rule
Is made by him. Relax! For living
On terms like his needs no forgiving.
Once we received with open hands
The *faits accomplis* of our glands,
And that's why no one ever changes:
The choice of being shy or wild
Is forced upon you as a child.
It's something that the womb arranges
(If not the womb, the family –
At least before the age of three).

2

Does mathematics make you weary?
I can't resist a simile
Drawn from an appropriate theory
(Since similes should make you see
What otherwise is just asserted,
So that your judgement is exerted).
The gnomon is a constant: where
L shapes are added to a square
That square remains the same. A Roman
Is always more or less at home,
A Celt is still a Celt at Rome,
And all experience a gnomon.
From character there's no escape:
Experience can't change its shape.

3

And so our life stays in proportion –
Although experience extends
The ways we feel its deft contortion
Of all new means to the old ends:
The Presidential Lunch Companion
Whose hunger rivals the Grand Canyon
(Public, permanent and deep,
A national property, not cheap)

Was once a tot who showed her knickers
To catch an absent father's eye;
Bishops were babies who were shy
(The windy ones turn into vicars);
And those who liked to crawl in dirt
Invent machinery to hurt.

4

Tim as a child was quiet and stable.
He dressed up in his mother's skirts
Or played with flour beneath a table.
He bellowed mildly at his hurts
And sometimes tidied up his messes.
When he was told he formed his s's
Not with a curl but with a bend,
He blushed and promised he would mend.
You'd think that adults would be worried
By children happy on their own,
Who don't know better till they've grown,
But parents sometimes don't seem hurried
To finish work that's half-begun
And remedy an only son.

5

It wasn't very much to sigh at,
Nothing to make a boy complain,
Simply a dozen years of quiet,
Stagnation of the blood and brain.
Nothing there was he ever wanted
That wasn't immediately granted.
Such honeyed treatment has its sting:
He never wanted anything.
No siblings whom he could confide in
Challenged his private universe:
No elder sister like a nurse
With naughty secrets he could hide in,
No younger brother in his care
With whom he had to fight or share.

6

His father wasn't over-reckless.
When gilts were low he kept his head.
Mother inclined to wear a necklace,
Although she cooked and made the bed.
Tim came to learn they were not upper

By things like when they ate their supper.
Yet on that scale they were not low:
A comfortable fact to know.
Treated indeed by his relations
In those pecuniary ways
Which liven dull school holidays
(And, later on, the long vacations)
He felt that money grew for him
If not on trees, then at his whim.

7

At school he could not stand correction.
He found the swimming-bath too cold
And played for truces and protection
By reading Joyce at twelve years old
While chasing round with those much younger
And owning an immodest hunger
For every well-loved master's praise
(Reserving, though, the right to laze).
Later, the need for approbation
Made him excessively polite:
He never disagreed, despite
An urge to shock which sublimation
Converted to a milder trait
Of clamming up when *tête-à-tête*.

8

You know the sort – who treat a question
As though you aimed to catch them out,
As though it gave them indigestion
To be in any sort of doubt,
Who guard the cleavage of their answer
As close as a retired fan-dancer:
Smiles are the flowers of their talk,
Cool and reserved, with lots of stalk.
They do not mean to be mysterious
And haven't very much to hide.
Their silences are due to pride,
The need to seem relaxed and serious
When all the time they're scared as hell
You'll nail them with a *J'en appelle*.

9

The gnomon works. Those layers of living
Accumulate towards the grave.

Our naked selves are unforgiving
As they grow tall and learn to shave,
Are visited by mild afflictions,
Toothache and sex and social fictions,
Carrying keys or diaphragms,
Taking soft drugs or hard exams.
Beneath it all our Shape still trembles,
Unchanged by the absurd disguise
Of what we do to it. Its eyes
Stare dumbly out and it resembles
Nothing so much as a caged beast,
A butchered Banquo at the feast.

10

You'll say this story lacks coherence:
It hasn't got a sense of place,
Tim has no physical appearance.
What are his clothes like? Or his face?
The social background's pretty hazy.
Is it the poet being lazy
Or is it that he doesn't care?
Are there no facts that he can spare?
I must insist the poet retails
Only the goods he wants to stock.
Go to life's warehouse to unlock
That gloomy inventory of details
You need to validate the truth:
Put down the book and hire a sleuth.

11

If you're still with me, here's a label
It's possible to stick on Tim
(Try just a little, if you're able,
To close your eyes and picture him):
You'll find him aged nineteen at Camford
With his rough edges smoothed and chamfered,
Hair lying longer on his skull,
Silent still, but much less dull.
An undergraduate! That's better,
For few of them can seem miscast
When you enquire into their past.
All are free spirits to the letter.
Like workers threatening to strike
Or Chinamen, they're all alike.

12

I tease? Of course, but don't you tend to
Refer to groups and types like these?
And are ashamed? And then pretend to
A quizzical mock journalese?
Pity the foot-loose processed student:
The mind says 'should', but money 'shouldn't',
And then whatever he does well,
Odds on it's something he can't sell.
No wonder in studio or scrimmage,
In Castro beard or ancient car,
With racquet, fur-coat and guitar,
He seeks to fix the witless image
Created for him by the press.
It makes him feel he's a success.

13

Tim wasn't quite like this. I'm sorry
If I misled you, hampered your
Half-hearted chase after your quarry
With such a trivial hackneyed spoor.
The truth is that the hunt dismays me.
I need perspective, but it pays me
To keep a field or two ahead,
A brace of stanzas still unread.
I hear the breathing of the reader
As slow and heavy as a snore
But close, like steps outside a door.
It is a game of follow-my-leader?
And are there prizes in the race?
Charades, perhaps? A paper-chase?

14

Ah, yes. I scatter and you follow.
The scraps are quickly scanned and gone,
Like secret messages spies swallow
Or Christmas bangs with riddles on.
My story's somewhere, don't you doubt it:
How could I keep things up without it?
The many roots, the single trunk;
The separate scratchings of a monk
That slowly lend illumination;
The shifting of one's little stock
When playing patience round the clock;

171

Industrial negotiation:
Most steady purposes bespeak
A sometimes circular technique.

15

Now Tim had left his latest lecture
With notes upon *les Symbolistes*
Idly scrawled as in a deckchair
Upon the outside of a creased
And second letter from his mother
Which asked why he'd ignored the other,
Now sandwiched in his copy of
The Student's ABZ of Love.
Though he was reading Modern Languages
The proper study of mankind
Is – woman. Tutors must not mind,
With such a rival, if work languishes:
Why slave to clear up others' doubt
Of what *their* lives were all about?

16

But still, if art v. life's in question,
A questionable gulf remained,
For youth is open to suggestion,
To literature's ideals enchained.
Frowning, in beads, with sheepish jerkin
(A Hobbit's view of Rupert Birkin)
The shapes that he drank coffee with
Exemplified this forceful myth.
The talk was steamy as a sauna
And hearts were worn upon each sleeve,
Encouraging you to believe
The Grail was just around the corner
In the bewitching shape of grass,
A guru, or a piece of arse.

17

The last, of course, is most enticing:
We want to eat and have our cake
And thus we nibble at the icing,
Politely longing to partake.
Such reticence creates an aura,
A novice out of each adorer
And sacred texts which must be read
(Accounting for Tim's *ABZ*).

He was a victim of convictions
Forced upon Nature's masterpiece
By intimations of decease:
So too we all subscribe to fictions
Written, and published, by our hope
That we'll outlive our envelope.

18

Even the lecture he had been to
Confirmed love's sublimated role.
The lecturer, though he didn't mean to,
Expounded just the rigmarole
To stir a boy's romantic bowels,
Giving the sense of Rimbaud's 'Vowels'.
Alpha to Omega: not odd
The sonnet should end up with God!
It plays with colours like Dumb Crambo,
Contriving to convey a hint
Of the erotic with each tint,
What we expect, perhaps, from Rimbaud.
I'll give a version, somewhat sham
(Since very free), in lipogram.

19

'A: swart as Alabama mammas
Aghast at Arrabal's drama, tar,
A Madagascan sans pajamas,
Black mass, and Sagan's dark *cafard*.
E: perfect teeth, sheets, eggs, tents, cheeses,
Endless Decembers, new deep-freezes.
I: vivid tiling, prickling hips,
Lightning in Spring, pink smiling lips.
U: just cut turf (smug thumbs-up suburb),
Burst thumb (such pus), bush's plump bud,
Sputum (lung's mucus), tumulus, cud,
Fungus, butt's scum, surf's rush, surf's hubbub,
O: ghosts, ohms (off/on), porno book,
Photo-room's glow or God's cool look.'

20

Perhaps I've lost you here. Well, never
Mind. If it really made you blench
At least give marks to the endeavour
And hurry quickly to the French.
You'll see then what I thought essential,

173

Considering the low potential
Of closely rhymed tetrameters.
The rest is silly, but it serves.
From head to tail a girl's suggested:
Fetishistic tresses; how
The pavilioned splendour of the brow
Shades a hard mouth; the double-breasted
Pastures where a man might graze;
The *petit trou* in metaphrase.

21

One kind of girl Tim met completed
This picture of inanity,
Their talk, but not their senses, heated,
Their ideas, not their actions, free.
Their sublimation meant adoring
Tied like a dinghy to its mooring.
A dance was 'perfectly divine',
Which meant the men were cool, the wine
A good deal cooler and the rhythm
Hot. Safest in art, they froze
In all the postures of the rose,
But there was nothing doing with them.
'Perfectly divine' – how odd!
A party was their flawless God.

22

Others had burned bra *and* bikini,
Tending to deprecate the bust.
In garish dresses by Fratini
They warmed their ankles and men's lust,
Or claimed the female was a martyr
Through being brainwashed by 'pink data'
And that the best way to be dressed
Was in frayed jeans and Woolworth vest.
With minds made up (but not their faces)
They had men squirming at their whim
(And that, I fear, included Tim)
Of offering in public places
The bouncing cheques of a desire
To light the blue paper and retire.

23

But Tim had left his latest lecture,
As I've already said, his mind

Aflame with sexual conjecture.
You're right: it would be too unkind
To itemise his actual progress
With every sort of highbrow ogress
Who haunted the academy.
It must be done in simile.
Sublime as jokes by Arthur Askey,
Secret as Open Scholarships,
As frequent as the sun's eclipse
And prompt as Fischer meeting Spassky,
His assignations were not bold
And left him (and his partner) cold.

24

Now such emotional immunity
Unleashed a hunger for dis-ease.
Each face became an opportunity
Where eyes could test their power to please,
Glance up from unread book and wander,
Noting which of the blondes were blonder,
Between each sip look gravely round
As if no beauty could give ground
With tacit promise of contagion,
As if no exploit of the flesh
Could tangle him within its mesh
Or be a quest he could engage in,
As if to life he felt he ought
To offer nothing but deep thought.

25

Ah, self-delusion! Common error
That in the sum of human kinds
Provides wrong answers! A sort of terror
The unsuspecting hero finds
To come from within himself, a spectre
Using the psyche as reflector.
But just as signs rely on posts
My verse needs characters, not ghosts:
By luck, one sitting near his table
Watched Tim with patience somewhat like
An aged angler after pike
Or a lost demon from a fable
Needing a soul to be rehoused,
A grave Mephisto stalking Faust.

26

His face was long and age had hollowed
Away his neck so that you saw
Performance of muscles when he swallowed,
While every movement of the jaw
Like a gaunt preacher's in a chapel
Showed off a monstrous adam's apple.
His eyes and motives were opaque
And frequently he nibbled cake.
The hand to mouth was automatic,
The eyes attentively on Tim,
And all the time the rest of him
(Just like this narrative) was static,
Relaxed as if he had all day
In which to pounce upon his prey.

27

Manipulators never hurry.
They like a sedentary pace.
Their choice is sometimes arbitrary
Depending on their victim's face,
A safer tie or shirt that's cleaner,
A modesty in his demeanour
That seems to show he might be used
Or propositions not refused.
No need to ask why Tim was chosen.
There's always someone to be caught
As groping arms touch, though unsought,
A fleeing shape that's pinned there frozen,
As will in action must take aim,
Or a statistic someone's name.

28

'My name is Quancy. You don't know me
But I know you. (May I sit down?
Thank you.) I asked someone to show me
Where one drinks coffee in this town
And here I am, you find me drinking
It! I did so, little thinking
That you'd be here, but it was you
I came to find. Yes, yes, it's true!
I work in ATI. Dear Richard,
Your cousin Richard, told me to look
You up. What *is* that curious book?'

Tim blushed, and then began to fidget.
He coughed. He smiled. He dropped a fork.
Did anything in fact but talk.

29

Quancy was not put off. How little
Responses to one's gambits count!
Enthusiastic, noncommittal,
It matters not, and no amount
Of tactful fencing ever really
Wears an assailant down who clearly
Has it in his mind to stay.
Tim wanted him to go away
And sat there in a hopeful silence
Meditating various crimes
With headlines in the *Camford Times*:
'Man dead in café. Shocking violence.
Expert in Renaissance art
Stabbed with a teaspoon through the heart.'

30

But all to no avail. The chatter
Detained him, powerless, like a spell.
Nothing else much seemed to matter.
The adam's apple rose and fell
And Quancy's cake-strewn conversation
Dominated the occasion:
'You write, I hear? Oh yes, I've seen
Reviews in the student magazine.
Quite a talent for analysis.
We all thought so. I liked the one
On Dali and the visual pun
(Elephants into swans and phalluses
And so on). Yes, we see these things
In London. Genius has wings.'

31

To reach the very heart of the matter
In words so casual and brief
Shows you how genius can flatter:
Surrealist painting was the chief
Of Tim's few interests. Amazing!
There is a subtle art in praising
Which only demons tend to know
And Quancy knew. As flowers grow

In marshes, so in his conversation
Bloomed all the favourite names: Delvaux,
Man Ray, Max Ernst, de Chirico.
Small details showed his obligation
To Tim's reviews, and his respect.
How could Tim possibly object?

32

Indeed, it almost made him curious
To find out more of Quancy's game,
Whose interest could of course be spurious,
Simply a smokescreen. All the same,
Even as he sat and glowered,
Tim saw that Quancy was high-powered
And if not absolutely high,
Someone at least in ATI
Who might assist him with employment –
For undergraduates a ditch
Not quite the last of ditches which
They don't, though, view with much enjoyment
And which as time goes on they find
They somehow have to bear in mind.

33

From it they wage against society
Polite but suicidal war.
Full-scale attack has less propriety
Than quiet infiltration, for
Positions often yield to meekness
And opportunists build on weakness:
The enemy holds every card
And simple victory is hard.
So, those adept at odes to Pyrrha
Send spies into the BBC,
Forsake the Bullingdon and flee
In mufti to the *Daily Mirror*
Where, mastering an alien mode,
They cheer their lagging troops in code.

34

Comrades who demonstrate together
Change sleeping-bags for evening dress,
And parlour Trots in Afghan leather
Apply to write for the *Express*;
Swots who are shy and over-solemn

178

Turn agents for a gossip column;
Shagged socialites begin to search
For openings in the Catholic Church;
The academic Winter Palace
Takes in its annual Bolsheviks;
Plump organ scholars in a fix
Carry a torch for Dirty Alice;
While student poets roll the cues
For readers of the TV News.

35

The crump of truth was not too distant
For Tim to start to dig his trench:
The warning guns sounded insistent
To someone who was reading French,
Since literary information
Doesn't provide a sound vocation.
What *can* one do with Rimbaud as
A special subject, when one has
Annotations interlinear
To show one what the poems mean
And yet, oneself long past eighteen,
Has still to face one's Abyssinia,
Even (the thought was frightening) one's
Dérèglement de tous les sens?

36

So Quancy mentally had ticked him
Off already on his list
Of convert, mortgagor and victim
To Life the great monopolist
Of single lives. Now in this history
Quancy is something of a mystery.
Into Tim's world you've seen him glide,
Sallow, serpentine, bow-tied,
Peripatetic emissary
Of Art Treasures International,
An institution with a pull
Among art-lovers who are very
Rich, but never rest until
Someone has made them richer still.

37

And there we may as well abandon
Him since his initial bid

Is made. He has a leg to stand on.
So has the story – at least a lid
Which you can open, if you fancy,
To see what more than Tim or Quancy
Can possibly be found inside,
Or what the ensuing pages hide.
The scene is changed. We move to London,
Where we shall meet some others who
Will re-enact their parts for you.
All that they've done must now be undone,
The links that go to make the chain
Be put together once again.

Chapter Two

The boss

1

In a gracious street off Piccadilly,
Just far enough removed from where
The buses roared and newsboys shrilly
Proclaimed the progress of a scare
(A P M's threats of resignation,
The closure of a railway station,
Industrial spying by Japan,
A fall of shares or Princess Anne),
Gracious, that is, but somewhat seedy,
With antique showrooms ('Genuine')
That cads disposed of heirlooms in,
Some cut-price travel for the needy,
Teashops for talk, gowns for the svelte,
And Turkish baths for those who smelled –

2

– Seedy, perhaps, but with a cachet
Lent by its Georgian façade,
(A grey and gold, like papier mâché
Quainter for fading, slightly scarred
Like a Van Dyck that one retouches
To heal the canvas in a Duchess),
There lurked the marble and plate-glass
Of ATI. It had some class,
Most passers-by would have admitted.

A single oil was easelled in
The window, velvet deep as sin
Unrolled beneath it over fitted
Wilton, Wilton inside and all
Indeed was Wilton, wall to wall.

3

Across its pile, in pairs, were walking
Four feet expensively encased.
A couple of yards above them, talking,
Two mouths in which cigars were placed
(Whose taste competed with each syllable,
Since throats with smoke or words are fillable:
Tobacco may supply a tale,
But first the teller must exhale).
'You see, Hingeby – ', the first was choking,
Oblivious to this rule whereby
No conversations satisfy
When interrupted by his smoking.
'You see, Hingeby – '. Again he tried,
And once again the sentence died.

4

Now Hingeby need concern us little.
Neither'd said much but nonetheless,
Obese, patrician, noncommittal,
Hingeby had spoken much the less.
His eyebrows signalled hidden power
To make whoever failed him cower.
His smile, benevolent and wide,
Contrived to hide what lay inside:
The fangs of a financial viper.
He rolled his cigar from left to right
And right to left, almost alight,
Regular as a windscreen wiper.
It showed that he was listening,
As a clock's tick betrays a spring.

5

Just listening and waiting. Only
One with a firm sense of the role
Of money to convert the lonely
From frigid hells of self-control
To the blest calm of expectation
Knows how to wait, his compensation

181

The ripening fruit of all desire,
Life's index creeping ever higher
And dividends of independence
Accruing in the shape of others,
Lawyers, agents, masseurs, mothers,
To dance attention and attendance,
Pleased to be underprivileged,
Given one glimpse of what's gilt-edged.

6

And Hingeby *was* gilt-edged, his silence
Oozing ingots. That fixed smile
Disguised with gold intrinsic violence
Like a crude barter-system, while
His balding head glowed yellow like an
Ecstatic hermit's on an ikon.
His spectacles were solid gold
(And his impatient eyes were rolled).
Slopes of his chest gave the illusion
Of pinnacled lapels the shade
Of one of the rarer kinds of jade,
Of old Welsh slate, or a contusion.
His cuffs shot pearls, and white gold drew
Rings that his fingers struggled through.

7

No wonder people felt diminished,
Fidgeted, mumbled, blushed with shame
And left their sentences unfinished:
'You see, Hingeby – '. Always the same,
The reasonable explanation
That suffered an abashed truncation,
Complexion slowly turning puce,
The tongue ashamed of its excuse.
Thus Harold Distimuth, beginning
With perfect credibility,
'You see, Hingeby – ', or 'Hingeby, you see – ',
Was soon reduced to futile grinning,
Wild easing of his collar and
Abandonment of all he'd planned.

8

The upshot of the conversation
(If something so one-sided could
Be given such an appellation)

Was to reveal that matters stood
A trifle shakily in areas
You can't afford to find precarious
If, like Harold Distimuth,
Your *raison d'être* is to put
Suggestions to financial giants,
Noughts on the balance-sheet in black,
Customs officials off the track
And everything over on your clients,
Pull the wool and grab the loot
And be, still, Harold Distimuth.

9

He could make packets on a Titian
By bribing all the auctioneers.
He'd launch a 'limited edition'
Of fairly obvious Vermeers
So lonely thousands spent their savings
On worthless prints they thought engravings
Or found an expensive lithograph
Fetched, when they sold it, only half
Of what they'd paid. He dealt in flowery
Kitsch, posters and Art Nouveau,
Or built up your portfolio
With someone else's L. S. Lowry.
His dealings were pure legerdemain,
His only motive naked gain.

10

At ATI itself the gallery
Maintained a reasonable flow
Of cash, enough to pay the salary
Of those who kept it on the go:
Nico, his young assistant; Mary,
Superefficient secretary
Who cooked the books and answered calls
And hung the paintings on the walls;
Quancy for wheeling and for dealing,
In salerooms devious and calm
With legal guile and deathbed charm
When rich art-lovers faced the ceiling;
Old Fredge, who kept the door; and Tim
(No one had found a job for him).

11

But there was other money owing
And there were other fees to pay.
Where there is reaping there is sowing
And every dog will have his day,
From specialists in tax-evasion,
Unfriendly experts in persuasion
And all professionals in art
Down to the mere impure-in-heart.
For many bribes were made to tyros:
Perks to restorers, tips for Earls
And necklaces for office girls
Who weren't content with pinching biros
And needed sanctions for their wiles
In lifting confidential files.

12

Much went to Hingeby (in his opinion
Not enough) for he was king
And Distimuth simply a minion,
For a time in favour, obliged to bring
Gifts to the gifted, and beholden
To load with gold the already golden.
'You see, Hingeby – '. It was a sigh
Laden with doom for ATI,
The unimaginable spectre
Of failure and of Hingeby's frown,
Of the whole venture being closed down
(Or at the least a new director
Replacing Harold Distimuth
And he himself given the boot).

13

Well, well. The interview went badly
And Distimuth was in a hole.
Sympathy is required, but sadly
We find that motion of the soul
Frustrated by the man's excessive
Self-esteem. He *was* impressive,
Surely? And Hingeby understood
He'd do much better if he could?
That no one else had finer talents
For all those small artistic crimes
Reported in the *Sunday Times*?

No one a greater sense of balance
Between being cautious and being brisk,
Between inertia and risk?

14

Perhaps. But Hingeby left behind him
Distinct disquiet. Nothing was fixed
But Distimuth knew where to find him;
Would he please do so? Soon? He mixed
A double Dutch and vermouth, trying
To hold the bottle steady, sighing.
He took his glasses off and sank
Into a canvas chair. And drank.
Hingeby was gold, but he was leaden.
Life did not glow for him but drained
Him of all colour. Money pained
Him like an ache no drug could deaden.
He had to have it, like a child.
His face was pale. He never smiled.

15

This master-copy of the Ego
Sported a drooping black moustache
That made him look like an Amigo
From the Sierras in camouflage,
Or if not a bandit not much smarter
Than Marlon Brando as Zapata.
His eyes were drilled beneath his brow
Like open portholes in a prow.
His hair was greasy as *rillettes*
But combed in wings above his ears,
Innocent of the barber's shears.
His jowl was razored by Gillette, a
Swarthy blue (tough bristles win
The daily game of steel and skin).

16

Individualisation
Of capital's most common slave
Needs little detailed information.
We know how types like this behave,
Or do we? He certainly did badly
At what was asked of him at Radley
And spent his commission in the Guards
Learning how to shuffle cards.
But did you know he practised judo

185

And sukiyaki in Gerrards Cross?
Commuters and salads he could toss
With equal ease. It may seem pseudo
(A black belt in the green belt), but
It helped to minimise the gut.

17
Alas, it didn't make him happy,
Nor lovely either. Nor his wife.
Relations were distinctly *frappé*.
Her look was wounding like a knife,
And he was wounded. So he carried
Scars to show that he was married,
Daring the girls he met to wince
Or turn the frog into a prince.
One look? One smile? A hand that snugly
Slipped into his for comfort? It
Was not to be, we must admit.
In every sense he was too ugly.
Unbid-for in the catalogue
Of love, the frog remained a frog.

18
'Mary, Mary, come to dinner –
Deploy your power to console
One virile lonely would-be sinner
Crushed by the weight of his drab soul
Who needs to live a little faster,
Who needs a slave to prove he's master,
A quiet accomplice in his task
Of answering what he dare not ask,
The body's single stumping question!
Lead me back gently from the brink!
Restore me, and restore my drink!
Restore the power of suggestion,
Yield me the grandeur of your sex:
De minimis non curat lex!'

19
These words were felt but were unspoken,
The girl in question was unmoved,
The silence in the room unbroken,
His melancholy not improved.
Mary, sublime in her sweet face's
Quite ordinary office graces,

Came in and out with papers and,
Demanding that he set his hand
To various protests and avowals,
Held out her folders for his pen
To scrawl his personal amen,
Oblivious of the silent howls
Of grief and lust that came from him
As he deployed the signing limb.

20
His eyes were black as two black coffees,
The canine gloom of his moustache
Suiting a kennel not an office,
His breath like something from a marsh.
How could poor Mary be expected
To love a person so dejected,
So bland, acquisitive and grey,
So humourless, so *ennuyé*?
She concentrated on her letters,
The expression on her face quite blank.
She sent the bond and filed the bank,
Calmed creditors and needled debtors.
These missives were superb – *quand même*,
They owed it all to IBM.

21
How can a silent invitation
Make clear that something is afoot?
Such failure of communication
Must be deplored. El Distimuth
Was not her cup of . . . well, tequila.
She knew him for a double-dealer,
A squeezer of the elbow and
A too-long shaker of the hand.
But did she know how very deeply
He needed now to be redeemed
From being exactly what he seemed,
A man who valued far too cheaply
All that was rare, and held too dear
The vulgar traffic of this sphere?

22
And would she think it a disaster
If a man's credit balance sank

On her account, or heart beat faster?
No one would notice, to be frank.
She hadn't got a classic figure
(Some of the curves could have been bigger)
And yet she had a certain style,
And little hands and what a smile!
Who knows what longings filled her diary?
For no one's life is what it seems
And poise can be a stage for dreams
Athletic, airborne, lithe and fiery,
Fully designed to compensate
For perfect years of sitting straight.

23

Now what's your usual daydream, reader?
A useful shape behind a desk
Or something sultry like Aïda,
Mysterious, doomed and statuesque?
Fright-wig and beads? A hint of faerie?
Or sweet uncomplicated Mary?
Suppose you called at ATI
Offhand and unexpectedly
To ask (perhaps) the price of Hockneys:
Which would make you tremble more,
The lightness of your wallet or
The twinkle in her eye? (Knock-knees
Commonly denote restraint,
Whether in front of girls or paint.)

24

Six o'clock. She wondered whether
Her downcast boss would ever go.
Nico and Tim had left together
At half-past five, slowly, although
They'd never been in such a hurry.
Quancy was in the depths of Surrey.
Outside the door she heard a wheeze:
Old Fredge was shuffling with his keys.
Six o'clock. Rub, and the genie
Of all your wishes will appear.
The hour is magic. Freedom's near
And Distimuth and his martini

Not something that you want to stay
And watch. You need to get away.

25

Six o'clock. The air seemed scented.
Excitement, working like a yeast
Upon the hurrying crowd, invented
The hurt imaginative Beast
On whose extended palm might settle
The fragile promise of a petal
As in his garden's wilderness
He wandered in a grave *tristesse*,
Uncertain how his hairy power
Might be transformed and so disclose
The healing spectre of the rose.
All London at this darkening hour
Roared in a silent rage to be,
For a night, both maimed and free.

26

Experimental gins and tonics
Were being lifted to the lips
Of eager youths and weary chronics,
A few in gulps and some in sips
But all with nausea masked as relish,
For alcohol serves to embellish
The blank walls of the evening
With its sprayed messages that sing
Of love. Out in the dusk, commuters
Scurried along the walls like rats
With leather zips and little hats,
While girls and foreigners, like looters,
Rifled arcades for mugs and packs
Of Nude Bezique and Union Jacks.

27

Let's leave poor Distimuth contriving
A similar assault upon
Material things. For since Arriving
(The experience of Napoleon
Comes to one's mind) is not a frequent
Conclusion to, nor is it sequent
Upon that enemy of doubt,

189

The common act of Setting Out,
We may be sure that he will never
Contrive to sober up, relax
And save the day behind our backs.
His Moscow beckons. And his clever
Conspiracy is brewing, though
Softly and elsewhere falls the snow.

Chapter Three

The bet

1

And what of youth? What great decisions
Were quietly being anatomised
And then performed? What bold incisions
Were made in their anaesthetised,
Incurable and sterile futures?
What gaucheries were healed in sutures?
What student skills ready at last
To diagnose the suffering past
(Eager, having learned their lessons,
To wheel the memory that survives
Into a corner of their lives
For a convenient convalescence),
Oblivious of what agonies,
Called out: 'The next experience, please!'

2

For Tim, the safe imagination
Offered its usual substitute
For every risk of gratification:
It claimed, unwilling to dispute,
The independence of ideas
Whose objectivity must free us
From all responsibility
Of thinking them. And so we see
Friendship frustrated by politeness;
Desire restrained by the sharp tug
Of feared rebuff; the rueful shrug
Of an inevitable triteness
Blunting the spur of sympathy.
It seemed enough simply to be.

190

3

The figures in his landscape waited,
Patient, circumambient
And indistinct, all orientated
Towards that effortless event
That held them to its humble centre
While still forbidding them to enter,
Kept them like supers in a play,
Required, with nothing much to say,
To come and go (or to appear to)
While at the forefront of the stage
The hero could with ease engage
At once the spotlights of the theatre
And the rapt audience's applause,
Greeting his modest bows with roars.

4

A cheering role, but goodness gracious,
Wait a minute! Not so fast!
Isn't this strategy fallacious
Isn't the audience and cast
The *same*? That urge to smile and fidget
When visiting with cousin Richard;
That cool pretence of nonchalance
At Mary's penetrating glance;
That need for instant self-removal
When Quancy looms; that tendency
In conversation to agree –
Dropped cues won't get you the approval
Of actors you upstage, and you've
Got no one else who *can* approve!

5

With Nico, Tim for once suspended
All his social terrors. Soon
He found that he had been befriended
When during one long afternoon
Each told the other of frustrations
Aroused by thwarted expectations.
Tim wondered why he had been hired
(When *were* his services required?)
And Nico felt that *his* assistance
Was operating in a void:
They were, in short, underemployed,

And Distimuth preserved his distance
The better (as we know) to cheat
And at the same time be discreet.

6

So Quancy said Tim was 'a treasure'
Simply for making cups of tea
(Which Fredge did better). He would measure
Attics already measured three
Or even four times since he'd been there.
He wondered what was to be seen there,
But wisely shrugged and held his tongue:
Those attic walls were never hung.
So Nico learned that to assist is
To ask, assuage, assort, assess,
To make a statement to the Press,
To spend an afternoon at Christie's,
Frame the accounts (or prints) to take
To the auditors (or to a sheik).

7

At this point I can hear your query,
Discreetly framed but deeply felt
(Felt, that is to say, in theory –
As eyes can swim and hearts can melt
As in true sentiment they ought to
Unless, as I suspect, you're bored to
Tears): 'If Distimuth's a crook,
Then what of Nico? In our book
He's the Assistant Crook.' Not really,
I hasten to assure you. Some
Activities he thought quite rum
But (and I mean this 'most sincerely')
Like Carter with the Pentagon
He knew a fifth of what went on.

8

Nico had welcomed Tim's arrival
Since *two* young men with nothing much
To do might guarantee survival.
(A tyro with a BA! Such
An image-builder wasn't serious,
The motive certainly mysterious
But no more so than many things
Performed by firms whose underlings

192

Were underprivileged.) He reckoned
He'd been around too long to fire
And Tim was not a chap they'd hire
To take his job. So in the second
Week the friendship was begun
Of twenty-eight with twenty-one.

9

Nico looked somewhat like a spider,
All arms and legs and hairy-faced.
His pinstriped trousers were much wider
Around the ankle than the waist.
His basement flat in Canonbury
Was painted brown and smelled of curry.
It had no chairs and was equipped
With smoking candles like a crypt,
And lest the darkness constitute a
Danger to the groping guest
There was a light-show which expressed
The feelings of a small computer
In glowing landscapes made of cubes
And portraits of some neon tubes.

10

This programme would at times illumine
In changing gleams of mauve and green
Activities more purely human
Than those performed by a machine.
The passions novelists call tidal
Welled up before it. Like an idol
It glared upon, yet deigned to bless,
In various stages of undress,
His victims. When he bit a shoulder
It winked some ultra-violet winks,
Beamed at a thigh and when the jinks
Grew higher, fused and began to smoulder
(Except when, rolling on the rug,
The serving priest pulled out the plug).

11

Was Nico glum? He was. Small wonder.
What girl of honour genuflects
In front of (or on top, or under)
A fluorescent god of sex?
Once they would suffer it, once only,

Leaving poor Nico just as lonely.
He sought, and found, but did not keep
(And frequent changes are not cheap).
Tim met them and commiserated:
Such beauties! He was thunderstruck!
It seemed the rottenest of luck
To win the girls yet be frustrated
In your quite reasonable prayers
For more than ephemeral affaires.

12
There was the hopeful lady painter
Who thought he'd further her career
(Her appetite grew slowly fainter
And was discovered to be queer);
A poetry-secretariat groupie
Already partially loopy
Heard 'Dead Ewes' and went insane;
A lonely au-pair fresh from Spain
Turned out to be a week-end tourist.
Widows he tried and divorcées
Who then remarried, a Japanese
Who made love like a manicurist,
A secretary high on hemp,
Another in every sense a temp.

13
Then there was this extraordinary
Girl who like an illness moved
Through London. 'As a commentary
On a lost text, which might have proved
Divinity to the lapsarian
World, now rouses the grammarian
Only,' Tim suggested, 'so
Has love become a thing we know
About but do not *know*. Her chemic
Beauty gives men back the text
In its simplicity, perplexed
For ages by an academic
Version of the passion, bred
In the sterile margins of the head.'

14
'Eyewash!' growled Nico, whose obsession
With that aforesaid pulchritude

194

Could not contrive its full possession
And did not anyway include
Ingenuous idealisation
Of the sort contained in Tim's equation.
'Her body's simply alpha-plus
And her behaviour infamous!
The combination is desirable
For what it promises: the full
Enjoyment of the possible.
A pity the body's not acquirable
On terms to which (or otherwise
We'd try) the likes of us might rise.'

15

How could an ordinary human
Being play such different roles?
To Tim, an aspect of the Numen;
To Nico, several tempting holes
Concealed with poise about her person.
To Tim, a subject to write verse on;
To Nico, an object of desire
Confined to purchasers in higher
Income groups. Of course, the feeling
Was much the same: they were harpooned
By their obsession, and the wound
Showed little sign of quickly healing.
In seas of rage they thrashed about,
One lickerish and one devout.

16

What of their friendship? Its survival
In such conditions was assured.
Each thought the other not a rival
But a fellow-sufferer to be cured.
What was the cure? A valid question.
You swallow pills for indigestion
And pack a boil with soothing lint
Or a cracked arm into a splint:
The cure is easy to discover.
Can you be sure that aching hearts
Are *quite* relieved by other parts?
That love's achieved by being a *lover*?
Both so believed, denying hence
Their several experience.

17

For Tim was still the grave idealist
And consummation all he lacked,
While Nico in his role as realist
Was ever hopeful of the act
That always let him down so badly.
Reader, do not view this sadly.
Only the direst misanthrope
Conducts his life without such hope.
Don't we all feel that somewhere waiting
Upon us is our destiny?
A choice or act to set us free?
Some think they find it meditating
On Skiddaw or in discothèques,
While some discover it in sex.

18

You may have seen the girl in question,
Mistaking her for other girls
Whose lidded eyes held no suggestion
Of vague derangement and whose curls
When shaken out failed to astound you
With thoughts of hair being all around you,
Whose legs looked merely like supports,
Designed for dancing or for sports,
Inclined to kick, or strut, or dangle,
Not strangely move as though her path
Were mapped by Venus at her bath,
The hip relaxing at an angle
For whose delight in the effect
We praise its fleshly architect.

19

'That girl' was how they came to know her.
Smiling at parties, glasses full,
They felt themselves so far below her,
Felt her so unavailable,
That they would smirk and blush and stammer,
Rating a social beta-gamma
Until some hugh with cleaner cuffs
Came and completed their rebuffs
By talking her away. Impressive
Stomachs cornered her. An arm
Held out with confidence and charm,

Partly polite, partly possessive,
Demanded her. And yet, alone,
She walked and smiled and was her own.

20
And now, I think, you may find apt a
Small reminder that we last
Saw Nico in the previous chapter
Around five-thirty sneaking past
The room in which his poor superior
Distimuth was feeling wearier
Than he had ever felt before,
Sneaking away through the front door
No less, with Tim in tow. Starvation
Becomes a serious threat to those
To whom the gourmet guides propose
Their rosettes and discrimination
Whenever a lengthened cocktail hour
Shortens the time left to devour.

21
Six o'clock. I have already,
If you remember, logged its mood,
This moment of the evening heady
With expectation and imbued
With appetite. It is sufficient
To remind you how we are conditioned:
The hour is struck, and in a wink
The middle classes pour a drink.
And if by chance the next hour passes
In light and profitable chat
Extolling this and damning that,
Swirling the ice in empty glasses,
It will be time, it will be time
(I won't say 'dine': it doesn't rhyme).

22
Now Tim, of course, was a beginner
And Nico seven years ahead
In the art of hunting out a dinner
Worth what you pay for it. They fed
In grills with plastic chandeliers
Or little dock-side trattorias
Or anywhere where instant fame

Had not corrupted a good name.
You know those fashionable places
Where it's imperative to book
But no one has the time to cook,
Which welcome all the well-known faces,
Attempt to hide the *table d'hôte*
And charge for hanging up your coat.

23

Pretensions wholly self-defeating
Most restaurants carry off with verve.
We suffer in the cause of eating
More agonies than we deserve.
We pay the earth for each warm squirmy
Display of kitchen taxidermy,
Fermented secretions of the cow,
Dissected birds, part of a sow
Or smaller slices of its babies.
These days there's greater virtue in
Native simplicity, less sin
In hedgerow lore like Richard Mabey's
When only berries pass our lips
And gourmets change from ribs to hips.

24

Come with me, then, to *Adam's Palate*
And eat as our nude forebears did.
Mangold soup and groundsel salad
Will only set you back three quid.
And those who don't mind little creatures
May dine at *Romany's* which features
Campfire Soup and Poacher's Grill
With fiddling thrown in (the bill
Not least). It says in Egon Ronay:
'It's better (if you have the heart)
To venture to the *à la carte*:
Hedgehog in Clay, or Throttled Coney.
Try Towpath Pudding (enough for four).
It's only two pounds fifty more.'

25

And then *The Trenchermen of Harlech*
Offers the cooking of the Celts:

Amazing how a squeeze of garlic
Improves the champ and skewered melts.
It's easy to digest the nettle
Provided it has time to settle,
And all the most nutritious parts
Of animals, like lights and hearts
And various glands, are, so they tell us,
By far the cheapest. Not so here.
In fact you'll find them very dear.
The management is always zealous
To charge for its civility
(And then some more, for VAT).

26

But still, I can't pretend this sort of
Thing was quite their line. In fact
The macrobiotic was still unthought of.
The regional and ethnic lacked
Such desperate and wholly gruesome
Embodiment. Our hungry twosome
Made for a place called *Albert's*, where
A fillet could be ordered rare
And be so, where you found fresh spinach,
A whole blue Wensleydale with lots
Of celery, some little pots
Of sticky chocolate mousse to finish,
And sometimes, for the regulars,
Ten-year-old Léoville-Lascases.

27

There the debate, renewed with fervour,
Took on a more dramatic turn.
It might have seemed to an observer
That some grave topic of concern
Engrossed the pair, they looked so solemn.
What could it be? A daily column
Exposing gaffes with snorts of prose
Was not more urgent, medicos
About an ulcer less divided.
Now most dilemmas of that ilk
(Whether to cure by knife or milk)
Inevitably *are* two-sided:

Shall it be bold incisiveness
Or a more leisurely address?

28

In short, the issue reached such major
Importance in their lives that they
Resolved forthwith to have a wager
About which means would win the day.
Agreed upon the diagnosis,
They differed on the strength of doses
Needed to bring the patient round,
And here their difference was profound.
'That girl,' claimed Nico, 'like all others,
Would fall to any seducer who
Has both the urge and wit to woo.
They have the example of their mothers
To show them that the act is not
Apocryphal: they *were* begot.'

29

He was for showing her no mercy,
Only the weapon of his choice.
Tim's counter in the controversy
Was to propose the human voice
As being much the more convincing:
Not only nicer, but evincing
All the substantial qualities
Of what our noble species is;
Agent of body, mind and spirit;
The passions' representative,
Singularly moved to give
Them shape. What neutral ear could hear it
And not for certain recognise
Their sweet rhetorical disguise?

30

A bet it was, then, a cool fifty
(More than they could afford, but then
Nico was reckless, Tim was thrifty
And both as single gentlemen
Might risk behaving like Edwardians
With gestures to a hidden audience
Or, as the claret reached their toes,

A pair of Restoration beaux
Who dally in a world of whoredom
To prove that vice is exquisite
For those with manners and the wit
To hide its cost and utter boredom).
Certain that he'd clear the bet,
Each thought the other in his debt.

Chapter Four

The bid

1

No sooner was the bet decided
Than one of those events occurred
Which make one think that life is guided
By some strange force, unseen, unheard,
That finds it passably amusing
To make what happens seem confusing
And organises these events
Into a giant coincidence.
Tim was choosing from the trolley
And happened to glance up: outside
The restaurant he saw there glide
An ancient taxi in a jolly
Colour resembling cherry jam.
It looked just like a lacquered pram.

2

From one side stepped six feet of flannel
Wearing a sneer that opened in
A blank face like a secret panel
Leading nowhere, and a chin
Like a worn step. From the other
Fell one who might have been his brother,
Sporting a blazer and cravat
And a strange curly kind of hat,
Gasping with laughter. Together moving
Like badly-rehearsed comedians
They opened the rear door. At once,
In a manner faintly disapproving,
Giving her skirt a little swirl,
Out stepped, pale and aloof, 'that girl'.

3

The diners goggled as she entered,
Flanked by the Blazer and the Sneer.
Everyone's attention centred
Upon the girl as she came near.
Forks were raised with roasted meat on
That cooled before it could be eaten;
Sorbet melted in the spoon;
Noodles, missing the mouth, were strewn
On neighbours' laps; some men, unable
To stop themselves from turning round,
Tipping their chairs, became spellbound
And had to hold on to the table
To stop themselves from falling. All
The restaurant was in her thrall.

4

A word from Blazer and a waiter
Showed them into a darkened booth.
'The menu, sir?' 'We'll see it later,'
Replied the Sneer. His voice was smooth
As eggs. He gave a common glottal
Catch (a cough): 'Bring us a bottle
Of something cold with bubbles in.
And make damned sure it's genuine.'
He ended with some imprecation
Better left unrepeated, then
He briefly smiled, and sneered again.
That done, a buzz of conversation
Broke out at once on every side
As suddenly as it had died.

5

'Isn't that . . . ?' 'Yes, it is, it's Polly . . .'
'Polly who?' 'I know her face.'
'Not Polly Passenger?' 'Yes.' 'Golly!'
'What's she doing in this place?'
'I can't imagine.' 'She likes slumming.'
'Don't you find her dress becoming?'
'Yes, what there is of it.' 'Is that
Prince Charles wearing the little hat?'
'What's the car?' 'It's a De Soto.'
'No, it's a taxi.' 'It's superb!'
'I see they've parked it on the kerb.'

'Is someone going to take a photo?'
'I hope not. Is my collar straight?'
'I must be looking overweight.'

6

Picture the girl: her hair was Goya's,
Out of which her forehead blazed
Like light. Her eyes, those dark destroyers,
Like a Modigliani gazed
You into a trance. How to respond? You
Pleased her by finding it beyond you.
Amused to see your gauche dismay,
She narrowed them, and turned away.
Slender nose, a little slanted,
Ears the unfolding of a rose,
Neck and shoulders in a pose
Gainsborough would have gladly painted:
Every feature in its place,
Rhyming the poem of her face.

7

A strange feat of contemporaneity!
Nico and Tim were riveted
At this appearance of their deity.
Upon their plates the food lay dead
(The bill however was alive: a
Little murder with a fiver,
Six singles and a noisy mound
Of trouser-heated change was found
To be required by the sadistic
Waiter who straightened out the warps
And bore away the paper corpse,
Which leaves me with the final distich,
No time for more, a good pretext
To move on quickly to the next).

8

How to get rid of Sneer and Blazer?
How *could* she sit with those two twits?
What gallant action might amaze her?
Flowers? A duel? Fainting fits?
Leaping upon the table? Jocular
And knowing grimaces monocular
(i.e. winks)? Such thoughts flashed through

Our heroes' minds in swift review
And left them glum. It seemed that little
Could be accomplished there and then.
They felt a bit like jurymen
Who should have stuck out for acquittal
But played it safe and acquiesced
And voted 'Guilty' with the rest.

9

But even cowards get their chances,
Like MPs waiting to be bribed
Or girls with platform shoes at dances.
The twits in question had imbibed
A good deal of the harry lifters
Which sinks down to the bladder swift as
A Bentley's petrol gauge, a leak,
Or mercury after the week
Of regulation English summer.
That's what happens when you drink:
Without a bladder made of zinc
(Which sadly the Celestial Plumber
Struck off the specification) you
At times like these must find a loo.

10

Which Sneer and Blazer did, upsetting
A chair or two on stumbling out.
'Now's our chance,' hissed Nico, getting
Up from the table. 'The first bout
Begins! Keep calm, my boy, and follow
Me.' Tim stayed behind to swallow
The last dampness of claret in
His empty glass and square his chin.
He then felt ready for whatever
Nico might have in mind. He took
His bearings but he did not look
To see where Nico'd gone. He never
Noticed till too late that he
Had gone not to Polly but to pee.

11

This left Tim moving irrevocably
Towards her table, where she sat
Watching the waiter pour the bubbly,
While Nico was already at

The gents. He clearly saw his mission
As dealing with the opposition
Before he moved in for the kill.
A hopeless prospect that, but still,
Isn't it true that life is action?
Well, he had acted. Whereas Tim,
In reflex like a second limb,
Proved the power of attraction,
The area of error and
The vagaries of chance's hand.

   12
As for his own, it was extended
Uncertainly towards a chair
At Polly's table. He intended,
Smiling, careless and debonair,
To grasp its back. And this intention
Itself (I hardly need to mention)
Was something he proposed anon
To make a firm decision on.
At least, he felt the said proposal
Was something to be considered in
The circumstances, well within
The powers he found at his disposal,
If only he had time to *think*
(Perhaps with something more to drink).

   13
The gap between him and the table
Became a narrow chasm whose
Dim dizzying depths left him unstable,
The carpet rose to meet his shoes
And bore his weight without volition,
His fingers shrank from their petition
As from a bowl of worms. The chair,
Though getting nearer, was not there
But in a timeless limbo, swelling
Inside his head to monstrous size.
He felt upon him all the eyes
Of diners, silently compelling
Him to trip. He wished they'd look
The other way. His fingers shook.

14

Now Nico meanwhile had discovered
Something that he'd not bargained for.
As yet he scarcely had recovered
From the strange shock of what he saw
Or rather didn't see. What was it?
What sounds emerging from the closet
Brought to his ears with muffled force
Yet unequivocally, like Morse,
Their obscene message? Flabbergasted.
Nico continued to pretend
To wash his hands. When would it end?
He was amazed how long it lasted!
How shameless and how public were
The passions nothing could deter!

15

The drab convenience of a cottage
Will suit a love that's not sublime.
The hidden scrabblings and frottage
Signalled an act there's always time
To bring off and stay undetected,
Even (as now) drunk and expected.
The memoirs of the great are full
Of the quick grope and lightning pull
In the unlikeliest of places.
'Hang on a mo,' the boys would cry
And off they'd beetle. Friends would sigh
And wait for them to show their paces
In corridors of trains, on stairs,
With waiters and commissionaires.

16

Sunday leaders still remember
That Honourable Member who
Stood for – well, any *other* member.
Divisions found him in the loo
(Though he obeyed the Whip's instructions,
Was politic in his seductions
And thus paired-off). Gossip recalls
An editor with restless balls
Whose quest for talent for his organ
Led him to many a writer chum
Whose claim to fame was that his bum

Had once been lightly cupped by Morgan
Forster, whose bum in turn, &c . . .
He printed nothing by a hetero.

17

Nico's thinking changed direction:
If Polly, waiting thus, was not
Therefore their object of affection
(Which seemed to be each other) what
Could they be doing with her? Or she with
Them? They weren't so nice to be with.
He dried his hands and rapped upon
The door: 'All right!' he said. 'You've one
Minute precisely! DC Vincent
Of the Metropolitan Police
(Vice Squad). I must insist you cease
What you are doing upon this instant.
We've organised a general purge.
Adjust your clothing and emerge.'

18

He paused and listened. All was silent
(Save for the swearing of the chef:
The wall was thick, but he was violent
And several of the waiters deaf).
So far so good. His task was lightened
If they were genuinely frightened.
He issued orders, then went out
And stamped importantly about.
No sound emerged except a hiccough
(What else is there to say when caught?
'Officer, I was taken short'?
'Here's for your trouble'? 'That's no pick-up,
That's my nurse. Victims of strokes
Require assistance in the cloaks'?).

19

Nico nipped back and softly muttered
In a foreign accent through the door
(The words were welcome that he uttered):
'Here! I tell you! I want no more
This sort of trouble, understand?
The man-police, he with his panda
Car on walky-talk. Believe
Me, it is safe now if you leave,
But turn right, back door through the kitchen.'

Nico's instructions were obeyed
In double-time. The escapade
Concluded with a scamper which in
Ten seconds smashed ten glasses, shook
Sugar from shelves and scorched a cook.

20

The twits, too conscious of their folly,
Weren't drunk enough not to be scared:
Their swift abandonment of Polly
Showed Nico just how much they cared
About (a) her, and (b) theirs truly.
So, deprecating such unruly
Manners as the pair betrayed,
And with a little smile, he made
For the restaurant proper, hardly thinking
Of what his friend had meanwhile been
Engaged upon. But in the din
Of conversation, laughter, drinking,
He once more turned his mind to Tim
And what might have become of him.

21

Time is accustomed to the failure
Of real events to alter her.
They merely, like rude marginalia
On an old text, tend to occur,
A comment on corruption, never
For long accepted, like the clever
Solution of a simple crux.
And rarely in the swirling flux
Of time's equivocal dimension
Actions stand out like islands in
The boiling waters, origin
Of cities and all frail hopes. I mention
Such a banality by way
Of making progress by delay.

22

For if this chapter feints or lingers
It only mirrors time and her
Caprice. You saw Tim's trembling fingers
About nine stanzas earlier
Reach for the chair at Polly's table:
Surely by now he has been able
To clinch the action? I'm afraid

Not. By no means. All is delayed.
A dreadful stasis settles, crippling
Fingers, story, time and verse.
It couldn't, in terms of pace, be worse.
You'd be much better off with Kipling
Or Samuel Butler or Tom Hood,
Someone who can be understood.

23

It's no good saying that I ought to
Know clearly what is going on.
My characters have not been taught to
Accept me as a hanger-on.
They hide their thoughts from me, refusing
To share their hopes or be amusing.
They change their minds or disappear,
Or turn out not to be sincere.
What I would like to happen isn't
As a consequence, you see, what *did*.
Like measuring the pyramid
I've cooked the evidence and listened
At doors. However, let's pretend
This chapter's somehow going to end.

24

One way would be if Tim succeeded
In his attempt to grasp that chair
And consequent events proceeded
As if he were as debonair
As such an act implied. His folly
Might reap a strange reward and Polly
Melt for a moment to a smile.
Together they might rise and while
Nico looks on in stupefaction
Go from the restaurant through the night,
A goddess and her acolyte.
Such a solution has its attraction.
And so – the author interferes,
And music thunders in Tim's ears.

25

The theme was happiness and glory,
The senses were the instruments,
The variation *con amore*
With ostentatious ornaments,

A grave *notturno* elevated
And calmly recapitulated
Through Eliotic labyrinths
Of streets, odours of hyacinths,
And moonlit figures of sleepwalkers
At large in the dead city where
Every perspective led the pair
Past open doorways from which glaucous
Eyeballs stared out as if through the
Lamenting protoplasmic sea.

26

And everywhere before him drifted
The mocking and elusive shape
Of Polly. As the shadows shifted
She seemed intent on her escape
Yet still beguiling and alluring
Like a magician's doll, ensuring
His bondage to her carapace
And its contrived hypnotic face.
We'll leave them here (Nico pursuing)
Lost in a temporal cul-de-sac.
Shall we now go discreetly back
To see what Quancy has been doing
Somewhat less discreetly? Turn
The page, dear reader. You shall learn.

Chapter Five

The bait

1

The house called Summershoot stood smugly
Upon the crest of a small hill.
Victorian towers that once were ugly
Were mellowed now – and ugly still.
Its spacious rooms were buried under
Free-standing piles of saleroom plunder:
Here a column, there a bust,
And everywhere an inch of dust,
Mirrors in gold frames staring at you,
Elephants' feet to stumble on,
Armour, a carved harmoniphon,

Dog-irons, a revolving statue.
You found you longed, while standing there,
To get back to the open air.

 2
Lord Baltrap owed his ancient acres
To dull industrious forebears who
Were foundrymen and boilermakers
Enabling steam to carry to
An ignorant Empire's furthest borders
(In triplicate) its monarch's orders.
Adept at engineering boats,
They turned their skill to getting votes:
Out of the stoke-hole and the steerage
The pale disfranchised lent their voice
(The papers hailed 'the people's choice')
And when the Palace gave a peerage
Took cuts in wages to donate
(Unwittingly) this large estate.

 3
A part of it was old. Beneath an
Exterior of Gothic stone
Was smothered an Elizabethan
Heart of brick – but it had grown,
Like everybody's good intentions,
Corrupt with magnificent recensions
Whose heirs delighted in the fake
Like icing on a cardboard cake.
Small wonder that with swingeing taxes
The present Baltrap made the most
Of ways a lord could play the host.
His stately oaks succumbed to axes
And from his car-parks there were tours
(With headphones) of rococo sewers.

 4
But such a large scale interruption
Was hardly worth the tiny fee.
Better the wages of corruption
(Granted that one's mortality
Was not in any case in question)
As means to unimpaired ingestion
Of tidy sums. And this explains

211

Why in pursuit of easy gains
The feckless Baltrap, bald and tweedy,
Inevitably overdrawn,
Could here be seen upon his lawn
Perambulating with the weedy
But nattily-suited Quancy. How
They met need not concern us now.

5

The late September day was sunny,
Casting deep shadows in the yews.
Quancy was naming sums of money
That Baltrap scarcely could refuse:
Behold the twitching of his whiskers
And popping of his eyes. Hibiscus
Showered its gay confetti on
The pair. They passed a myrmidon
Clipped from a bush who gave his blessing,
And down an aisle of croquet hoops
Flowers in little nodding groups
Acknowledged Baltrap's acquiescing,
While Quancy's adam's apple fell
And rose, like an exultant bell.

6

'Who knows,' Quancy was heard to murmur,
'What may be found in lofts among
Tea-chests, brass idols made in Burma
(Or Birmingham) and such far-flung
Outposts of culture that were plundered
When your rapacious grandsires thundered
Across the globe, bundles unbroached
Since Queen Victoria approached
Her grand climacteric, &c?
Sit back. Do nothing. I know a man
Perfect in every way. Began
In life an East End shopfront letterer,
Went on to banknotes, but loves art,
Paints the old masters *à la carte*.'

7

It's true. He did. The chap could dabble
In any period of paint.

His fakes were indistinguishable
From genuine: he'd do a saint
In gold leaf or a whore in charcoal,
Sketches of pets or patriarchal
Desert temptations, Dutch still-lives
Or portraits of the artist's wives
(Or of the artist's aunts or nieces),
Murals of mayors in roomy furs,
Elizabethan miniatures,
Fairy dells or altarpieces.
Give him a bottle or two of scotch,
He'd even tackle the *Night Watch*.

8

And when he was completely blotto
And therefore really up to par,
Another cognac saw a Watteau
Or possibly a Fragonard
Take gradual shape beneath his trembling
Brush. On gin he'd do a Memling.
A schnapps tended to make him squint:
Fine for a Dürer aquatint,
While grappa brought on Titian's *Pontius
Pilate washing his hands of Christ*,
A work that wasn't overpriced
Given he did the hands half-conscious
(Though some de Koonings he had sold
Had been completed while out cold).

9

Quancy could not resist a chuckle
At Baltrap's puzzled, willing face.
He broke a branch of honeysuckle
With which the more easily to chase
The insects from his scented toupee
And lend élan to his wild whoopee
At all the business they'd discussed
Capering round a mouldy bust
Of Priapus (a garden deity
Whose likeness in his evil leer
To Quancy was distinctly queer
And lent an air of simultaneity

213

Or strange coincidence to what
Was not in fact a garden plot).

10

'A rape, a rape! His *Rape* will suit us!
We have the painting, provenance
And now – a purchaser!' Arbutus
Scattered at his manic dance
And dutifully lurking servants
Gawped in surprise at their observance
Of what could only be at best
Unusual behaviour in a guest.
Later, when dialling long-distance,
Quancy was calmer and explained
The situation in restrained
Important tones: 'Baltrap's resistance,
Never a threat, is overcome!
We have him underneath our thumb!'

11

From Summershoot to Piccadilly
The GPO provides the means
Whereby two voices, willy-nilly,
May cross through wires and small machines
That link the ear and lips together
Without distraction from the weather.
Sometimes a voice, as voices do,
Will interrupt with: 'Are you through?'
And often it can be a trial
Simply to get connected to
The number of the person you
Originally tried to dial.
But this time Quancy clearly put
The gist across to Distimuth.

12

The gist is really all that's needed.
I've thinned the details here and there,
As from a bed too densely seeded,
To give the leaves a bit of air.
Let's leave them now to grow (a sceptic
Would say my method's not proleptic,
But when the fruit begins to peep

Nature will know the time to reap).
They say that art is imitation,
But what is there to imitate
When characters predict their fate
And hide? Time for the Dedication!
I'm sorry that you've had to wait:
It's 1800 lines too late.

13

*T*o you, clear-headed, lean, sarcastic
*O*bserver of the Government,
*M*aster of the hudibrastic
*A*nd self-styled 'poet by accident'
*T*hat out of vacant hours not vanity
*T*ook pen and ink to save your sanity,
*H*appily I dedicate
*E*ach line of this that I relate.
*W*ere civil servants panegyrists;
*P*oets of low life, diplomats;
*R*oisterers, ministers; kings, cats;
I doubt we'd have lugubrious lyrists
*O*r such dull politics – instead
*R*ulers would think, writers be read.

14

But those days won't return. The nation's
Been jilted on its single date
With destiny. This dedication's
Two hundred and fifty *years* too late,
Launched like a bottle from an island
(Or political careers in Thailand)
In desperation. All I want
Is the mere inkling of entente,
Like yours between the Court and tavern.
For you, whose treaty had set free
An era of prosperity,
Preferred a drink to the mind's ravine
And used your happy verse to bless
The science of forgetfulness.

15

To keep the mind in a good humour
Just like one's wife, was your advice,

Not to dissect it like a tumour,
Gravely examining each slice
For evidence of everlasting
Bliss to come, like quarry-blasting
Inviolate and veinless rock
Or chipping with an alpenstock
To understand the promontory
From which with idle pleasure you
Might simply experience the view.
Well, Mat, it is an ancient story
But one you told extremely well.
Thank you – and *vive la bagatelle!*

16

Poets adore a divertissement:
They are the hooligans of wit
Not intellectual policemen,
And all the poems they commit
Make shocking reading. Every sentence
Is met with gleeful unrepentance.
Most of them are doing time
For loitering with intent to rhyme
Or being found in the possession
Of little sense. Since words began,
A close conspiracy to scan
Has led to many a false confession,
When po-faced readers cock an ear
For what's not meant to be sincere.

17

And if one's mood is not inflated
One's budget will be: lengthy verse
Simply by being understated
Must be capacious, like a purse.
Even the leaves on which one scribbles
Grow more expensive, like the sibyl's.
Small margins, now, for deathless myths,
But not for W. H. Smith's.
Better write limericks and qasidas
Upon the backs of envelopes.
You too were broke once when your hopes
(Living in style among ambassadors)

Incurred for an enormous bill
Pure governmental overkill.

18

In custody you wrote that salma-
gundi of tetrameters,
Your 'loose and hasty scribble' *Alma*,
Which almost no one, it occurs
To me, now reads, the more's the pity,
Although it's cool, relaxed and witty.
On every later poet's fun
With riddle, innuendo, pun
Or idle use of the persona,
You had, let's say, a prior claim
And may yet seize your dated fame,
For time accords a rightful owner
(To whom all property reverts)
The final gift of just deserts.

19

But dear me, talking of reversion:
When will we get back to the point
We'd reached before this last excursion?
The thinnest slices from a joint
Have the same shape of lean and every
Same slice stops at the bone. A reverie
Departs from some obsession and
Travel's enjoyable unplanned.
And so, please tolerate the notion
Of wearing shackles to be free,
Inconsequentiality
As a vital principle of motion
And all my empiric English pains
To shift these Russian quatorzains.

20

Which are, to one so handicapped, a
Kind of habit. Let us conclude
This somewhat insubstantial chapter.
We're none of us now in the mood.
For though it's not obligatory
For every verse to tell the story
Some, I expect, are wishing that

There was more narrative, less chat.
Let's stop – and see what's going to happen.
Write cheques too frequently, the bank
Gets shirty. Any water-tank
Will empty if you leave the tap on.
So put this down and take a rest.
Go for a walk. Or get undressed.

Chapter Six

The breakfast

1

Naked is how we come and naked
Is how we dance back to that world
Whose sense is only what we make it
When the still body, tightly curled
In rooted embryonic panic,
Lies like a hostage to titanic
Oblivion-demanding night
While all our spirits carry light
And reason to a strange created
Inner stage where actions are
Disordered, all phenomena
Overdifferentiated
And everything taken to extremes:
I mean, of course, the world of dreams.

2

Where now we find the sleeping Mary,
Her profile on the pillow in
Her childhood bed (a solitary
Bottom bunk in origin,
Now somewhat prettified: the other
Was slept in by her younger brother
Two rooms away) and her still brain
Alive in its occult terrain
Where passions act without rehearsal
And the strict will in full control
Tells the mind's cameras to roll
On scenes whose lure is universal
Though they were never looked upon
Save by an audience of one.

3

What did she see? An endless mirror
With figures passing in and out
Of it, and so becoming clearer.
At first each visage was in doubt
And might have been her own, reflected,
But when the melting glass bisected
The blurred insignia of the face
It put the figure in its place
And gave a name to it. On meeting
Within her dream each mirror-shape
Making reflection its escape
She moved her lips in silent greeting,
But naturally no one heard.
The figures passed without a word.

4

The first was corpulent and sinister,
Wearing his eyebrows like a threat:
Walter Retlaw, Tory minister
Who put the country into debt
By pushing with patrician bonhomie
A cut-throat system of economy.
With him was Samuel Leumas who
Appeared a deeper shade of blue
If that were possible, his features
Contracted to a line of pain
Subtended by a weary brain
That also drafted Retlaw's speeches
Where eloquence and hatred joined
In every slogan that he coined.

5

The two were followed by that solemnest
Of jesters, Graham Maharg, who played
The easy game of being a columnist
Of whom his readers were afraid:
In bed-sits, semis, mews and manses
They cowered at his fads and fancies.
From his front pocket peeped the fine
Orectic bust of Enid Dine,
Her coiffure shiny as a Sheaffer,
Her mouth agape as with the need
To say extempore the Creed

219

Or take, with grace, a Popish wafer.
Instead, she could be heard to sing
Better-known highlights from *The Ring*.

6

Then from another (left-hand) pocket
Glared Sir Ron Norris, union boss,
Nostrils like an electric socket
(Though hairy) arguing the toss
At annual negotiations
About industrial relations.
Graham Maharg knew when and where
To animate this puppet-pair.
If short of copy (and even more so
During a national alarm
When comedy could do no harm)
He slipped a hand into each torso
To praise or scorn speech or introit
At festive Blackpool or Bayreuth.

7

The mirror yielded further figures:
Escaped industrialist Mark Kram,
The teeth of Eric Cire, the sniggers
Of Sidney Yendis, the pure ham
Of Noël Leon, arch and cosy
Much-travelled Ysobel le Bosy,
Robert Trebor doing time
For little kidnapped Emily Lime,
Lord Droll holding a lighted taper
Beneath his nanny for a joke,
And many more. When Mary woke
She found she'd dreamed the morning paper
Where all put in a daily stint
And acted out their lives in print.

8

But still the night was not quite over
And there was one more face to dream.
Like love eluding Casanova,
A radio star, *Enigma*'s theme,
Its actual lineaments were traceless
And in her dream this face was faceless.
The kiss was casual and direct,
Surprising, chaste and circumspect,

Imbued with sadness not surrender
Like the full moon above a hill
That must in time be gone, and will
Perhaps not come again, a tender
Contact and its brief eclipse:
A silencing finger on the lips.

9
At which she really woke, a mystery
To her, but not to you, I think,
Who have been following this history
By scanning rows of signs in ink:
The things which tend to make us tenser
Are often struck out by our Censor
Who leaves it to the guilty Id
To hoard the facts it would forbid.
Were you or I to know who kisses
Us in dreams, who chases us
And whom we chase, voluptuous,
Along the edge of precipices,
We might improve our self-esteem
But then, there'd be no need to dream.

10
At breakfast all the world lay folded
In black and white against the milk.
Singers sulked and generals scolded
(Those in khaki, these in silk),
Some crooks were jailed for wielding axes
And others for avoiding taxes
While others still were knighted for
Their murdering or avoiding more.
Life thus proclaimed itself, profusely,
To Fairlea Crescent, Number 4,
Where, single and awake once more,
Mary sat down and ate her muesli:
Toothpaste and cereal combined
To put the kissing out of mind.

11
'Mary, *have* an egg,' her mother
Pleaded. 'Look, there's one just done.'
John said: 'I wouldn't mind another.
I can't keep up my strength on one.'
Every family's breakfast chatter

221

Is much the same: it doesn't matter,
And working girls have other things,
From hard facts to imaginings,
To think about. Her present worry,
Her cross, dead loss and albatross,
Involved attention from her boss:
'Sorry, Mum, I've got to hurry.
Mr Distimuth said he
Would very kindly call for me.'

12

'Hallo, hallo,' said John. 'What's cooking?
Lifts to the office in his car?
Pity he isn't better-looking,
Or aren't you so particular?'
'John, that's enough,' his mother chided.
'Finish your toast. Your tie's lop-sided.
And look: it's nearly ten past eight.
Get on with it or you'll be late.'
Being a widow in East Pinner
She didn't mention Distimuth,
Fearing that something was afoot
Beginning with lifts, moving to dinner
And after-dinner mints and verse
And after-dinner-something-worse.

13

And Mary thought so too. They neither
Spoke but moved about the sink
In silent contemplation, either
Washing or drying. What we think
We never speak; in conversation
We never think – dismal equation!
She took the paper to the loo
To do there what she had to do,
And found, somewhere between the Sporting
And City page, a photograph
Clearly designed to make you laugh,
A gem of straight-faced news reporting
Which showed that Polly Passenger
Had danced with a new follower.

14

Tim's name, of course, was printed slightly
Wrong. The camera caught him on

The hop, grinning, with an unsightly
Lick of hair. His forehead shone.
His posture was, to put it mildly,
Ape-like: bent knees with one arm wildly
Flung, performing the latest dance
With unconcerned extravagance.
(What it was called, I've no idea.
You may supply the name yourself:
'The Hump', 'The Limp', 'The Curious Elf',
'The Trots', 'The New Orleans Brassière',
'The Dalglish Skip', 'The Eiderdown',
'The Standing-Still', 'The Lord George-Brown'.)

15

But what the photograph omitted
From its trimmed margins was the glum
And static shape of the outwitted
Nico, still of course Tim's chum
But also now his deadly rival,
Painfully struggling for survival.
He'd had his moments of success,
Acquired that girl's West End address,
Hovered about, and at one juncture
Stepped forward with strange readiness
(When on the kerb in mild distress
She stood before her Fiat's puncture)
To pump the tyre *he* had collapsed
(After some minutes had elapsed).

16

That failed to get him in the paper
(Which didn't matter all that much)
Nor in her bed (which did). Each caper
Betrayed a faulty sense of touch
In dealing with love's paraphernalia.
Nico was half in love with failure
While Tim was twice in love with – what?
With youth? with love? but surely not
With Polly Passenger, a person
He could be hardly said to know,
Always half-drunk, the lights too low.
(Remember, when relations worsen,
The friend you are unfriendly with
May not be actual, but a myth).

223

17

And Mary's view of Tim, how valid
The Camford graduate grotesque?
Would the reality have tallied
With what she saw across her desk?
The vowels, the smile, the stoop, the shyness,
The knowledge of Plato and Aquinas,
The curious hat bought in Torquay,
Quotations from French poetry:
All these, and more, were blossoms grounded
In roots of personality
Already difficult to see
In nature's soil, so how well-founded
Could be the feelings which required
His playing satyr to her naiad?

18

Feelings which in her dream produced
That soft inevitable kiss
Anonymous and unrestricted
Upon the lips' parenthesis?
For Tim had shown no inclination
To any sort of conversation
(Still less to play it by the book
And start with the old-fashioned look
That shows with tact the way you're leading).
He didn't tease like Nico nor
Was he, like Distimuth, a bore.
It must have been the boy's good breeding
That kept him distant and polite,
Yet he could dance, it seemed, all night!

19

And here was Distimuth already
Sounding a fanfare from the street.
She grabbed a scarf, feeling unsteady
Upon her (help, still shoeless!) feet.
'Bye, Mum! Bye, John!' she called out, slipping
Into her green suede brogues and zipping
Her matching green suede shoulder bag
Stitched in dark umber zig by zag
(The bag contained a key, a diary,
Some bijou tampons for the curse,
A tube of mints, a comb, a purse,

A letter warning of the expiry
Of library tickets, a Penguin Jeeves,
Lipstick, and paper handkerchiefs).

20

Lashing a girl to bogus leather
Inside pressed steel provides a good
Excuse to be alone together
Since giving lifts, it's understood,
Is kindly meant. Some such idea
Was Distimuth's while changing gear,
Clutching and moving Mary's knee
Gently and absentmindedly
Down into top, thereby revealing
Much more of it than anyone
At ATI had ever begun
To see (though once when she'd been kneeling
With proofs of some new catalogue,
Fredge had peeped in, his eyes agog).

21

'Today, my dear, I lunch a client
Who's of great consequence to us,
In Middle Eastern oil, a giant
Among collectors. Make a fuss
Of this one, won't you? Do it discreetly.
I trust your savoir-faire completely.
I'm having a bit of lunch sent in,
Braised carp and duckling from Tientsin,
Snow peas and noodles, and a bonus
Of baby crab. We'll drink champagne,
Or maybe Corton Charlemagne.
There's still some left. The best coronas
Of course, and coffee as only you
Can make it. That should see us through.'

22

Lifting eight fingers from the steering
Wheel in unctuous emphasis,
He smiled one of those unendearing
Smiles that require paralysis
Of upper cheek and jaw and narrowing
Of lips: the whole effect was harrowing.
His gaze, intent upon the road
In steely concentration, showed

No kindness, warmth or even pleasure
In the said luncheon he'd rehearsed,
Though as he drove and they conversed,
His hand descended at its leisure,
Patronising, plump, inert,
To smooth the folds in Mary's skirt.

23
Ugh, I can't bear it! Do let's leave them.
Mary can handle him, I'm sure.
As for these lines, it's hard to weave them
Around a scene that's so impure.
I need, in this extravaganza,
Occasionally to give my stanza
A little rest, to let it breathe,
Especially when emotions seethe
Without some corresponding action.
The car was hot, the journey long.
I see no reason to prolong
Her torture for your satisfaction.
You know what Distimuth intends.
His client waits. The chapter ends.

Chapter Seven

The bargain

1
Time is an index to life's thesis.
Forward and backward stretch the weeks.
We squint in awe at their caprices:
Clusters of hours, the months in cliques,
Dense paragraphing where one reckons
Minutes by inches, pages seconds,
The years alone in heavy type
Like bachelors, with dog and pipe.
Time sidles up when you're not looking,
Pressing your hope into your hands,
Shows you the glossy future, lands
Of exotic promise, checks your booking,
Issues passports, labels, pills,
With the glib tout's deceitful skills.

2

Before you know it, all is over,
The moment's moving shores recede
And there, unchangeable as Dover,
The past confronts you like a deed.
Did Tim suspect the trouble brewing?
Surely he knew what he was doing?
I mean, of course, not his pursuit
Of love, but what as a recruit
To Quancy's current shady dealings
He found himself required to do.
For Quancy took the canny view
That innocence and finer feelings,
Though almost useless, would in time
Provide a cover for their crime.

3

And so we find that it was granted
To whom else but our hero, Tim,
To find the painting that was planted
Expressly to be 'found' by him
At Summershoot. He was ecstatic
When searching in a dusty attic
To come across in an old trunk,
With candlesticks and other junk,
Rolled up in paper, a quite sizeable
And battered canvas. Then and there,
Unrolling half of it with care,
He knew at once that recognisable
Grotesque, satiric, volatile
Augustan master's unique style.

4

Instant fame in all the headlines!
The papers sent photographers,
Broke up the news, extended deadlines.
The Times created such a fuss
That, hot for space, its arts reporter
Had 'Court News' made a column shorter,
While Tim, being questioned on *Tonight*,
Found even Robin Day polite.
In all the limelight Tim was modest,
Truthful, factual and concise.
Hard to suspect someone so nice

Who said himself: 'You know, the oddest
Thing is that this cornerstone
Of Hogarth's art is quite unknown!'

5

He told how Baltrap's father, eager
To fill the rooms of Summershoot
With something better than the meagre
Sticks he'd got, went in pursuit
Of heiresses as likely spouses
Who'd bring as dowry ancient houses
Crammed full of varnished paintings, rich
Tapestries, silver and what-not, which
Would give the Baltrap name a flavour
So far lacking. He explained
How such a bride was boldly gained
And just as boldly lost his favour,
How they removed to separate wings,
Apportioning their various things.

6

Baltrap himself confirmed his parents'
Long estrangement and the fact
That with a vengeful proud forbearance
His mother'd never quite unpacked
Some of the spoil she brought when married.
Their whole relationship was arid
Save for the presence of their son
Who found the odds two against one,
And so on. What a dreadful story!
It had, no doubt, some lineaments
Of truth, and served, at all events,
To map that murky territory
Across which scholars, armed, roughshod,
Mile by hard mile would have to plod.

7

But then, such scholarly geography
Designed to plot a simple route
Is very different from biography
Which needs to settle, not commute.
Baltrap's mother showed small fondness
For his young stubbornness and blondness,
First tearing captive butterflies
Then watching his own salmon rise,

But when he (to be strictly truthful
One should say when his *wife*) produced
A pretty son she was induced
To love this newer gentler youthful
Baltrap. And so they took to one
Another: age and youth had fun.

8

The tweedy Baltrap grew more tweedy
And more like his rapacious dad,
Became, as fortunes dwindled, greedy
For more than he already had,
And wondered how he could arrive at
Possession of his mother's private
Fortune. She, sensing this, bypassed
Him in her will, and firmly cast
Her by now twenty-year-old grandson
In the absorbing role of heir
To her estate. So debonair,
So idle, so refined, so handsome!
A pity he took his au revoir
By being burned up in a car.

9

Yes, he was coming from a horse show
(He didn't ride, but liked to look)
And drove his low-slung orange Porsche
Into a lorry he mistook
For open road. So he was swizzled
Out of the fortune, being frizzled.
And all were sad but not surprised
The body wasn't recognised
(Much the best method of departure,
Conveying the personality
With a discreet immediacy,
Swift as a bull's eye from an archer,
Permanent as a foundation stone,
Into dimensions quite unknown).

10

The painting's provenance, as Quancy
Had exclaimed, was water-tight:
It would have needed necromancy
To bring to the enquiring light
All links the chain contained, each section

Furthering the firm connection
Through family and through bequest,
Through private sale and fastened chest
(Time makes the demonstration fainter
But no less credible for that),
Through patron and through plutocrat
Back to the only source – the painter!
But still, the dangers were untold:
The Hogarth must be quickly sold.

11
Just as assassins need usurpers
To lend direction to their skills
And every fabricated purpose
Incontrovertibly fulfils
Existing appetites, so London's
Cosmopolitan abundance
Of all the rich and ignorant
So constituted an affront
To sober taste that men with talents
For rectifying (like Distimuth)
Unfair apportionment of loot
Acted to preserve a balance
Between the rolling and in need,
Between extravagance and greed.

12
The latest buyer cultivated
By the precarious Distimuth
(Who for the fake he had created
Needed a shady deal to suit)
Was Lebanese. He'd made his millions
In oil's dark jets and blood's vermilions,
Staining his country's smoking shore
With the materialist décor
So favoured by emergent nations.
Faud Warallah he was called,
Five feet tall, completely bald.
He'd murdered most of his relations
And occupied (plus personnel)
Three floors of the Hyde Park Hotel.

13
That lunch you'd heard was in the offing
Took place as planned, a feast at which

230

The greasy pair enjoyed their scoffing.
The sale went off without a hitch:
Desert hyena bent on culture
And patient mercenary vulture
Bared tooth and talon and ransacked
The stinking carcase of their pact.
At first the sum was hard to swallow
(A brace or two of grouse moors would
Have cost as much, it's understood)
But Quancy's write-up in *Apollo*
As 'quintessential English verve'
Restored the snob Warallah's nerve.

14

But that's the beauty of the bogus:
It makes us all conspirators
(With knives, perhaps, beneath our togas)
And so light-headed. What else does?
The drunkenness of our pretending
That happiness is never-ending;
Theories of spirit built on dope;
The realist's last and secret hope
That the cold world reflects his prowess
In so conceiving it: all this
And every kind of artifice
Establishes the fault as ours.
Yet still we love it. And that knife
Has been deep in us all our life!

15

The tongue explores what it has never
Cared to explore before; each hint
From purist critics (who endeavour
To crush all writing) reaches print;
Strikers protest at undermanning;
The ingénue is quietly tanning
Parts you will never look on; books
Exposing the history of crooks
Pay whacking royalties to numbered
Swiss accounts; each girl not kissed
Becomes a female chauvinist;
Litigious husbands, quickly lumbered
With Right of Access, in some pique
Turn into fathers once a week.

16
Driven to the limits of endurance
The senile mayfly promises
To rationalise his life insurance;
The drunk who thinks he's what he says
He is turns into Otto Klemperer
Conducting Gilels in the 'Emperor';
The Catholic novelist's receipt
For sex and guilt and self-deceit
Is signed by J. B. Page in vivid
Green; the poetess with legs
As purged of hairs as hard-boiled eggs
Visits the beaming surgeon; livid
Moralists are crucified
By dons who say: 'I nearly died!'

17
The pair shook hands. Cigars were lighted.
Despite himself, poor Distimuth
Showed by his sweat he was excited,
While the squat butcher of Beirut
Remained impassive as a beetle,
His features smooth and bland and foetal.
Within the glass was shifting sand,
Tomorrow and tomorrow and
The day after, the summer shortens,
Bringing the year about our ears,
Fate comes and clicks her little shears
And threads are snipped, of no importance.
If life and works, then why not verse?
Can the next chapter show much worse?

Chapter Eight

The bequest

1
Oh yes, much worse, for all and sundry.
The weather rarely turns out well,
For when it darkens it gets thundery
And figures in the aquarelle
Splash across pavements hunched and holding
Briefcases over heads or folding
The Guardian into makeshift hats.

232

Commuters, critics, bureaucrats,
Citizens of a busy nation,
With soles of insufficient shoes
As soft and damp as fillets, choose
To make their way to some libation
And as the warming liquors glide
Dry off by getting wet inside.

2

In fact it actually *was* raining
The night the Hogarth was displayed:
Lamborghinis aquaplaning
Along from Hyde Park Corner sprayed
Couples already growing chilly
From hailing cabs in Piccadilly,
Late-night shoppers in arcades
Sheltered until they drew the shades,
Those who had left their work were jealous
Of those who hadn't and were dry,
And drinkers kept a weather eye
Open to see if their umbrellas
Still safely glistened by the door
Like some bizarre marine décor.

3

O alcohol, you know the heart is
(Like cocktails) better for being stirred!
The pubs were publishing, and parties
Imparting, their confident, absurd
Advertisements of cheer. Deception
Lurked in every bland reception,
None more than that at ATI
Where now a livid crumpled sky
Wept over victim after victim
As, shaking raincoats, they advanced,
Smiling and eager to be entranced
(Thus bearing out this stanza's dictum
Which says it doesn't matter who's
Invited if there's lots of booze).

4

The earliest to come were wealthy,
Their having nowhere else to go.
Only their bank accounts were healthy,
Only their party spirits low.

233

Deep from a Daimler climbed Lord Wembley,
The first at any such assembly
(Solid as a cornerstone,
His presence guaranteed its tone).
Chairman of every Arts Committee
And arbiter of union strife
He'd left the academic life,
Oozed intellectual self-pity
And offered judgement (as he swirled
His whisky) on the real world.

5

Then came Sir Peter Hingeby, bringing
An Under-Secretary or two
And, with a naked lapdog clinging
To her, Lady Astarte, who
In her youth had paid to sit for Sargent.
Her withered bosom clinked with argent,
A complement to Hingeby's gold,
Well setting off what she had sold.
There followed company directors
Like Stuart Millions and Les
Scrip who with lies and promises
Had feathered nests (other collectors
Without resource to tax-loss quids
Could never match their reckless bids).

6

Faud Warallah and his henchmen
Were there, of course. A burly Swede
(Something in glass). A pair of Frenchmen
Who had demolished in their greed
About a tenth of Paris. Buyers,
Collectors, hangers-on and pious
Scions of old families
Who knew what may be somewhere is
(And came to ATI to see it)
Were there that night: who knows what lessons
They might imbibe of deliquescence?
Old Pictures equals Cash. So be it.
(And someone from the Government
Was there to find how much was spent.)

7

Then there were guardians of museums
For whom the plenteous spirits harmed
Already much-harmed peritoneums.
A portly publisher was charmed
By girls with orange crewcuts. Scholars
Were overheard to talk of dollars.
Taxis drew up with heated clocks
Debouching doyens of the Box.
Here was Lord 'Titian' Gaumont shouting
Friendly abuse at Crispin Swine
The critic who, obese, malign,
Looked ready for a Sunday outing,
With rustic sideburns to his jaws,
A walking-stick and cord plus-fours.

8

When Swine took off his wet galoshes
His feet steamed gently in the air
Like vegetables under cloches
Bulging to tuberous growth. The hair
Upon his head grew somewhat sparsely
As, on a ham, a sprig of parsley.
He gave his coat to Fredge to hold
Who brushed politely at the mould
On its lapels. 'Good God, man, gently!
I've had that coat since '21.
I got it from Augustus John.
It's worth a great deal!' 'Evidently,'
Said Fredge, noting the curious weave
And what remained of the left sleeve.

9

Together Swine and stately Gaumont
Pressed their way into the throng,
Swine open-mouthed as if a moment
Would see him bursting into song.
The beautiful were there: vivacious
Scented priests made goodness gracious.
Students, unstudious of their looks,
Flashed eyes that were not made for books.
Models in clothes looked melancholy
And some half out of them looked cold.
Nico was laughing, for behold:

235

He was accompanied by Polly,
Freshly fallen to his snare
When Tim was occupied elsewhere.

10

But do not think a bedroom drama
Had yet been played between these two.
No shining zip or creased pyjama
Had yet been loosed in earnest. Who
Was known to get that far with Polly?
To act too early would be folly.
The dangers were immense. The bet
Required a cautious etiquette.
So Nico laughed, coolly dispensing
Pale alcohols in glasses from
A tray and moving with aplomb
Among the guests. Of influencing
Events beyond their natural scope
He now had (wisely) little hope.

11

He gave one glass to Swine, who drank it,
Put the glass aside and walked,
Warm in his purpose like a blanket,
To Harold Distimuth who talked
Apart with Wembley and Warallah.
A rigid smile, unusual pallor
And restless movements of the hand
Gave Distimuth the air of bland
Insouciant terror, paralytic
Greed and vicious wariness
Mixed all together. Nonetheless
He turned to greet the baleful critic
With artifices to appease
An expert who was hard to please.

12

Swine had spent his life acquainting
Himself and then the world at large
With what was known of British painting.
It was a duty he'd discharge
With glee. He wrote profusely
About the watermarks of Fuseli,
Knew to the week when William Blake
Was running short of crimson lake,

Compiled the authoritative text on
Rowlandson, could date a Dadd
By knowing when the man went mad,
Could tell a Palmer from a sexton
And spotted any kind of fake
Through varnish umber and opaque.

13

And Distimuth was well-acquainted
With Swine's aforesaid acumen.
The man would know when it was painted
Or, rather, he would work out when
It *wasn't* painted. Not to mention
What clues a little close attention
Could soon uncover in the way
Of technical naïveté.
Why, you may ask, *have* the reception?
Why not let Warallah whisk
The thing away? Avoid the risk
Of such laborious deception
Being, at a stroke, seen through?
Avoid, in short, this hullabaloo?

14

Of course it all was Faud Warallah's
Fault: he should have lugged his haul
Back to some ministerial palace
To grace a gleaming stucco wall
As yet undoodled on by mortars
Or the bored pencils of reporters.
What Distimuth was never told
When the said fake was being sold,
What during the negotiation
Never a hint of had emerged,
The reason Warallah now had urged
This public show, the explanation
Of his unusual desire
For the great work, will now transpire.

15

The Hogarth had to be the pivot
Of Lebanese acknowledgement
Of British support: Warallah would *give it*,
Free, to the UK Government
In hope that bonds might be unbroken

Or possibly as a minor token
Of friendly ties as yet untied
But likelier now, as nationwide
(Warallah thought) a wave of pleasant
Feelings about the Lebanese,
Replacing earlier unease,
Would surge when news of this great present
Was made in print and on the air,
Catching the people unaware.

16

So he had just explained, with Wembley
Delighted, squeezing his pudgy arm:
'Magnificent!' But Harold, trembly
And nauseous beneath his calm
Thin smile and sallow heavy-lidded
Gaze, coughed, politely considered
The possible objections, thought
Of none – and knew that he was caught.
For up came Swine to hear Warallah's
Offer: 'What's this, Distimuth?'
He cackled. 'Are you going to put
It into expert hands? Hell has
No fury like a scholar warned
That weaker colleagues were suborned!'

17

What could he say? The critic's talons
Had sunk in deeply, and were sharp.
This Rhadamanthus of the salons
Stood loftily upon the scarp
Of his own judgement. Doubtful pictures
Submitted to his scornful strictures,
In doubt no more, were quickly damned.
Basements of galleries were crammed
With canvases that he'd demoted.
Famous careers at his behest
Were summarily reassessed,
And when his merest qualms were quoted,
Rank upon established rank
Of reputations promptly sank.

18

And he already was suspicious
Of Distimuth's elaborate fake!

238

Would he find out it was factitious?
What grave pronouncement would he make?
The Hogarth, you may guess, was badly
Lit, but who would not have gladly
Wished it much worse? An extra layer
Of varnish? And a silent prayer
That Swine would somehow be distracted,
Impeded by the chattering throng,
Clutch at his throat and fall headlong?
But no, he didn't. How he reacted
May best be told by focusing
Our own attention on the thing.

19

The painting showed a painting, firstly,
And next a man without a wig
With arms akimbo, looking cursedly
At what was clearly infra dig.:
This painting showed *another* painting
Of a young lady loudly fainting
Amidst a crowd of rakes and flirts
Wearing slight sneers and hooped silk skirts.
This second painting was being painted
By what appeared to be the same
Man who stood outside the frame
As if to disown the girl who'd fainted.
'It's me! But be that as it may,
It's not *by* me!' he seemed to say.

20

The canvas was of course quite sizeable,
Being a kind of Chinese box,
The inner subject recognisable
As Antelope's *Leap of the Fox*
(That can't be right, a slip of the fountain
Pen), as Ilex' *Top of the Mountain?*
As Axel Slope's *Slip off the Rock?*
Lick of the Rope? Rip of the Sock?
Lack of a Pick? My wits are failing.
At altitudes like this my luck
Is almost invisible, like Puck.
I'm feeling dizzy. Am I ailing?
All aches and I peep: 's a rip-off, a lark!
Excellent paps! Riper, they'll arc!

21

Dash it, you must know who I'm after.
He wrote of fools and country seats
(No, not Yeats – there's too much laughter).
He's quite a little chap (not Keats),
More of a classic (no, not Pindar).
His heroine is called Belinda.
(Wait while I pour another glass
And let this silly moment pass.)
She trumped her partner with a singleton
(As you might say) who in a fit
Of amorous inspiration lit
A pyre to put her stolen ringlet on:
Ah, love! What fetishes we use
In the false boast of self-abuse!

22

Her honour thereby was diminished:
Thus her hysterics, and that bright
Accusing glare (though not quite finished,
Needing a spot of Chinese White
To lend a highlight to the shining
Eyes) and that stretching half-reclining
Pose, a sofa usefully
To hand! The painter, you could see,
Was doing all that he was able
To add fine detail with his brush:
An azure tear, a deeper flush,
A splash of coffee on a table.
For even Hogarth clearly faked
Made other painters look half-baked.

23

*W*hat are his several contributions,
*I*n ink or pigment, to our art?
*L*ooking at doubtful institutions
(*L*aw or marriage) with that tart
*I*ncisive detail which enables
*A*ll sketches to convert to fables.
*M*aking a moral riddle out of sin
*H*e draws a nation gross with gin,
*O*r in the beer and beef of England
*G*ives xenophobes the chance to quench
A thirsty fear of the starved French.

*R*ascals and parsons intermingle and
*T*hereby betray one origin:
*H*uman nature, which makes us kin.

24

But sometimes less than kind. Our critic
Grinned from ear to ear, began
To promulgate his analytic
Hatchet-job. (O ruffian
Of reputations! Grudging growler!
Self-satisfied and hateful howler
Down of doubtful daubs! O fierce
Exposer of spurious portraits, pierce-
r of priceless polychromes, paladin
Of plain unvarnished picturehood!
Under your command they stood
Like mighty djinns before Aladdin:
By others worshipped, but by you
Superbly told what they could do!)

25

At least, he made a start, parting
His lips and drawing in a breath
(But then, it's always easy starting,
The view more common than the death).
His revelation of corruption
Was subject to an interruption
That no one present could foresee,
Whose unpredictability
Meant that Lord Wembley drenched a waitress
Who dropped her tray on Tim who leapt
On Lady Astarte – all except
A dour young skivvy from the caterers'
Turned from their drinking and their talk
(She went on polishing a fork).

Chapter Nine

The blame

1

For there upon a little table,
Flashing a fine mascara'd eye
As full of meaning as a label,

Holding her half-full glass up high
Then dropping it, stood who but Polly?
('There's going to be a scene. How jolly,'
Said Gaumont.) Polly's usual poise
Was somewhat countered by the noise
That issued from her lips, viz. screaming:
'The picture isn't yours! It's mine!'
Her mouth became a scornful line
And Nico wondered, was he dreaming?
This girl had been, seconds before,
Frosty, aloof, his paramour.

2

Now, like Belinda, she created
And everyone looked on in awe.
Distimuth was fascinated
As by some pale conquistador
Whose sudden presence at an altar
Once made an Aztec's hatchet falter:
Was this, he wondered, a reprieve?
Or was it only make-believe?
Hingeby by now was so suspicious
That he was more or less resigned
To ATI's imminent wind-
ing up, and with a sudden vicious
Wrench of Distimuth's left arm
He murmured so – with usual charm.

3

For what tycoon could risk a scandal
And trade for peanuts his good name?
The game was hardly worth the candle
(Nor was the candle worth the game)
And as he watched the writhing Polly
He knew at last the utter folly
Of trusting Distimuth. The girl
Was mad, of course (starting to hurl
Her clothes about), but what a muddle!
Distimuth himself looked lame
(Also for somebody to blame).
Quancy to Nico in a huddle
Muttered beneath his breath: 'My dear,
You'll have to get her out of here!'

4

And yet the scene seemed strangely fated.
'The painting's mine, the painting's mine,'
The swaying shape reiterated,
Pale, hypnotic, serpentine,
Like some auditioned songstress destined
For short-lived stardom in the West End,
Insistent shoulders, powdered spine
And voice's low and throaty whine.
Baltrap stepped forward, agitated:
Something about the voice and face
Was far above the commonplace
And made him feel associated
In ways as yet still unexplained
But which were somehow pre-ordained.

5

And somehow not to be resisted.
But still, such pain! Such *mauvais gout*!
'Not yours to sell!' the voice insisted,
And one white patent-leather shoe
Hit Distimuth upon the forehead
Leaving a really rather horrid
Bruise. What happened then no one
Can now remember, but the fun
Came thick and fast. 'Perhaps it's stolen,'
Someone daintily volunteered,
A man whose neat moustache and beard
No bigger than a semi-colon
Was promptly punctuated by
The other shoe as she let fly.

6

'No longer will I knuckle under
While *he* sells off his precious loot!
The painting's mine, with other plunder
That he's acquired from Summershoot
Left by my grandma!' With this veto
She stayed no longer incognito:
Warallah's henchmen lunged and gripped
Her dress, from which she promptly slipped,
And so they saw the lady vanish.
Her wig was trodden on the floor.
Her clothes lay scattered: through the door

There slipped a figure slight and mannish,
Short-haired, shouldered, epicene,
Eye-lashed, breastless and obscene!

7

'I don't believe it! God, it's Percy!'
Breathed Baltrap, as 'she' disappeared,
Leaving behind a controversy:
Some people fainted. Others cheered.
An artless few paid court to mammon
And helped themselves to more smoked salmon.
But none was able to agree
On what exactly she or he
Had done or said or why, by aiming
All that abuse, appearing in
Such an extent of cryptic skin,
Throwing his shoes about and claiming
The picture they had come to view
At its much-heralded début.

8

'It's Percy!' cried Lord Baltrap, blotting
The tears from his moustache – his grief
And joy left him in shock, garotting
A finger with his handkerchief,
Tight-lipped in the extreme confusion
And breaking of his self-delusion.
Well! After this, could there be more
Surprises? Singly from the door
Polly-Percy's pursuers slowly
Returned: the slippery naked prey
Had managed somehow to get away,
And now attention focused wholly
With awesome disbelief upon
The famous Hogarth – which was gone!

9

'Oh, no!' groaned Distimuth. One minute
There was a painting in its frame
And now the frame (with nothing in it)
Showed only the dead artist's name:
The canvas had disappeared. 'How awful,'
Said Wembley. 'Worse than that – unlawful,'
Chuckled the critic, Crispin Swine,

Taking another glass of wine.
'Did no one see it go?' asked Gaumont.
No one had, of course. The air
Was buzzing. Hingeby said: 'The affair
Was from the very start ill-omened.
And I consider that the theft
Has *nothing* to do with me.' He left.

10
Distimuth in apoplexy
Sat down on a canapé.
Quancy thought it all quite sexy.
Warallah's men were furious. They
Fingered their guns in silent menace.
Said Gaumont, vaguely: 'Once, in Venice
At the Biennale an event
Like this occurred. Some of us went
To open a restored palazzo.
There we were gawping from the bank
Of the Grand Canal: the whole thing sank!
No one knew whom to blame.' 'Is that so?'
Warallah muttered. 'Isn't quite the same.
Is fishy. *I* know who to blame.'

11
Accusation, remonstration,
Loss, discomfiture, surprise:
It hardly bears examination.
We'll tactfully avert our eyes.
For ATI the consequences
Lay not in shame but in expenses
And Baltrap, too, had been outdone
By these strange antics of his son
Who'd claimed his birthright without mercy
(Killing himself the fatted calf).
Why, you may ask, the tender half?
Why Polly Passenger, not Percy?
After the crash, alive, in luck,
He'd tried the part out – and it stuck.

12
He had his will without resistance:
To disappear was his one chance
To alter his entire existence,
So he had led them all a dance,

Finding himself more fully human
Living a new life as a woman.
But money, money: who can do
Without it? I can't, nor can you.
And nor could 'Polly'. He would rather
Reconstitute the gross façade
Of gender, blow the whole charade,
Than stand by weakly while his father
Continued with this rotten swizz
Of selling stuff that should be his.

13

So said goodbye. And goodbye, ladies,
Goodbye, sirs, and others! Who
If he knows how long his masquerade is
Going to run will see it through?
The man of sense will tiptoe quietly
And close the door on the unsightly
Mess. For here today and gone
Today is perfect oblivion:
No lingering, no lines to garble,
No fidgeting from gloomy friends
Who say, when asked, 'It all depends,'
No wit, no worry and no marble,
No tears, no explanations, no
Crescendo on the tremolo.

14

For shysters are at one with stoics
In fading firmly from a scene
That threatens to require heroics
And battles with the unforeseen.
The lucky yokel flattens ogres
Only because he isn't bogus.
Suffering's for the self-aware
Whose calculation that they dare
Not dare is like the bat's antennae,
Instinctive, automatic, fine,
(Though powered by a high-pitched whine).
In real life there isn't any
Ending that we apprehend,
For when that happens it's the end!

15

Whenever their accounts are settled
The greatest crooks are not around.
Just when their victims are most nettled
They hold their tongues and go to ground
(Cf. God's lame attempt to straighten
The serpentine career of Satan,
Or Lodovico's to extort
Iago's reasons for his sport).
The same with masters of the phoney
Who never live to face their lies:
Silent are Giordano, Wise
And *Eoanthropus Dawsoni*
(I mean, of course, that Piltdown gang –
Including the orang-utang).

16

Who loved a girl whose son was christened
Georgette, but wed a girl called George?
Who could not hear but always listened?
Who bored the farrier at his forge
And promised he would live for ever?
Who thought the truth had to be clever?
Who, preaching greed's exhausting price,
Reached forward for another slice?
Who, loving nature, joined the army?
Who filled his pistol full of blanks?
Who changed his dollars into francs
And back again? Who said: 'Don't harm me,
I am a poet'? Who, in short,
Hasn't avoided being caught?

17

Dear reader, surely you have noticed
The quantity of pages left?
The thunder of the anecdotist
Is thereby stolen. Welcome theft!
About the end I'm noncommittal.
Most of my characters have little
Left to live for: Distimuth
You may imagine destitute,
Nico reduced to being taken
By friendly Quancy out to dine
(And on long Shropshire walks with Swine).
Baltrap returned, quite badly shaken,

To Summershoot and in disgust
Bequeathed it to the National Trust.

18

Warallah went and bought the Hayward,
Feeling he'd aimed, perhaps, too low.
The Blazer and the Sneer and wayward
Polly made their escape, although
Their taxi's engine was so sluggish
They were arrested with their luggage
In Lower Bond Street, covering
With stolen canvas Polly's Thing.
('Here, here, what's this? Let's see your driver's
Licence, then. Nowhere to put
It, have you? No? Something's afoot,
That I can see. No, sir, no fivers
Please. If you've done something wrong,
Money won't help. Now come along.')

19

Mary and Tim became redundant
And time fell ripe into their hands.
The opportunity's abundant,
Beyond these pages, for romance.
Only a realist dismisses
The prospect of some cautious kisses.
But would you have it so? We can't
Be sure without a confidant.
I wasn't there myself. A candid
And exact appraisal's not
Yet possible. I tell you what:
To save you leaving empty-handed,
Let us *suppose* they met again
By chance. And dreamed again. And then . . .

VII
1973–1982

Annie upside down

What a position! I might as well be dead
  And suspended in the sea
My feet treading the blue laid out beneath my head
  Like infinity.

I never thought the sky could press so hard
  Or rock needed my hair
As roots for the blood to pound through, with my feet starred
  Against the air.

It's the whole earth turned inside out like a sock
  And me just hanging on.
It's no more than a sixpenny magnet: give me a knock
  And I'd be gone!

Didn't they use to bury you upside down?
  I've felt like this in a cellar
Bending for coal. But then I wasn't snagged like a clown
  Or a wounded umbrella.

It's the wire that's got me as it pinches wool.
  Isn't there someone coming
Whistling up the mountain for sheep who could give me a pull?
  My head is drumming.

Once from bits on fence and thorn I wove a
  Skirt, something for free.
Revenge! There never was a wall I couldn't get over:
  Now it's got me.

Where are Owl and Hugh, those gentle boys
  With deep pockets and a stone
For the dark pool in the wood where the eels made no noise
  Swimming alone?

How I ran after that pair just to be taught a
  Way to catch fish, and froze
As they held me by the bare heels with my hands in the slimy water,
  Tickling my toes!

Harry Tidy and Peter Shape would grin
  To see me on my head,
Who keep their balance as they keep their money in
  A feather bed.

251

And poor Tim Molehouse who for a whole spring
    Called to me from the garden
Might beg not for my finger for his mother's ring
    But for my pardon.

Why should he think it sinful not to marry?
    As if I belonged to him
One bit more than I belonged to Peter or Harry.
    Unhappy Tim!

There's many in their farms have shut their doors
    When I walked down the hill,
Though never did I once look back or without cause
    Wish them ill.

God help them with their sanctimonious drivel!
    They shall be stunned as an ox is
And shovelled into the black field under slabs that swivel
    Like pencil-boxes.

There let them gape as they have gaped from birth
    And gaping let them rot,
Each open mouth a rim of bone clogged up with earth
    Like a buried pot.

The soil shall not take me, caught up in my snare
    Like an old hanged ferret.
I am for the sun and the dissolving wind: the air
    Shall inherit.

I must weigh more than I thought. If I had wings
    I wouldn't be in this mess,
Slumped in the sack of my body and gloomily thinking of things
    To hate and confess.

Just like the redstart building I'd be gone
    With a moment on the stone
To check my heartbeat and an eye for danger. One
    Is too much alone

Where pairs are rooted. Clumsy arms and legs
    May be love's second-best,
But look how wings brave gravity to lower eggs
    Into the nest!

I saw the tell-tale twigs on precipices:
    Amazing! But why therefore
Should *I* be fastened to the tilted hill with kisses
    I did not care for?

I've had my arms round necks I saw too clearly
    For any kind of rapture:
No passing longing for the ordinary is really
    Worth the capture.

Best to avoid it. Single as the peak
    Which every restless eye
Strays to when valleys are damp there's nothing that I seek
    More than the sky.

Faces in rooms have too much of their own
    Individual life,
Never the same when you look again, silently grown
    Hard as a knife.

I've flown in dreams so perfect they'd convince
    Me I might really try to
Waking, if only the old earth didn't say: 'Why, since
    You've nowhere to fly to?'

I have no wings but only this dead skirt
    Peeled back like a glove
As once I had when I was young and nothing hurt
    So much as love.

The years fall out of your pockets, something comes in
    To your head like a passing thought
And can't be set to rights once it's got inside your skin.
    There: you're caught.

Hitched to the ribs of a field like so much mutton
    It's a wonder the crows don't come.
I might have thought of somehow trying to undo a button
    But my arms are numb.

Now I have had enough. It's all very well
    To hang here for a time.
At first I could have laughed: head over heels pell-mell
    Like a pantomime!

Let me be upright now and take a bow.
    Where's my fairy queen
To wave her wand and say that she understands just how
    Patient I've been?

Surely someone will come and fetch me and gather
    Me up and set me down

And all the escaped sheep will come running with their blather
    From their green town?

And the mountain will surely swing back in a while
    To point in the right direction
And I stagger about on the grass with a dizzy smile
    At my resurrection?

Surely the air after all this time has kept
    One secret, however old?
I can almost hear it, and I would stay to hear it except
    I am very cold.

Just a whisper would do it, the wind among
    The branches where we stood
Once listening for the mouse's and the eel's tongue
    In the dark wood.

Or water falling as if for all time
    Out of the rock, so cool
And calm the silent threads seemed almost to climb
    From pool to pool

And the eye moving upwards to lose that downward sense
    And all the elements weave in
A strange stillness and mysterious excellence
    I could believe in.

Such a secret would be worth the wait
    As birdsong after a night
Of horrors. There's hope for things to happen, though too late.
    And they might. They might.

The Duke's castle

I dreamed of the castle. Flying about
Were loosened trees, and I in my shirt
Saw sheets of water begin to shout.
I dreamed of the castle flying about:
Its turrets put the owls in doubt.
In my singing shirt I flew unhurt.
I dreamed of the castle. Flying about
Were loosened trees and I in my shirt.

Silence of chimneys ordered the air.
You were not there though bells were appealing.
I saw my childhood in rooftops where

Silence of chimneys ordered the air
To stand quite still and let me stare.
A tower of smoke became a feeling.
Silence of chimneys ordered the air.
You were not there, though. Bells were appealing.

The castle said nothing. Someone was calling
'Come back, come back.' I cried in my sleep
And asked the castle to stop me from falling.
The castle said nothing. Someone was calling.
The stones looked ready for my sprawling.
I shouted: 'What *is* there for me to keep?'
The castle said: 'Nothing.' Someone was calling.
'Come back, come back,' I cried in my sleep.

The Duke's pagoda

Tomorrow I will order stones
Beside a lake that is the shape
Of all desire, the lengthened ace
Unshadowed by its border,
No rose to break the perfect rim
Or water falls from wall to wall
To veil the cupolas and still
The single carp. And there
In tiers of rose and grey will rise
A wedding of Greece and China
From which the landscape seems to fall
As stair by stair turns round.
And nothing could be finer than
The way the walks direct the eye
To each of the six corners,
While from the topmost balcony
Showing like trumpets through the trees
The towers of Amboise will be seen
In the still hours of grey and green.

It stands in peace where once were nests.
Lights flicker in avenues
Where I can walk about, and then
About again, towards the stones.
It will suffice to turn my thoughts
Upwards, though at the pinnacle

Where can I look but down? And down
Again, and down the turning stairs
Must at the end of perfect days
Walk. The hills are lit
Beyond the window slits that turn,
Movement in stillness like a love
For everything unknown, and I
Still exiled with a summer frown,
The evening birds against my ear
Secure in leafy thrones.
All sullen beauty may be charmed
By the mysterious blood of building.
Tomorrow I will order stones.

Spirals

(179–)

   . . . and so I still hold up my head as
Far as the stiffness of my neck allows
And the dead weight of this nightcap worn to warm
A hairless head in pitiless November,
Still prefer no man's reason to my own
And say so readily at all times, yet
To you, my Friend, whose pie we have consumed
In this my humble lodging with much wine
(Trod in a Golden Age it seems, afterwards
Shipped while the unhappy Monarch still
Retained his head, though little else, the Palace
Lately stormed), to you, I say, I owe
Apology. I have no cellars for
Your *complots*, as neither for such old Bordeaux!
My steps (you counted them?) go up, not down.
   But I am flattered to be sought like this,
A Patriot still, I do admit, and somewhat known
In greenness for a pert Republican
With little good to say for King or Church.
Although (and here perhaps I'll let you smile)
You found me dozing with my feet in mustard,
Fingers a-twitch upon this folio
That has not left my knee in all this time,
Open at Exodus, a coffin's size.
You did not think I dined on Holy Writ,

Yet pastry crumbs have lodged between the pages,
A serviceable table for your kindness,
With gravy on these very words of God
That I was reading when you first came in:
'My face shall not be seen.' A daunting text!
Well, I am not ashamed. A text is not
A Bishop. Bishops, alas, may still be seen.
And God who fed his prophets will not grudge
An old philosopher a slice or two.
Yes, I am flattered that I have a name
Still worthy to be added to those others
Proscribed by our mad frighted Government
Who will, I know, persistently confuse
The speculatist and incendiary:
Priestley, you say? No, Priestley is not here.
Hardy? Thelwall? Holcroft? John Horne Tooke?
Whom some, I dare say, can admire. Brave men!
They are not exiled by the mob to spend
Their latter days beside a pretty water
That links the Catskills to long Chesapeake.
You say a thousand warrants are made out?
It seems to me that that is quite enough.
I would not wish to swell the dizzy list.
Forgive me to have ate the pie and now
Decline your ardent wish, but I was glad
To talk awhile with you and hear the news
Of the arrests and pamphlets, and the Trial
Of Reason soon to be attempted by
Our tailed and cloven-footed Ministers,
Happy not least, like them, with meat and crust!
If I had straight declined, my fast had not
Been so agreeably broken, I dare say.
You will forgive me then, my dear old Friend?
I do not think that Reason will succumb
Unless it be starved out, and who would rule
A land of corpses? I have kept this frame
Barely alive, but living is enough.
I shall not bargain for the people's bread
Or play the Law out like a shining fish,
Nor willingly would you rely upon
A dotard careless of all petty woes
By mankind self-inflicted, weak in arm,
Dreaming of secrets never to be shared

With idle cobblers and orators.
What, shall the rabble have my ear? Rather
My stone, my toe, or my incontinence!
I'd hang upon your project as on Sinbad
Hung the Old Man of the Sea, a parasite,
Unfed, uncertain and unpunctual,
Except perhaps in being thus confined
To one known spot, the window as you see
Target for halfpence, highest from the street.
(I've papered up the cracks, though, and have here
A jordan nearly full for my revenge).
    And why should men thus listen to their fellows
In times when misery distorts their tongues,
When hunger lends the fraudulent excuse
For violence, and truth's apprentice to
Expediency? In the best of times
It is a curious journey, hard and long,
And simply wishing will not get us there.
We shall not reach that eminence alone
Though each must find the pathway for himself
Nor help his brother to it with a gun.
Your cellared muskets keep their messages
Only for what they puncture: from the lips
Of the unsmiling dead their ignorance
Escapes and becomes the spirit they surrendered
To all the simple hungers, much too late.
How is that spirit nourished and repaired
But by the influence of natural objects,
The steady state of Nature shining out
As does a candle in a mine, small scope
(Yet pure) of subterranean artisans?
My own researches tell me all the time
That what we see assists us to see more,
Little by little, though the whole is dark.
As God proclaimed: 'My face shall not be seen.'
And what we try to see, precious beyond
The greed of governments, may not be taxed,
Stolen, corrupted, forfeited or lost.
    We'll have an illustration: here's a flame
Teetering on its tower of mutton-fat.
Look for a moth. The room is full of them,
And those that are not burnt or webbed will fly
Towards it, sure as our planet hugs the sun.

258

There, you see? Ah no, I fear you didn't.
The sluggish jelly moves too slowly in
Its pulleys of gristle. I have plans to make
Some kind of swift mechanic eye, with plates
Of silver turning in darkness on a wheel.
No more of that, but closely watch the moth.
Its path is indirect and spirals inwards,
Not equably as Archimedes' spiral
(A cylinder coiled up) but plunging in
As Descartes found, the vector angles round
The pole proportional to logarithms
Of the successive radii (the coil
Of elephant's trunk, since roughly conical).
You're with me? Still looking for the dazzled moth
Or for your claret? The quickness of the wing
Deceives the eye. I know it works with snails,
Whose tracks at night observe the rising moon.
These creatures do not look ahead of them
But seek a light they see somewhat abeam,
Adjusting their path continually to
This constant angle. So it is with Man
And his poor spiritual illumination,
Sought not directly but with reason like
The snail or moth, plunging at last to truth!
The time's not now, and will not come just yet.
The mind moves slowly in its glistening track
With all appearance of obliquity,
Requiring gods with appetites or with
The heads of fish; worshipping any shape
That fear dictates or custom renders dear,
The totem's beak, the bosom of the hills,
Even the commonest odd-toed ungulate;
Requiring weakly to be led, to scrape
The forehead at the shrines, to guard the secret.
     The secret's in our hands! At least in mine,
I'm sure of it, and I'm familiar with
Its teasing shape, whether in text or shell.
You will remember, Friend, our youthful scorn
Of the confusions of these mosaic texts
And our analysis, as of a star,
Of the emergence of the single God
Unhappy in his fable as in a cloister
(There is no word in Hebrew for a Goddess).

259

We wished him married for morality
And for his greater peace of mind. Poor jest
Of riggish youth! Oh yes, I might still grant
That YHWH bears a cruel resemblance to
The Babylonian YA, yet in this shape
He brought to men (significantly closer
As in a geometrical progression)
A truth, the flame and centre of the whorl.
My years of study in philosophy
(The prism and the forms of animals,
My struggle with fossils, even my lost decade
Of gases) reveal to me the pattern of
What in our youth we scorned. My theory
Explains exactly why Moses is neither king,
General, priest, prophet nor magician,
But simply one of the constant angles of
Our spiral quest. When God said: 'Thou shalt see
My back parts; but my face shall not be seen,'
What was it but a recognition of
Our spiral-equiangular of truth,
The snail's way, the moth's way, and ours?
We see the back parts, sure enough, as did
He in the blinkered cleft: a passing glory
Which is to our poor eyes the shadow of time
Upon the world itself, the hem of Nature.
    And I have seen the vision, too, myself,
Seen it askance, obliquely like the snail.
You'd hear of it before you go? You're kind
To humour me. There is not much to tell,
Though it was that which changed my life, or else
I would not put you off so easily,
My blood now being cooled but pumping still
To serve my will with steady revolution.
You knew my patron gave me the wherewithal
To take my passage on the *Adventurer*
And catalogue the fauna of the voyage?
We'd parted months before, you to collect
Subscriptions for another journal (which,
I now forget) and I to Charmouth for
The fossils. It was the year of broad-arsed Bridget
And the hackney feats. Which year was that, I wonder?
I have no head for years. We sailed from Bristol.
Long months of patient work. Hot sun, bad food.

260

Then we were wrecked, most unexpectedly:
Some business with an anchor and some rocks
Which blame could never fully clarify
Though later a whole bench of admirals
Sifted our testimony. The ship sank
And we were thrown upon the southern sand,
My cabinet upended and its trays,
The spiralled Nautilus, the Conch
And other specimens rejoining their
Own world, as I now feared I never would.
I nearly lost an eye, this breach from cheek
To scalp so longed to bare my fizzing skull.
Most sank. Many were beached already dead.
We mouthed in silence with our blackened tongues
Till one, the meanest deck-hand, found a fruit
That loosened his, and spoke in measured speech.
    And so we walked each one despite his wounds,
Mine not the greatest, though the pain was deep,
Till we came to the very nape of the mountain where
They lay so thick a blind man could have picked,
Moving his hands over the abundant sprays
Like a saint blessing the heads of children. One
With his guitar (all that remained unsmashed)
Plucked from its waist a sort of minuet
Which with its strictness mocked his purple mouth,
Lent it a smile which all of us returned
Who were not sleeping. The sounds moved over the trees
As shepherds wakeful on the Cotswold pastures,
Nudging the birds from soporific perches
To fan their colours in the glades and lodge
Again when the music ceased. I was still curious,
And reached the peak with all my pain forgotten.
And there it happened. Do not ask me what.
I cannot say what it was. Each footstep stirred
A melancholy shriek from vines that trailed
Up a cathedral's height to a green mist,
And drifting down were scattered veils of light.
I did not doubt the benevolence of that
Untrodden place. We lived. And were five years
Upon the island, where every shape betrayed
The trailing hem of Nature. Nothing was asked,

Nothing vouchsafed which I could learn or teach
In the ways of men. You were not there, my Friend,
And well may smile and shake your threatened head.
So you may die and feel that it is noble
To take us to the brink of civil war
To break a Bishop or a King or two.
It seems I have become a misanthrope
And see no future in the race, and yet
I have my work and it is noble, too,
Though reaching beyond the human, vainly perhaps
As these poor daughters of the ransomed earth
Wooing the sons of heaven . . .

Well said, Davy

He went to the city and goosed all the girls
With a stall on his finger for whittling the wills
To a clause in his favour and Come to me Sally,
One head in my chambers and one up your alley
   And I am as old as my master.

I followed him further and lost all my friends,
The grease still thick on his fistful of pens.
I laced up his mutton and paddled his lake
In the game of Get-off-me and Just-for-my-sake
   And I am as old as my master.

I sang in his service a farewell to sorrow
With rolled black stockings, the bone and the marrow.
The Law was a devil to cheat as you pleased
As we knelt on the backs of the city girls' knees
   And I am as old as my master.

So back to the country where birds are squawking,
With possets for pensions and witless talking
Of walloped starvelings and soldiers' fortunes
From his nodding bench in the smothered orchards
   And I am as old as my master.

Age turns the cheek of a buried scandal
In a nightmare of cheese and a quarter of candle.
When the servant is privy he's good as a guest,

The first to be carved to and last to be pressed
    And I am as old as my master.

Country or city, no pleasure can last:
It's farewell to the future and beckon the past.
Though he that we drink with is sometimes a fool,
A single grey tooth may furnish a smile
    And I am as old as my master.

A secular sermon: Bel and the Dragon

Beneath the diagrams of light
That shaped this city and its kings,
Beneath the painted roof of night,
Beneath the towers and the stones
Lie all the kings and their black bones
    And their gold rings.

Where beneath tombs each son lay down
Beside his father and gave birth
To history and lost a crown,
Beneath the pavements and the sands
Extend the barren nameless lands
    Of the old earth.

And the stars spell, as stars will,
A tale of the spinning of the years
Out of a warring of the still
Centre of our certainty
And the illimitable sea
    Of our old fears.

Marduk and Tiamat, hero and snake:
Great hands that tore the serpent through
And beat the waters down to take
The tablets of our destiny
Out of impossibility
    And make them true

Became the judge, became the god,
The god of Hammurabi's laws.
Yet still the snake the hero trod
Moved in the temple of the kings,
Moved in the shadow of all things
    And was their cause.

And the god smiled in silence and
He too in the temple of the kings
Received the supplicating hand,
And his quiet triumph became a style,
Smiling in silence, a golden smile,
   A god with wings.

Bel out of Marduk, mighty Bel
Stood in the temple with the priests
While on its plinth the Snake as well
Moved in the glistening of its powers,
The gold, the pavements and the towers
   And the long feasts.

For the stars spell, as stars will,
That the strange patterns of the sky
Reveal that all is change until
No end, and nothing is complete
And may be greater for defeat
   And does not die.

So all is change, and Bel with Snake,
Snake against Bel, carry their armed
Complexities, make and remake
Their battle in the souls of men,
Propose, retire, engage again
   And are unharmed.

How should we live except by this
Long struggle, this duality?
Why find a new hypothesis
For what may mock and may inspire
The acts of men and their desire
   So to be free?

For thus we bring the bread and wine
Daily into the temple where
It lies and is consumed, a sign
That the two presiding images
Are living powers and eat with us
   And hear our prayer.

And what we pray for is the peace
That gods have had and men may know
When mind presents his masterpiece,
The circle closing on its round

Or sound answering perfect sound
   And senses know

How in the light the dark remains,
How in the whole the part is proved,
How they have triumphed in their chains
And lost their bid to rule alone,
How out of Many may be One
   Who is unmoved.

And the stars spell, as stars will,
Pride of the temples and the schools
Where priest begotten of priest to fill
The temples and the palaces
Turns from the truth of images
   To rites and rules.

Priest upon priest who walks and sings,
Priest upon priest in false meekness,
Priest upon priest, greater than kings
Who learn from them the key to dreams,
Who learn from them the thing that seems,
   Who learn their weakness.

And all the offerings sustain
The pride of priestly family,
The gold, the wine, the wheat contain
No meaning that is not the least
Of simple meanings, to a priest
   Who should not be.

And the stars spell, as stars will,
A prophet of another land
Who will expose the priests and kill
The gods by ruse and violence,
Break what he knows has no defence
   With his own hand.

O images, O images!
You stand between the earth and sky
Greater than both, and all that is
Is not so great as what men fashion
To comprehend their fear and passion
   And justify

The small lives that they daily hoard
Against the dark, O images!

265

What learned doctor can afford
To put down images? What king
Will put down images? What thing
　　Is not, that is?

For all that is is not so great
As what men fashion in their need,
And all men need, early or late,
The life of gods and images,
Though there be some deceit in this
　　And priests must feed.

Or else the tombs must crack and all
The stars in the speechless dark stand still
And the waters will rise again and fall
Never, and kings for all their gold
Will be as the stars which will grow cold
　　As stars will.

The kiss

Who are you,
You who may
Die one day,

Who saw the
Fat bee and
The owl fly

And the sad
Ivy put out
One sly arm?

Not the eye,
Not the ear
Can say Yes:

One eye has
Its lid and
Can get shy;

One ear can
Run out and
Off the map;

One eye can
Aim too low
And not hit;

One ear can
Hug the air,
Get too hot.

But lip and
Red lip are
Two and two,

His lip and
Her lip mix
And are wed,

Lip and lip
Can now say:
'You may die

But not yet.
Yes, you die
But not yet.'

The old lie.

The voice

I am the pulse of a new language,
The code of the invader.

I am the touch of white,
And thus I ask admittance.

I am the trace of a dim thunder,
The fear of the sentry.

I am the sound of black,
And thus I enter.

I am the dead kiss of damage,
The voice of the rebel.

I am the taste of red,
And thus I establish myself.

I am the reign of the little robbers,
The struggle of the settler.

I am the birth of pain,
And this is my time.

I am the breath of the heavy lover,
The stillness of the occupied.

I am the smell of death,
And I shall leave as I have entered.

The wilderness

A memory of Oscar Silverman in Buffalo, 1962

Displaying a wicked smile through his morning cigarette
Like a benign Demon King wistful for home cooking,
Smiling his big smile of seduction and authority,
Oscar said: 'Today I'm going to give them *Henry IV*
And you can be Hal. Can't you?' I supposed I could be.

Yes, I was Hal. And Oscar ceased for an hour to be
Professor of English and Chairman of the Department.
He sat on a desk and chatted to the Seniors,
His charm unwearied, his enthusiasm without reserve,
The big collapsed roué's visage alive with naughtiness.

And Shakespeare's dialogue confirmed their impression
Of a visiting stranger in an armour of self-control,
Wrapped in his own atmosphere of curiosity and judgement
With an alien humour and a palpable timidity:
I was a useful assistant and the old man's foil.

Fifteen years ago it was easy to be the empirical Hal.
I was angler and non-swimmer on the bank of that river
Which shifts us so slowly but certainly along, noting:
'I believe the wilderness will be new to all the party.
The Miss Bertrams have never seen the wilderness yet.'

As though we really were required to escape being in character,
As though life were designed to parade its ridiculous threats,
Like a sober doom, at once glamorous, sedate and sinister!
And there was a justice in the role I played, endorsing
A poetry of implication, disturbance and restraint.

They told me it was the coldest place in America, and sure enough
A colleague got frostbite just walking across the car-park.
In the year of the Cuban missiles, under campus ivy I wrote:

'The wilderness is what we see from broken shades.'
But I was secure as Pope 'descending' to the gaieties of Horace.

I had located a role for the broken city about me
Like the Lisbon earthquake, sitting in our green apartment
On the corner of LeBrun and Winspear, not explaining myself,
Dreaming in the prose style of Gibbon of the violent landscape,
Ice crusting the trees, cars smashing in the streets.

But Oscar, that kindly master of the academic ceremonies,
Had something else to tell me if I had listened.
There is a life of all lives to be lived that will contain us,
That draws us to its centre with no kind of calculation,
Native, beyond art and of a power to forgive our rejection.

It is without honour, no punched card or map of it
Exists to be consulted and the city has not heard of it.
It has never been rehearsed and cannot be explained,
And though you may begin to define it by knowing the wilderness,
Its easy habits may well take a lifetime to learn.

And so he must have known as he sat on the edge of the desk,
Betraying confidences like a shopper in a tea-room,
Giving assurances like a doctor with his bag on the bed,
Appealing for support like a crafty baby with a toy:
The students listened, as did his ignorant accomplice.

'A goodly portly man, i'faith, and a corpulent;
Of a cheerful look, a pleasing eye, and a most noble carriage.'
Here was a humour indeed, a man confronting the wilderness,
Knowing the good places to eat, guardian of the wonderful papers,
His two daughters, and the many kinds of apple.

In the hotel

Where was it, then, that I saw my dead friend?
The hotel with breakfast beneath a curving stair?
The hotel under the eaves and the spouting gutters?
The hotel of darkness? The hotel of black marble?
The hotel of dead water with its dripping
And lead wounds and stumps of extempore plumbing?

All our days flourished in their bound ledger!
The accounts are kept open for the unforeseen
Yet absolutely necessary expenditure.

Sleepless we think, we are driving in our sleep
To arrive in the end at the commercial hotel
With its frail balcony above the empty streets.

Sleepless, are yet asleep and not asleep,
The room is airless, change piled on the washstand,
The pipes sighing all night with water or air
In whichever hotel it was that I saw my friend,
Where we ourselves must wake on the final day
In the last and least remembered hotel of all.

In the corridor

Francis, it *was* you yesterday, though I knew you were dead,
    Smiling and nodding your head
As though your long-kept secret could wait a little while
    To be recounted in style,
Fondly amused at my pain and excitement at seeing you there,
    At seeing you anywhere
When I thought, when I knew, the historical you that really mattered
    Had been so cruelly scattered.
It must have been you I recognised as much as the once alive,
    Unless those who survive
Go on and on as they did investing the shapes of friends
    For their own strange ends
With the voice and significance of what affects them most.
    Like an over-insistent host,
'Francis, what *happened*? Tell me. Tell me how you escaped,'
    I silently mouthed and gaped,
Eager and simple for a startling truth. I was so compelled
    To what seemed to be withheld
That I moved along the corridor towards your stillness
    As doctors deal with illness,
Reckless of answers that the only cure requires,
    Immune to its desires.
But of course the darkness shielded you from inquisition
    And I froze in the position
Of one whom the dead night's noiseprint has suddenly caught awake
    Like one frog in a lake
When all else is slow mist rising to meet the moon
    And the first light all too soon
Shocks us to a reappraisal of that brief deep
    And self-satisfied sleep

Which is our charmed life. In the corridor
   My bare feet on the floor
Were rooted even as I thought I began to tread
   In drawn and willing dread
The several thousand and worn stitches that lay between,
   Its invisible brown and green.
You will forgive, I am sure, that craven breaking of the spell
   Though you may have wished to tell
Secrets that only such silence and respect of fear
   Ever allow us to hear.
Francis, now I have seen you once more, knowing you are dead,
   Though nothing at all was said,
I know that for you the future has ceased at all to exist
   And will not be much missed.
Only our sorrow for you will come again and again
   And goes some way to explain
Why there is fit passage for its evidence of our fears
   In a few words and tears.

Nocturnes

1
The fingers press
And they release
The hopes which else
Would stifle us.

Such brief soundings
Are like endings
Not beginnings:
Hopes are dead things.

2
Let us, as the sun grazes
The hedge, renounce the prospect
Of new happiness.

Even the tawdry relics
Of our own past hopes
Are lost for ever.

All that certitude of novelty,
That determination to do without
The timid and the shoddy.

The portraits are of interest
To no one. They are indeed
Like ourselves.

3

Admitting that it is one of the
Minor though loved surfaces of my
Brief days as a nomad of matter
(One dear body and the cloudy blue
Sphere itself come to mind as greater)
I sit above it with fingers spread
As if to heal the straitened world of
Elephant and forest which offer
Their wounded sounds into the smiling air.

4

The room is giving the fire its attention
And the fire is self-absorbed:
A studied Brahmsian *nobilmente*

Of knots and boles and bark,
Textures too fine to lose, although
The burning must continue.

Flower, stone, pomander:
The light and warmth are wasted
For the room is empty.

5

Low moments are like slow movements
Where joy succeeds, *presto possibile.*

Succeeding is not success, to be sure,
Merely a dialectic of structure.

The natural ebullience of an ending
When we sense, with relief, that ending is final.

Sonata

The body leaning slightly back, the arms held firm and straight
As if she found those first deliberate chords a heavy weight
Impelling sound to herald, like the raising of a curtain,
A massive concentration on the things we find uncertain,
And with a noble carelessness of what she there might find,
She starts upon her journey to the centre of the mind.

At first the notes are confident of all they understand,
As if the sum of human purpose lies beneath each hand.
The cadences of concord cross the measured page in pairs
As calmly as a couple might descend the morning stairs
Or children playing in a garden weave the air with thirds
As though for simple happiness their calls were those of birds.

But then her eyes perceive ahead a shift in the notation.
An *allargando* of regret, bereavement's modulation,
Reveals the theme's distinction to be that of comprehending
How every ravishment contains the sourness of pretending
That in our perfect virtue it may chance to last for ever,
If destiny so smiles upon our singular endeavour.

Its falling minims lucidly declare the fight will fail
To win ourselves the closure of the lucky fairy tale.
The sober music now decides the battle has been done.
Its message to the pianist is that nothing has been won.
Not even sheer persistence in the struggle for expression
Ever deprives the darkness of the fullness of possession.

Descending octaves falter as the left hand turns the page
Revealing flocks of quavers beating wings against their cage.
The fingers fumble wildly in their effort to release
The soul that mocks their movements from the prison of the piece.
She offers it the freedom that its dumbness cannot learn
Though she bargains for its ransom, trying all the keys in turn.

The music turns to panic only stubbornness denies,
As if the fingers' questions forced the vagueness of replies,
Until with all the righteousness of having come so far
It thunders to exhaustion at the final double bar.
Her hands remain a moment on the flat and silent keys
And then she slowly places them together on her knees.

Her head is motionless and bowed, hair faintly disarranged.
The silence holds suspended everything her hands have changed,
In muted echoes from the mind of what the air has lost.
Her feet have quietly drawn back from the pedals, ankles crossed,
As if conclusion could admonish how the sound behaves
When granted independence from the locked and blackened staves.

This moment is what you or I, had we been there to hear,
Would call the grave illusion of the will to persevere,
Since all except our love for her has vanished like a vapour
And nothing is at rest, or certain, save the printed paper,

273

For love demands a truth the music has denied in vain
And what it said contented us, and will content again.

Dozing

How much longer must I sit here
Waiting for something to happen?
The clatter of the exciting parcel
Is only the cat nosing through her door
In search of the relief her hardening kidneys
Refuse, the back leg drawn slowly through the flap
Extended behind her like a ballerina's
Who turns and turns, without a thought,
Through the repeated afternoons.

She dozes on the arms of the high fender, twitching,
Throat flattened trustingly on the padded cloth,
Tail drooping, body slipping sideways,
Till only her claws, which experience has anchored
To the warm raft of her dreams, sustain her,
And she is left hanging on like Norman Lloyd
In Hitchcock's *Saboteur*. As she climbs back
Her look is hurt, sleepy, resigned,
Like an arrested drunkard.

If I encourage her to lie on my knee
I will never move again! The bottle is out of reach,
The finishing cadences motionless on the turntable,
The amplifier's hum expectantly filling the room.
It is a moment for some truth to occur to me,
About chance, about hope, about stubbornness,
About how we are to face the unfaceable.
Notions I reckon too solemn for silence,
Too gravelling for tenderness.

Trio

A gardener's triumph! But it was planted at an angle
And has to be supported on its frail root.
Her hands run up and down its trunk like squirrels
And she loves it like a child between her knees.

A feat of balance! But it all takes place
Between tight-rope fingers and clown-mouth
On a journey in a wooden boat with a single oar
Occurring in the guarded space belonging to kisses.

A banquet for one! But he toys with his food,
Eyes closed, head tilted back in rapture
At the enormous table, the black table,
The table with three legs and a lid.

Syrinx

Most surgical of instruments!
Aeolian tube with rods and keys
Poised in the balanced hands to squeeze
The slender soul through its precise space,
Like a rare serpent of the desert south
Worshipped in its narrow place,
Drawing the soul from the hovering mouth!

A trickle that defies gravity, creating
Pools of articulated notes that fly
From each prestidigitating hand,
A shining elevated wand
Whose buttons the fingers do up so quickly!

It is like a telescope for the wind's song
Extended from the lips and tongue
As from an eye to which horizons are strangely near.

Then the silver body is broken in three
And the music survives in the ear.

Concerto for double bass

He is a drunk leaning companionably
Around a lamp post or doing up
With intermittent concentration
Another drunk's coat.

He is a polite but devoted Valentino,
Cheek to cheek, forgetting the next step.
He is feeling the pulse of the fat lady
Or cutting her in half.

But close your eyes and it is sunset
At the edge of the world. It is the language
Of dolphins, the growth of tree-roots,
The heart-beat slowing down.

Silence

Once again the instruments
Rehearse their elaborate departure
And the eyes continue to stare ahead
When all excuse for pensiveness
Is gone, the record long unwound;
Only the miles-off surf of the speakers
Establishing its vacant musty
Presence: not worth listening to.

Lily and violin

1

You buried them so lightly,
These crinkly globes and packages,
It seems a thought would wake them.

Slumbering in their soily shallows,
Folded waxen music of earth
That stirs like a waking shape.

The shape thinks them, breeds them,
As ink is splashed in crotchets
Across a furious page.

The instruments begin to sound.
Their warmth is the slow warmth
Of defined space, of paysage.

And the black and white of a late snow
Melts into laughter like small touching,
The giant's coloured beard.

2

A needle of lightning strikes
The black imaginary valley
As a tyro lily with inch of violet nib
Tries to scribble a message

As still as abandoned smoke
Soon to become the frail green
Of a grandmother's silk girlhood
Whirling and twisting in the snapped air.

And she encounters Herr Geige
Hiding tears beneath nobility,
The frayed sleeves of a maitre d'hotel,
Dripping traces of hot sugar
To cool in a bowl of clearest water
To thunderous applause.

   3
Prue, your bulbs are out a-walking
Quite without our knowing it:
The great lighthouse lily on its stalk,
Wing-cases askew, ready to fly;
The common hyacinths in waterproof shoes,
Green shawls and paper haircurlers;
The lily-of-the-valley standing still
In a sculptured fairy cluster.

Their earth, their pebbled bowls
Yield a fragrance like a great wine.
What do they think of this world with corners
They have so achingly woken up to?
Full of dry warm air, tobacco smoke
And the sound of the sublime K BN I TET?

   4
The violin's voyage through the still room
Establishes a momentary map
Of things distinguished and responsive to
Its movement: books silent and tight as slate,
An empty chair, a battle-row of pawns,
The glass monstrance of a forgotten claret,
And in a corner, stretching to be away,
The six soundless sails of a great white lily.

Strangely I wish, I wish I were not here,
For only the mind among them recognises
(How unwilling, how ungenerous!)
The vain deception of its call to action,
The wildness of its promises, how soon
It will all end, the deadness of the dead.

277

5

Here we are, then, half in and half out
Of what, being in such a position,
It is almost impossible to describe
Except in terms of the small events
Which shadow its embracing dimension
And please us by seeming to be other than it.

Like the sustained rich impure
Voluntary of the stroked string
Doubling itself and redoubling,
In motion still, although the sound
No longer reaches the ear. So that
We almost hope to be wrong in saying
With Duke Mantee that we expect
To spend the rest of our lives dead.

6

Afterwards we may not speak: piled chords
Are broken open with changes of key;
Logs in settling shoot a surprising flame;
A petal folds more slowly than night falls;
A face is lifted to catch the last
Ache of struggling body or air.

Afterwards we may not speak, since
Everything hastens towards its end
With an enlarging beauty. May not,
Need not, will not, we say, obsessed
Like vagrant creatures with consummation.
But it is all our dear illusion
Belonging to the experience itself
Which must not speak of afterwards.

7

I was reading of Samuel and Sara's cottage
With its talismans of jasmine and myrtle
Preserved in splashes of exclamations
When I saw you carrying away the bowls
Of lilies like the toyed leavings
Of a pampered flower-eating god!

Dead, are they? Dry already?
And was there nothing to preserve them
Except these simple marks shared
Across almost two hundred years

With the dreaming poet whose
Utopia was a failed commune,
His Arcadia an accessible breast?
It is you, Prue, my eyes follow, not lilies.

8

After their brief incarnation
The bulbs are returned to the garden
And the room is without life.

Sounds have now no shapes to charm
Beyond this clutter whose collapse
Extends beyond a year.

The spring was counterfeit
Like the excited emotions
Of our own first flowering.

Before experiment was experience,
Before discovery was recognition,
Before the event became activity.

And we are left now with our patience,
The sleeping of beauty unaroused
The silence between the movements.

Waiting for the music

This is the news: two sounds
At a guarded melodious distance
Follow each other wherever
Either chooses to go.

And all our lives we are
Waiting for the music,
Waiting, waiting for the music.

Scanning the instructions,
Hand reaching for hand.

Waiting for the music.

Retreat

I should like to live in a sunny town like this
Where every afternoon is half-day closing
And I would wait at the terminal for the one train
Of the day, pacing the platform, and no one arriving.

At the far end of the platform is a tunnel, and the train
Slows out of it like a tear from a single eye.
You couldn't get further than this, the doors all opened
And the porter with rolled sleeves wielding a mop.

Even if one restless traveller were to arrive
With leather grip, racquets under the arm,
A belted raincoat folded over the shoulder,
A fishing hat, and a pipe stuck in his mouth,

There would be nowhere for him to move on to
And he would settle down to tea in the lounge
Of the Goat Hotel, doing yesterday's crossword,
And would emerge later, after a nap, for a drink.

You meet them in the bar, glassy-eyed, all the time.
They never quite unpack, and expect letters
From one particular friend who doesn't write.
If you buy them a drink they will tell you their life history:

'I should have liked to live in a sunny town like this,
Strolling down to the harbour in the early evening,
Looking at the catch. Nothing happens here.
You could forget the ill-luck dogging you.

'I could join the Fancy Rat Society and train
Sweet peas over the trellised porch
Of my little slice of stuccoed terrace. I could
Be in time for the morning service at Tesco's.

'I expect death's like this, letters never arriving
And the last remembered failure at once abandoned
And insistent, like a card on a mantelpiece.
What might it be? You can take your choice.

' "I shook her by the shoulders in a rage of frustration."
"I smiled, and left the room without saying a word."
"I was afraid to touch her, and never explained."
"I touched her once, and that was my greatest mistake." '

280

You meet them before dinner. You meet them after dinner,
The unbelieved, the uncaressed, the terrified.
Their conversation is perfectly decent but usually
It slows to a halt and they start to stare into space.

You would like it here. Life is quite ordinary
And the self-pity oozes into the glass like bitters.
What's your poison? Do you have a desire to drown?
We're all in the same boat. Join us. Feel free.

And when the bar closes we can say goodbye
And make our way to the terminal where the last
(Or is it the first?) train of the day is clean and waiting
To take us slowly back to where we came from.

But will we ever return? Who needs us now?
It's the town that requires us, though the streets are empty.
It's become a habit and a retreat. Or a form of justice.
Living in a sunny town like this.

Year of the Child

Furiously behind its frozen lens
The shutter moves. And catches the breath
That will not live to cloud it.

Winter has hugged the world to death
And still the shutter moves, a thin
Turnstile for populations.

Eyes stare at the eyes staring
Forever unblinking, the paper is printed
And the shutter is still moving.

Moving and not moved, the eyes close
And the paper recreates hunger
Like inflated currency.

We must believe it, for our anger
Is blown about the world, a ransom
Refused. The shutter moves:

Over the year's grave, and the child's,
One by one a million shutters
Darken just for a moment.

281

We seek the selfhood of the race
In the shared turbulence of beauty
That creates the human face.

And that face is winter. Is nothing.
Is our bad understanding. Is uncreated.
And the shutter is still.

Topkapi

I am the sultan. Jewelled, I sit on jewels.
My head bows with the weight of jewels.
My fingers curl open with the weight of jewels.

They bring me a bowl of emeralds the size of figs
To play with if I want to, and curds
To eat with spoons so diamonded
They rasp my lower lip.

I have a candlestick
With 6666 diamonds. The British Queen
Has sent me the jewelled order of her garter.

One day I will throw myself into the Bosphorus.

Sultan Ahmet Square

In Sultan Ahmet Square
The brass domes of the pots
In the boot-boy's box
Echo the domes of the mosque
On which one seems to step
As if to threaten Blefuscu
While on the leather are mixed
The browns and blues and blacks
That would let a Whistler daub
A dissimilar sky to the sky
From which now Allah leans
To admire his shining toe-caps.

Fuatpaşa Caddesi

On Fuatpaşa Caddesi
A man stands all day in the mud
With ten bedsteads against a railing.
They are for sale, but no one buys.

Down Çadircilar Caddesi
A man staggers as though inspecting the mud
With ten mattresses roped to his back.
He is taking them somewhere from somewhere else.

In the evening they drink warm salep by the bridge
And the cinnamon tickles their throats!

Galata Bridge

They stand patiently in doorways
Fingering their rifles like exhibitionists.
Eyes are averted from bayonets.
Crowds pass busily, resigned like brides.

They are required to look serious in case
Anyone pauses long enough to laugh,
And because their upper lips are shaven,
Leaving them vulnerable and naked.

There is a tank by the Galata Bridge
Which has not come down the steep streets
Nor over the bridge, which rocks in frail sections
That let through the dawn shipping.

It is positioned here mysteriously
Angled on its concrete eminence,
As though by a boy kneeling with a toy,
Breathing heavily, placing it exactly.

Mosque

One hand keeps a scarf to the mouth, the other
Holds the paired shoes lightly at waist level
Like the violinist's finishing flourish of the bow,
The eyes looking down in modesty and concentration.

283

Carpets layer the stone, careless, unstinting.
A patch of window shows rain, and a ship passing.
The dome muffles whispers like a yawn, and on
The grandfather clock are numerals like closed umbrellas.

Outside, the rituals of trade and government
Continue to gather and disperse the organisms
Which here have no place in the everlasting designs
That weave their studied intervals around you.

Except for a few flowers you may warily tread on
As you walk further and further into the silence
Or find repeated in the baked gardens of the walls
That reach their blue and orange to the dome.

Prayer

Prayer is talking to these beautiful inventions
And is agreed to be a performance
Best conducted in a professional silence.

Beneath the great hanging circles of lamps
On the rich carpets they settle themselves
And begin to practise their headstands.

Don't we recognise the pretence
From our own feinted applause?

St Sophia

Two figures there beneath the dome, walking with similar pace,
Turned as the other turned, forward and back, in that empty space.

Turning on the heel, looking about, casual but intense,
With everything that might belong to a stranger's cautious grace.

Eyes like hands went out to the marble and stone and precise gold
On the walls where the guarding images left a broken trace.

In the narthex, in the galleries, in the side-aisles,
Up and down, as drawn to each other as to that echoing place.

As though it were the whole world, and I saw the man was myself
And he walked there with the woman and the woman had your face.

284

Çiçek Pasaji

Here on the dirty edge of everything
The streets are dark, pleasure uncertain.
But the fish and flowers are bright
As the loud throats of the stallkeepers!

Pipes of bones, and wigs and shawls of tripes;
Fish like wet embryos of fallen angels
Head down or gills unhinged
Caught by a beneficent fisherman
At some willed apocalyptic abortion
Of all the other world; lights behind glass;
Tulips on fire; spices bright as pigments;
Hissing of cooking; globes of oranges;
Our tight fingers, interlaced in wool.

And in dark alleys, a flickering bucket,
The hopeful outcast's fire.

Being

Being not elsewhere now
I wouldn't want to be
    Other than here,
With wine still in the glass,
Watching the year pass.

Being not yet asleep,
The fire glowing steady
    And furred with ash,
I take what was meant,
Receive what was sent.

Being is a wish,
Tilting the final inch
    Against the glow,
That being, once removed,
Need never more be proved.

Being, though, as cold
As it surely will be,
    Proof will be pointless:

Better to treat with caution
The planetary portion.

Variation on Gautier

This black dress: it gives me joy
To see you in it, the cut of the shoulder,
The arms in repose, the hidden bosom,
Naked the pagan throat and chin!

The quilted pensiveness of beauty
Lies in the soft touch of the stuff:
I would not wish a conspiracy
Of any other compelling textures.

Not the severity of shame
Colours this formal fabric: no,
It is the chastity of art
That veils in dreams the frank and nude.

Its deep shadows are the attentions
Of many unappeased desires
Which attract to the body that denies them
The vestments of a secret devouring!

Ironing

1 *Handkerchiefs*
They are impressed, imposed in 16mo
And lastly collated, the fingers walking up
Their ladder of warm cotton corners like money.

Later, when they are needed, they are carefully opened
And stared at, as though counterfeit, in the frozen
Instantaneous disbelief of a sneeze.

2 *Jeans*
The board is hard between their legs
As they cling in abject fear of being
Thrown. Endurance is an ignominy,
Branded on the bum by a Gothic arch.

3 *Shirts*
Collars crease into smiles, the weak armpits
Are tickled and the empty wrists hang limply.

286

The heat relaxes and the stroking appeases
The possible flap and flutter of spooky sleeves.

There are mornings when we bound upstairs
And open their coffins simply to establish
That they are still lying in peaceable folds
Under pungent sachets of prophylactic herbs.

How may we exorcise them? Mirrors reflect
The innocent idiot smirk of a confident victim
Careless of their guile which requires him to tighten
The fatal noose around his own neck, too.

A mysterious present

Two bottles lifted chilled
From their shredded paper duvets
    With Gilpin clink,
Not the less rare
For travelling as a pair.

A face with white moustaches
Medallioned on their bosoms
    Gravely presides
An inch above the label
Where they stand on the table:

Gruaud-Larose, a fine
St Julien, its sobered
    Purple enclosed
In white and black and gold,
A dozen years old.

Good for a dozen glasses
Among four friends, with talk
    Of nothing much,
And guesses at who sent
Such a distinguished present.

Loyal companions, braced
And knowing each other's secrets!
    Where one goes
The other, hearing laughter,
Will gladly follow after.

Sorrel

Apologies to the snail
For gathering his dinner
   And perhaps tomorrow's,
With whom I have no quarrel
As fingers search for sorrel.

The leaves are stacked against
The thumb, ready to spring
   Apart again
As from the packed plastic
They dump their green elastic

And stir upon the table,
A dark dealt freshness,
   In gathered mounds
Of vegetable life
That moisten to the knife.

With butter in a pan
They fall to a khaki slime
   As sharp as a lemon.
Outside, it continues to rain
And the snails walk again.

Wasp nest

Be careful not to crush
This scalloped tenement:
Who knows what secrets
Winter has failed to find
Within its paper walls?

It is the universe
Looking entirely inwards,
A hanging lantern
Whose black light wriggles
Through innumerable chambers

Where hopes still sleep
In her furry pews,
The chewed dormitory
Of a forgotten tribe
That layered its wooden pearl.

It is a basket of memories,
A museum of dead work,
The spat Babel of summer
With a marvellous language
Of common endeavour.

Note: it is the fruit
Returning to the tree,
The world becoming a clock
For sleep, a matrix of pure
Energy, a book of many lives.

Humming bird

Blurred bright thing!
Most curious
Behaviour of
A dying planet!

Immobile as
A star we know
Has moved and will,
Hovering

Over the hot
Vegetation,
Alert and alerting
The observer

Like a footnote
Asterisked
To a cancelled
Paragraph.

Still the inert
World of matter
Reminds it of
Its origins.

A flower mocks
Its stolen colour
And is siphoned
For energy.

Everything spinning
Up and away!

289

The globe is drained
Into the air!

Thing from inner space

Lumbering, dreamy, pig-headed: like a smooth
Cauliflower or ribbed egg it would offend
If not armoured and decently hidden.

At six feet from the planet, on its best
Behaviour, we accept its grumbles.
At half the distance it becomes

A croaking tyrant, sweaty accuser,
Pilgrim of the meaty cradle, or simply
Blotto, a weak grin on its face.

There must be a way to confront it
With the daily theatre of objects and calmness.
How shall we begin? Gaily, happily . . .

Tame it with the juice of the dartboard grapefuit,
Raise it gently to four and a half feet, to
Eiderdown county, a harvest fired from guns!

Two voices

'Love is a large hope in what,
Unfound, imaginary, leaves us
With a beautifying presence.
Love always grieves us.'

So sang youth to the consenting air
While age in deathly silence, thus:

'Love is a regret for what,
Lost or never was, assails us
With a beautifying presence.
Love never fails us.'

Zuni owl

Squat owl pot with umber ears
And painted eyes, your wings alert
But thumbed down to comic handles,
The posture ruffled but dignified!

Your lip and phallic nose droop
To hide your only orifice
Noiseless when blown and just too small
To welcome liquids or reveal

The hurt spirit hiding there,
That lifetime's guardian in his break-
able body of earth, waiting for our
Forgetfulness, and his release.

Small

Small wit, small will,
Small call, small kill,
Small flight, small fall,
Small say, small small.

Small love, small lies,
Small purse, small prize,
Small view, small verse,
Small what, small worse.

Signs

Talking to animals? The animal novel?
To hell with the stable ego of gorilla!
We look for signs. And she does sign,
Though with a dark air of abstractedness.
'Beans hurry give me beans.'
O lovely behaviour of silksad gorilla!
Is coal or soot, immortal coal or soot!

Old things

The nest in the sycamore has outlasted
The night's wind, but was already
Empty, its twigs just as unuseful
As these on the lawn of the morning's damage,
Its role bizarre, challenging, symbolic,
Like a crown in a bush on a battlefield.

The old barometer has traced
The wind's descent on its cylinder
Of paper, the loops of ink lapping
Its chequered weeks like a prize miler,
The information, required or not,
Accumulating under the glass.

These things stir the heart with regret
For all our fruitless struggles and hopes,
The lost chances, the hoarded rubbish.

Uncertainties

These moments of waiting
For an unarranged meeting
Are full of the strangest uncertainties
As the mind delightedly shifts in its willing vertigo.

Imagine a book deciding
Upon this or that meaning
In that close second before you open it,
The loose print tumbling together, the hand on the doorknob!

What will be, will be.
Everything has its way.
What did you expect from the encounter?
Did you think your life would be changed like the end of a chapter?

Decision is a failing
To understand feeling,
How it responds eagerly to the response.
Books are beautiful but dead. Who is reading whom?

Or perhaps the event's reversal
Was designed by rehearsal
And the future is simply the tide you swim with
Turning page after page after page after page after page.

The wood

This wood is not a wood to hide in.
It is a place to run about in,
A place where both the shoulders show
At once and the thin trees inclining
One to the other make tangled arches
That you must brush aside as you pass.

Where you stop, six ladybirds
As it might be hibernating
In a tree's armpit. Each pair
Of wing-cases as closely folded
As the stiff glass and gold leaves
Of an old time-piece, not going.

Have you looked up and seen something
Disappearing that was not a branch
Or the quick bird that left it nodding,
Curious for buds? Something that left
The grey and violet air more conscious
Of the still space it occupied?

If you do run, the dead trees
Stirring in broken sleep beneath you,
All you do is find yourself
In a different part of the same wood.
And no one seeing you can be sure
That they have seen you. And no one is there.

Primrose

With one knee arched over the ditch,
Finger and thumb reaching for the base of the stem,
I can't recall what the word was I'd forgotten.

Perhaps it was something the heart thought,
Loud in its cave of blood. If so, no matter.
I know I'll remember. Perhaps when I least want to.

For now the flower speaks in my hand.
The deep yellow at its centre melts to the petals,
A perfect wash. Its memory is in its face.

293

Absence

What can the world worse arrange
Than its encounters in time and place?
Imagine a girl taking her horse
Towards the sun. Frowning slightly,
She pushes back the hair from her eyes.

A walker, striding with cut switch
The length of a cropped valley, the wind
Just strong enough for new lambs
To lean into, finds nothing to swing at
Except a patch of opening gorse.

When an Easter butterfly
Weaves out of it, giddy with hope,
His gloom is complete. There on the sward
Are clustered the shallow clear mud-ghosts
Of horseshoes. Which might be hers. But aren't.

Secrets

Secrets certainly have a power to charm.
In front of you, an ape; behind, a chasm.
Keep it happy, keep it happy! Its fangs are hideous!
You must be almost a day's trek from your hideout!
A secret will make it pause. A secret amuses.
Take off your skin. Do explorers have anuses?
What a joke! Show it the other hole,
The metal one. Bang. The point goes home.

Elsewhere, secrets have greater pathos:
Flushed wives prepare themselves on patios,
Guilt an excuse for talk. After eight
The appeasing Bacardi develops into a fight.
But see them next morning, garrulous in a café:
Each is a charmed ape. The truth becomes a cage
For trapped excitements. 'He suspects I have a lover!';
'You must take care'; 'She can't sink any lower!'

Yes, it's the telling not the tale. The box
Rifled, look at that smile on the face of the fat boy
As he passes in the corridor the most hated master
In the school. What does he know? It doesn't matter.
It's who he tells. Not his baby sister,

But someone to charm. Perhaps the baby-sitter,
Curled up with *Cosmopolitan* and a lacy
Thigh, who will sit up and take it like a lady.

God knows, we all like secrets in small doses,
But beware. If she tells you whom she dotes
On, you're next. And maybe you're a blurter,
Your whole world revelation and bluster?
Who's your confidante, then? What is it makes
You spill the beans to her? It must be the male's
Need for approval; to charm. Or out of the blue
That mother ape. Is it? I haven't a clue.

Amazing

So many numbered tracts,
So many pictured acts
And unexpected facts
    Saw I never;
So many bedroom arts,
So many private parts
And so few affected hearts
    Saw I never.

Such hiding and showing,
Such coming and going,
Such ahing and ohing
    Saw I never;
So many jobs for the hands
And explored hinterlands,
So many well-used glands
    Saw I never.

So many genuflections
Before soft erections,
So many false affections
    Saw I never;
So much thrashing and snorting,
So much fruitless exhorting
And such sad consorting
    Saw I never.

So little forbidden
To the bedridden,

So little hidden
    Saw I never;
So many immersions
In corrupt versions,
Such cheap excursions
    Saw I never.

Such drooping and dragging,
Such feinting and flagging,
Such sighing and sagging
    Saw I never;
So many waves and handstands
At cheering grandstands
And thumping bandstands
    Saw I never.

So many hopeless triers,
So many falsifiers,
So many downright liars
    Saw I never;
Such long thrasonical
And unironical
Erotic chronicle
    Saw I never.

So many greetings
And frequent meetings,
Such silent entreatings
    Saw I never.
So many on the brink
Of the fourth or fifth drink
Wasting their love in ink
    Saw I never.

Words

Tongue is surface, too, though hidden.
Talking is an act, though hated.
Hands are still that would be moving
Over and over, but in silence.

Words are meeting, perhaps, though mistaken.

Lips are doorways, though on chains.
Heads are tilted, as before kissing
Over and over, but in silence.

Touch is withheld, often, though wanted.
Language claims lives, though wasted.
Eyes do much that the body would do
Over and over, but in silence.

Linda

1

Linda, Linda, slender and pretty,
Biscuit girl in a biscuit city,
Packing the biscuits in paper boxes,
What do you dream of? How do you dream?
The cutters rise and fall and rise and cut
The chocolate, the coconut,
The Orange Princess and the Gypsy Cream.
The biscuits gather and the boxes shut,
But things are never what they seem.

In the school the bells are ringing,
In the playground girls are singing:
   Lily, paper, hard-boiled eggs,
   Mr Swain has bandy legs.
Linda, Linda, rude and sweet,
Skipping girl in a skipping street,
Singing and skipping all summer long:
   Worms in the classroom, worms in the hall,
   Mr Swain will eat them all.

The cutters fall and rise and fall
And biscuits are unending like a wall
And school is over and the summer's dream.

2

The day the sun invented flowers again
Her heart unfolded with the spring.
Paul had appeared and nothing was the same.

   The railway's on its sleepers,
   The river's in its bed,

All Berkshire is beneath us and
The sky is overhead.

Linda crossed the platform to the train.
Her warm little mouth reached up to his
And kissed and whispered his exciting name.

What was it like before we met?
What did we ever do?
Can't think of anything like it
Or anyone like you.

Weaving fingers find out that they fit
And all the secret pleasures they commit
Are like the touch of flowers in the rain.

3

A whistle from the primus:
The water's nice and hot.
I've got the milk and sugar
And teabags in the pot.
Sometimes there are sandwiches
And sometimes there are not,
But fishing is a fiddle
And Paul requires his tea.
He hasn't time to make it
So he leaves it all to me,
And there are always biscuits
(I bring along the tin.
I think it might be useful
To put the fishes in).
Fishing on the island, only me and him,
Fishing on the island all the afternoon,
The river flowing by us, full to the brim,
And the fishing is over all too soon.

When I packed the basket
Was there something I forgot?
It says *Plum* on the label
And Paul likes apricot.
I usually forget things
Though sometimes I do not,
But fishing is a fiddle
And Paul requires his tea.

298

He hasn't time to make it
So he leaves it all to me,
And there are always biscuits
(I bring along the tin.
I think it might be useful
To put the fishes in).
Fishing on the island, only me and him,
Fishing on the island all the afternoon,
The river flowing by us, full to the brim,
And the fishing is over all too soon.

The river's full of fishes.
You'd think he'd catch a lot.
I'll call out: 'Have you got one?'
And Paul will answer: 'What?'
Sometimes he will land one
And most times he will not,
But fishing is a fiddle
And Paul requires his tea.
And when his basket's empty
He holds it out to me
And grins to say he's sorry
(I love that silly grin
And I find it very useful
To put my kisses in).
Kissing on the island, only me and him,
Kissing on the island all the afternoon,
The river flowing by us, full to the brim,
And the kissing is over all too soon.

4

When we went down to Maidenhead
Paul had his clarinet.
I tried to do the steering and
We both got very wet.
But how he blew that liquorice stick!
The music on a thread
Rose like a nest of rooks above
His black and curly head.

There's a rookery at Dorney
But all the rooks have gone,
Flapping their wings like overcoats

299

They're struggling to put on.
I love their wild black music,
But all the rooks have gone.

We took a tent and Mum was mad.
Paul had his clarinet.
I had this spoon and china mug:
We made a fine duet.
But how he blew that wooden throat
Like a musical millionaire!
The black night-sound inside forced out
In squiggles on the air.

There's a rookery at Dorney
But all the rooks have gone,
And clouds blow over empty trees
Where once the summer shone,
And Paul and his black music
And all his love, have gone.

5
Linda went out in her wedges.
The day was average,
And masses of water were moving
Under Caversham Bridge.

Paul had promised to meet her
And take her on the river.
She looked again at her wristwatch
And gave a little shiver.

Well, wasn't he worth forgiving?
The hour ticked slowly on,
And she threw her Wrigley paper
Down at a frowning swan.

Several boys passed by her
And all of them managed to stare.
But Linda looked right through them
As if she didn't care.

You believe him if he tells you.
You think he's ever so nice
And it's hard to find he can never
Say the same thing twice.

Promises break like biscuits.
Nothing keeps for ever.
But time runs on and on and on,
Deep as the lying river.

6

Linda, Linda, older and wiser,
Far from childhood in a biscuit town,
Making biscuits where the Thames winds down,
Under the eyes of the supervisor,
Under the hands of the factory clock:
    Tick, tick, tick, tick,
      Crisp and crumbly, thin and thick.
The cutters rise and fall and rise,
Cutting out (surprise, surprise)
The chocolate, the coconut,
The Orange Princess and the Gypsy Cream.

But things are never what they seem.
The trains pass clanking on the track,
Distinct and jewelled in the quiet night:
    Tick, tick, tick, tick,
      In life's absurd arithmetic.
And Linda in the tunnel of her dream
All night is restless, staring back
As wisps of the dragon drift into the wind
And, smaller and smaller, Paul is waving,
Smaller and smaller, Paul is standing there.
And Linda dreams and dreams and dreams
Under the hands of the bedside clock,
Till bacon smells are in the air
And combs tug sleepily through morning hair
And nothing is ever what it seems.

Valentine

The things about you I appreciate
   May seem indelicate:
I'd like to find you in the shower
And chase the soap for half an hour.
I'd like to have you in my power

And see your eyes dilate.
I'd like to have your back to scour
And other parts to lubricate.
Sometimes I feel it is my fate
To chase you screaming up a tower
    Or make you cower
By asking you to differentiate
    Nietzsche from Schopenhauer.
I'd like successfully to guess your weight
    And win you at a fête.
I'd like to offer you a flower.

I like the hair upon your shoulders,
Falling like water over boulders.
I like the shoulders, too: they are essential.
Your collar-bones have great potential
(I'd like all your particulars in folders
    Marked *Confidential*).

I like your cheeks, I like your nose,
I like the way your lips disclose
The neat arrangement of your teeth
(Half above and half beneath)
    In rows.

I like your eyes, I like their fringes.
The way they focus on me gives me twinges.
Your upper arms drive me berserk.
I like the way your elbows work,
    On hinges.

I like your wrists, I like your glands,
I like the fingers on your hands.
I'd like to teach them how to count,
And certain things we might exchange,
Something familiar for something strange.
I'd like to give you just the right amount
    And get some change.

I like it when you tilt your cheek up.
I like the way you nod and hold a teacup.
I like your legs when you unwind them.
Even in trousers I don't mind them.
I like each softly-moulded kneecap.

I like the little crease behind them.
I'd always know, without a recap,
   Where to find them.

I like the sculpture of your ears.
I like the way your profile disappears
Whenever you decide to turn and face me.
I'd like to cross two hemispheres
   And have you chase me.
I'd like to smuggle you across frontiers
Or sail with you at night into Tangiers.
   I'd like you to embrace me.

I'd like to see you ironing your skirt
   And cancelling other dates.
I'd like to button up your shirt.
I like the way your chest inflates.
I'd like to soothe you when you're hurt
Or frightened senseless by invert-
   ebrates.

I'd like you even if you were malign
And had a yen for sudden homicide.
I'd let you put insecticide
   Into my wine.
I'd even like you if you were the Bride
   Of Frankenstein
Or something ghoulish out of Mamoulian's
   Jekyll and Hyde.
I'd even like you as my Julian
Of Norwich or Cathleen ni Houlihan.
   How melodramatic
If you were something muttering in attics
Like Mrs Rochester or a student of Boolean
   Mathematics.

You are the end of self-abuse.
You are the eternal feminine.
I'd like to find a good excuse
To call on you and find you in.
I'd like to put my hand beneath your chin,
   And see you grin.
I'd like to taste your Charlotte Russe,

I'd like to feel my lips upon your skin,
I'd like to make you reproduce.

I'd like you in my confidence.
I'd like to be your second look.
I'd like to let you try the French Defence
    And mate you with my rook.
I'd like to be your preference
    And hence
I'd like to be around when you unhook.
I'd like to be your only audience,
The final name in your appointment book,
    Your future tense.

Practical Alice

The warnings went unheeded
    That sounded from the heart.
We rarely wondered whether
    We might remain apart:
It seemed that what was needed
Was just to be together.

I swore the tender jargon
    Would never pass my lips
Nor eyes be bright with pleasure
    When talking came to grips.
I drove a cruel bargain.
I took you at my leisure.

The strain of meeting faces
    Broke in a kiss and charmed
A circle I could enter
    And hope to leave unharmed.
You walked with giant paces
About that silent centre.

I lost you when you travelled,
    Moving a shade too fast.
The fashion was for lighter
    Stuff, never made to last,
And as the thread unravelled
I drew the garment tighter.

I suffered your attentions
    But somehow never could
Unearth my finer feelings
    To find out where we stood.
With lots of good intentions
I stared at lots of ceilings.

To please your casual hunger
    I only had to try
To melt when you grew colder
    As the packed months went by.
You did not wish me younger.
I scarcely wished you older.

Though parting is a nuisance
    It's clear we'll never stay
Close as the fatal minute
    That ticked our lives away.
And now the handclasp loosens
And feels the space within it.

How many goodly creatures

When freshmen have thoughts of adoring
    And tutors are keen to impress,
When the wife of the provost starts pouring
    And the chaplain begins to confess,
When the poet has hopes of reciting
    And the wine buff sets out to unscrew
Who is it they think of inviting?
    Miranda, my dear, it is you.

When scramblers open the throttle
    And choristers open their lips,
When committees discuss a new bottle
    And scholars observe an eclipse,
When candidates come to negotiate
    And christians lay tea-cups for two
With whom would they rather associate?
    Miranda, my dear, it is you.

Whenever they call and can't find you
    You have to reveal where you've been,
And when they come round again (mind you,
    You'll always arrange to be in)
You explain why it is you can't meet them
    And doggedly talk the thing through.
If anyone hated to cheat them,
    Miranda, my dear, it is you.

When quarter-backs have to give quarter,
    When forwards fall back, when the eight
Steps not in the shell but the water
    And the master refuses a gate,
When the scrum-half sees none of the action
    And the wrists of the slips turn to glue,
What's proved to be such a distraction?
    Miranda, my dear, it is you.

But everyone knows he's a rival
    (They're queuing three deep at your door)
And no one has hopes of survival
    Or ways of increasing his score
Unless you have given your blessing
    Do they know if you have? Not a clue.
Who's happy to keep them all guessing?
    Miranda, my dear, it is you.

Classicists love the Acropolis,
    Lawyers are crazy for torts,
Economists value monopolies,
    Philosophers cherish their thoughts,
Eng-Litters are deep into drama
    And chemists are hot for a Blue,
But what is it punctures their armour?
    Miranda, my dear, it is you.

Donald has asked you to dinner,
    There's a party with Denis at six,
Here's Dave pedalled up on his spinner,
    The Peugeot that's waiting is Dick's.
By the end of the evening you're woozy,
    But still your admirers pursue.
If ever a girl wasn't choosy,
    Miranda, my dear, it is you.

306

When Adrian writes you a letter
　　You send a delightful reply,
If Rodney complains he's no better
　　You never suspect it's a lie,
When William weeps on your shoulder
　　You notice his brand of shampoo;
If anyone wished they were older,
　　Miranda, my dear, it is you.

Whose partings were never as tragic
　　As second-year rumours alleged?
Whose drawers are full of Black Magic?
　　Whose RSVPs are gilt-edged?
Who lists all her friends in her diary
　　With a detailed dispassionate view
Like a clerk in a public inquiry?
　　Miranda, my dear, it is you.

Bonzo & Co

Bonzo is a serious dog
Of quite some size and strength,
And other dogs are all agog
To hear him bark at length.

His barking is notorious
In Sussex, York and Hull.
Some think it meritorious.
Few ever find it dull.

And Bonzo is rewarded by
Their hypnotised consent
And articles wherein they try
To fathom what he meant.

So shall we join them later on,
Keeping our pencils sharp?
And shall we play the harmoniphon
Or the canine claviharp?

Oh what a blessing culture is!
It tells you how to live.

Remember, then, when feeling mis
What Bonzo has to give

And with them gather on the landing
From morning until dark
To listen with misunderstanding
To Bonzo's serious bark.

Examination

The wasted roses droop from stems
Defying time like lowered hems
    And legs tucked under.
The frowning beauty in a rage
Darkens the problematic page
    Like June thunder.

Could time restore what scribbles fail
Upon the sheet to make less pale
    What pure idea
Might send its fragrance out upon
The deadening oblivion
    She feels is near?

Three times one falling hand defines
The figured circle that confines
    Her inspiration
As racing sentences unlock
The startling secrets which might mock
    Its cruel notation.

The uprights regular at first
Join with her loops like rhymes in verse
    But slowly worsen
As she plucks out of agony
A flowering sensibility
    In the third person.

And petals fall like falling souls
From the bright hope of button-holes
    On beating hearts
Or like those fragile, half-grotesque
And crumpled papers on the desk,
    Her false starts.

Time after all has nothing left
And like a spendthrift after theft
  Of what for years
Was wildly longed for in a lover's
Waking dream, she soon discovers
  Her prize is tears.

Now the examination room
Is empty of both girl and bloom
  And who would think
That so much effort had been spent
On this small part of what she meant
  In so much ink?

Gone to ground

Veuve du Vernay in the gutter, flattened wire and querns of cork
Mark where candidates vacated (like the elders of the Kirk
Joining in a witches' rout) the holy temple of their rites –
Schola Magna Borealis – spilling gowned inebriates.
Prior to every paper, files of desks were sown with writing-books
Germinating inkily beneath the working rows of backs;
Pentels played superbly in the cradles of their moving fists;
Silent whispers to the ceiling charmed the peacocks, prayed for Firsts;
Fingers propped up profiles Buonarroti might have liked to carve;
Unimaginable beauties shut in pallor like a cave
On a friendly surface flowers and antihistamines had made
Brought to life the latent heroines of *My Last Duchess, Maud,*
Nineteenth-century victims of the poet's urge to wield his power
Over girls not fully understood, bold, self-possessed though pure
(When their knowledge faltered, Kleenex, sweets and mascots were
  employed).
Schools became a theatre where the memory and passion played,
Empty all the summer once the fustian black and white had gone
(Tennyson and Browning are allowed to lie unread again).
Down the High Street stroll unhindered naked knees and tartan
  paunch,
Cluny's closed and Honey's empty save for someone buying *Punch.*
All the mysteries enacted now are commonplace once more,
Sacred circumstances simply something travellers can admire.
Evidence is trapped unnoticed in the omnipresent lens:
Businessmen from Nagasaki freeze as one of them aligns
What remains of Magdalen Tower with an antiseptic grin,

CANDY underfoot and to the right a door of brass and green.
On the other corner Oxford Travel Agents are relieved:
Sheaves of booking stubs reveal where students' lives are now being
    lived.
Transalpino, Apex, Eurotrain and private bus convey
Heart-struck, star-crossed, shattered souls to gaze upon a different
    view.
Foreign cities heal with culture wounds that culture has induced,
Love forgotten as the banger jolts through fascinating dust.
Soppy sentimental disconnected drainpipes go their ways,
Finding in a summer's absence much inducement to be wise.
Term was going out to dinner, giving bear-hugs in the quad,
Heads together over just the quantity of work required.
Literature is what you make it and it's bound to turn to tears.
Now it's nature's turn to comfort as the dear ideal retires:
Thumbs along the autostrada bring an everchanging view;
Tents in Sligo echo with the savage wounding of a vow.
Human lineaments will alter since you make them what they seem;
Rocks and water are unyielding for their substance is the same.
Wordsworth told us once and we were almost willing to believe
(Keeping fingers crossed behind our back because we knew that love
Conquered after all each famous effort to be understood,
Offering the various shapes of dull eternity instead).
Passion doesn't bear examination – though perhaps it should,
Shaping as it does the source from which all mental life is shed.
Ardent alpha-minus and besotted beta-plus, God knows,
Can't be much preferred to grieving gamma, narcissist NS,
Given our agreement on the joy of unrequited love,
Caring only that its fatal feelings may be kept alive,
Never to be disappointed by their hope of being fulfilled
Like a conjuror's spectators who are eager to stay fooled.
Don't expect a tutor to stay moping in a tourist town:
Bright at the receiver you will only hear the dialling tone.
If you're passing through yourself, perhaps to bring me back some
    books
(Quantities I lent you: won't you need to put them in a box?)
Don't imagine I'll be waiting, kettle steaming, on the hour.
Did you call? I'm sorry! I'm afraid that's just the way things are.
Was my room locked and the tap not dripping, friendly, on the stair?
Did the scout look blank and turn away and give her tea a stir?
Did you interrupt the Lodge's cricket, stamp and tear your hair?
Hearing Strutt recite his lesson: 'Mr Fuller is not here,
Having taken up a new appointment as the top masseur

(Being handy, tender, ready, when the nape and hips are sore)
With the Russian women's swimming, pole-vault and gymnastic
  teams,
Keen, you see, on sport and travel when he isn't keeping terms.
Leave a message with the porter? Always happy to oblige.
Got a packet for him, have you? Hope it isn't very large.
Look, his pigeon-hole is full already: invitations, cheques,
Magazines and scented envelopes as soft as ladies' cheeks.
Come back in October (what's the phrase? – "the sere and yellow
  leaf").
Michaelmas, I'm sure, will see us all resuming normal life.'
Life! Ah, life, who always lives us so intensely at his will;
Life in lying chapters, promising that things will soon be well;
Life, who understands us all but keeps the secret in his book;
Life, the truest friend – who, once he goes away, will not come back.

The college ghost

For Hugh Sinclair

At 11.25, after a college beano
Designed to wish a retiring colleague well
(Who with a glass in one hand, a watch in the other
Like the pieces of Alice's mushroom, sat and then rose
To remind with smiling words why we shall miss him),

At that suspended hour of a summer night,
Having made my few farewells, collected my gown,
My black tie carelessly telling the approximate time,
The claret filling my toes, the toes my shoes
And the shoes knowing more or less the way to go,

I left the smoking-room and paced the cloisters
In the wrong direction, almost three sides where one
Would do, to find the passage to take me safely
To the only place where we regularly fall
Utterly unconscious without rebuke or danger

And came at once upon the college ghost
Lolling in a Gothic arch not far from the kitchens.
It had a gross nonchalant air, pretending
That it simply chanced to be there waiting for no one
Particularly, picking its non-existent nails.

311

Its face was puffy and indistinct, the eyes
Burnt holes, nose gone, the grin healthy
But upside down. It wore a college scarf
And a row of pens in its shroud like a boffin,
Slouched in its window in a May Week pose.

It watched me as I approached and it made its greeting,
Not deferent, not assertive, simply assuming
Its right to expect me to stop, as though our notes
Had crossed and whatever it was had there and then
To be settled and some confusion straightened out.

The night was dark and winy as a cellar,
The only noises the clacking of the flagpole
On St Swithun's tower and the thumping of my heart.
But I wasn't surprised. I felt it was an encounter
Fated at one or another time to occur.

I fingered the keys in my pocket, the inner and outer
Circuits, comforting brass and heavy for turning
The secret doors and great gates of the college,
Fingered them as though they were amulets
To keep at a distance the presence I found before me.

Behind and through it gleamed the broad green square
Of the lawn where all that summer afternoon
In various attitudes of conversation
Undergraduates had sat with early teas
Outlapping the lingering remains of lunch.

And the voice of the shapeless shape, if voice it was,
Drifted towards me softly, catching my ear
Exactly like a carefully-placed loudspeaker,
And its words were the words of all who had sat on that lawn
Through similar afternoons until such darkness fell:

'Though I am not often seen here, at least at times
When troublesome tasks last through daylight or take
You from page to page of assorted memoranda,
Nose down like a broker or a winded traveller
Frantic for the last train in a foreign city,

'Though I am discrepant and uncorroborated
As a reputation; embarrassing as the memory
Of insufficient words at parting; feared
Like a summons for a forgotten misdemeanour;
Still, I do appear, and appear to you now.

'It's precisely at times like this, when you are distracted
By well-being and owl-light from shutting your senses
To what I represent and am ready to communicate
That I eagerly seize my chance to materialise
Like an image on paper in a paddled tray.

'You reckon you can shortly make your escape,
Say more next time. So be it. That is your manner.
But for the moment, stay. I have something to tell you
That has been keeping but will not keep for ever,
Like Clipsham stone or a Pomerol, but not so nice.

'It concerns the conspiracy to keep me partly asleep
With promise of distinct pleasures belonging to
The forms of success towards which you propelled me,
Wise like an elder framing a constitution
Before he retires and dies a powerless legend.

'You gave me much that could not shame the giver
Whatever whoops of joy and sounds of breakage
Greeted your smiles, fond as a distant uncle,
When the package was ripped open, the contents spilled,
The crucial instructions immediately lost.

'But grammar burned bishops and nations fell to the prism.
I negotiated the quantities of blood required
To put into effect the decrees of the Ineffable.
I argued over heads that I knew were soon
To lose all interest in what they commandeered.

'I was present when the planet first took its header
Into the bracing briny of the impermanent.
I dignified the scribbled with the spacing of nuts and muttons.
I bowed in Washington, once the place was invented.
Through me the Greeks discovered Australia.

'Theories of diet dispersed tribes, infections
Accompanied stately truths like interpreters.
I took your towers for wit, your lawns for sorrow,
And made the friendships that reduced brown acres
Of imposing mahogany to the space of a handclasp.

'Even when the world in a more appealing tongue
Spoke of the price to be paid for a share of power,
It was to you I referred with a slight shrug
And perhaps a mock self-deprecatory grin
That could not decide if it cared for your approval.

'You gave it. And that was when I became a ghost,
Rioting invisibly in the halls and staircases
Of my consecrated youth, while everything true
And good fell from my fingers or from windows,
Drifting like laughter in the direction of the ivy.

'Now I appear to you because at last
I have rejoined you for ever. Life has made
Its choice. My affairs are finally quite complete
And there is nothing left in the world to alter.
Whatever you teach will make no difference at all.'

So saying, it boyishly scissored the stone sill
With a careless stretch of the arms and a hint of flannel
As the bells in the tower tensed to tell three quarters
And the moon behaved as it likes to do at these moments,
Nodding above the treescape like an impresario.

Which way it went I really couldn't say,
But it had gone. And so I slowly continued
My right-angled path through the heart of the college,
Less light of foot, but somewhat enlightened,
Slightly unsure of what I thought I had heard.

Darkness was all around me like a sixth
Sense, or the absolute quiet of certain music
That the hand trembles to play. And it was like
The world pressing on its pockets of resistance.
Like righteous claims of love. Or threats of war.

And indeed, I thought, the ultimate chaos will surely be
A predicate of just this irresponsible architecture
Of convinced laws and prayers that meddled for years
With the best of fateful intentions until the wind changed.
The words were in my head like an egg in a bottle.

Thoughts too late to unthink: I had the feeling
Of being betrayed by something of my choosing,
Something I had connived at, something belonging
To the projection of a long-suspected failing,
Haunted by the forces it exploits.

VIII

The Grey and the Green

(1982)

The grey and the green

I'm writing lazily upon
A day in late July, from Wales,
With nettles standing by the wall,
Grasses uncomfortably tall,
And in the grasses, snails.

With such abundance, I shall need
No theme, the theme is all about me:
The evidence in stone and oak
Of rampant nature's only joke –
That she can do without me.

However riveting her glance,
I turn my back for half a year
And flowers are standing from the slates,
Spiders are spinning like the fates
And funguses appear:

Wet lips and frills upon the plaster
Like fairies kissing through the ceiling
Show how the rain induced the roof
To cease from standing so aloof
And to respond with feeling.

Rain! It's always up there, busy.
Sometimes it patters like a mouse
Or drums in boredom on the pane.
It stops, and starts, then stops again
And eavesdrops round the house.

It drifts in clouds against the mountain,
Swells the streams and starts to pour
In torrents down the slopes behind
The house and in the house, to find
Its way out through the door.

Sometimes it thunders on the skylights
As though being poured out by a jug.
This brief but mesmerising rain's
Succeeded by the helpless drain's
Protracted glug-glug-glug.

The gutters weep whole afternoons.
The contents of the sky, displayed
In sheets across the fields, aim at

The grass as if to beat it flat,
A drop for every blade.

Within our fenced and sheepless plot
The grasses work their grassy wills.
Rye and timothy and dock,
They cluster at the step and knock
Against the window sills.

Natural things are what we were
And what we should become again.
Once we were nature as they are,
And lug about beneath our star
The matter we were then.

So should our culture (said the Romantic
German in that sowing season
Of the soul's freedom) rightly take us
Back to our paradisal acres
Through liberty and reason.

You can be sure I feel the pull
Of all nostalgic mythic Edens,
But oh, how very hard it is
To see that arguments like his
Lend their design much credence.

For liberty in our sense never
Kept house with nature in the raw.
I think of Milton (as I scythe
The tangled clumps of green that writhe
In freedom at our door)

Whose message was that temperance
Requires the energy it curbs,
As syntax shaping sentences
Is happier not with simply 'is'
But much more active verbs;

That civil order shows the fairer
When mastering the pulse of riot;
That good is known by evil, just
As love springs from the cease of lust,
From fretful chaos, quiet.

The rage of the homunculus
To nuzzle in the blinding yolk

Requires an absolute devotion
We must deny, and no emotion
Insists that we must choke.

So my firm mowing arm controls
A green and sprouting commonweal.
The populations of the field,
Clock and seed and fruitage, yield
To government of steel.

Down falls the crested hair-grass, reed
Canary, oat; the barley's comb
And timothy's thick tail; the tender
Tree-palace of the bent; the slender
Fox-tail and the brome.

Where something like a nursery stood
Of lecherous grasses yet unborn,
See now their ravings quieten to
A neutered peace I can sit through,
A deckchair on a lawn.

Where on my knee a book can rest,
Where on the page my hand can think,
Where in my hand the Edding edds
Through which the mind in humour weds
Passionless thought and ink.

The mind, it may be said, and what
Is that? The mind is grass, alas!
It's all or nothing, that's the trouble
(I ponder on that velvet stubble,
Pouring another glass).

It's either everything we must
Become, or it's a giant con.
It's something we're amazed at, some
Impulsion – or it's like a bum,
Something to fall upon.

Who would not rather be a mindless
Grass? Locked in that quilted field,
No need to feel that it's of use,
Pollen and root and primal juice
In a green tube concealed.

With no pretence at calculation,
Hope or fear or memory,
Its head reveals its simple needs
In tapered symmetry of seeds
Tip-toeing to be free.

Our heads have long ago exchanged
The simple green for black and white.
Our good is lost, we do not need it.
Or if we think we do, we read it –
If someone else can write.

From noisy theatres of life
Our heads are full of long retreats
Where self-appointed NCOs
Exhort us daily in foul prose
From even fouler sheets.

Sunday mornings are devoted
To the required responses, civil
Arguments and qualifications;
To self-sufficient explanations
And other sorts of drivel.

The paragraphs of prescience,
The columns on calamity,
Are always just a little late
And, though so true, congratulate
Their authors with a fee.

And what is written may be thought,
Suffered or performed somewhere.
We're told it is, but then the telling
Becomes the product it is selling:
How can we ever care?

In solipsistic boogie-packs
Of cultural bandage we skate deaf
Through tower-blocks of necessity,
Protected from their shouting by,
For instance, Brahms in F.

Such music tries to tell us that
The air is yearning to contain
Whatever consonance of passion
Happens to be the current fashion
Of disembodied pain.

Culture creates élites of failure
And heroes of those tortured wrecks
Who at its prompting are most prompt
To issue chaste denials, swamped
By the hopelessness of sex.

The adolescent grass is not
Ashamed, is never seen to blush.
No secret hankering occurs,
Nor each *amitié amoureuse*
Turns to a helpless crush.

It does not calculate or risk.
Pleasure's unknown and so is force.
It does not crawl across the bed
And is too steadfast and well-bred
To contemplate divorce.

Nor does it regulate in verse
Complete disruptions of its soul.
No sublimation of *tendresse*
Promotes an urgency to bless
Another's vital role.

For one grass of a certain kind
Is not much different from another.
Its blind asexual reproduction
Requires no tea-time introduction,
Has never heard of mother.

It's not quite envy that we feel:
The sturdiness, the ignorance,
The generosity, the stillness,
Show love as an absorbing illness
That makes a choice of chance.

And in that paradox we live
As in the aura of a crime
That we regret but made us rich,
Too conscious of a truth for which
There's always or never time.

Living a good way up a mountain
Above the natural line of trees,
We nurture saplings, ache for torn
Or wounded cedar, oak or thorn
And mourn fatalities.

Trees are annual calendars
And their expressive flags have taught us
To greet the spring. They're twiggy babels
For many birds; pencils and tables
To please our daughters' daughters.

The lifetime that they take to grow
Is rarely ours. We feel a bond
Like that with age: memorabilia
To be respected, grave, familiar,
A little feared or fond.

We note the fruiting of the rowan.
If it's the year for bullace or
For sloe, or how much higher stand
The valiant Blackheath walnut and
The Oxford sycamore.

But most regret in this last winter
The passing of an ancient ash
Which air, that changed location at
Unlikely speed, disturbed and flat-
tened with an unheard crash.

But now, although it leans upon
One hinge of bark, new leafage shoots
From stumps the guilty wind has healed.
It dipped its elbows in the field
And there established roots.

If only our unrooted lives
When felled could simply change direction
And all our tall assumptions both
Be trimmed and find amazing growth,
A perfect resurrection!

The tree has found a way of walking
Not as our childhood stories told us
Through sudden supernatural strength
But through first tumbling its full length
Then growing from its shoulders.

A saint might get to Bardsey by
A slow deliberate prostration,
And such a gradual pilgrimage
Would postulate at every stage
A halting in his station.

And we could take our time like this
Were life as long as it is wide,
With no regretful glances back
At all the branchings of the track,
A lifetime for one stride.

I have a notion, though, that even
So we could not much rejoice
At what we'd done or where we'd got to:
What *is* requires to know what's *not*, to
Exercise its choice.

Perhaps we need alternatives.
Perhaps we need to make mistakes.
The will unfortunately thrives
On possibility: our lives
Must rise – or sink, like cakes.

And now the bees are sawing flowers,
As casual in the endeavour
As if the petals on each stem
Had fallen open just for them
And the sun would last for ever.

And other creatures in the grass
Move in their leggy purposes:
A caterpillar scurries hard
Across the warm particular yard
Of hillside that is his.

A beetle, tilted in the green,
Gropes with his antlers for a purchase,
And even from my chair I see
Its blackness inching to be free
In tiny wavering lurches

Down there are even lesser beings
Who do not have the need to walk,
Nothing to make them climb or stretch,
Nothing to carry, nothing to fetch:
They simply hug a stalk.

You'd need a microscopic eye
To see them blind and massed and thronging.
Although their grassy life seems bleak
It is a vertical, unique
Achievement of belonging.

Few other sounds: the distant snigger
Of buzzards; the complaining tones
Of sheep; the crumpling of the small
Stream as it makes its shallow fall
Over the worn stones.

And always the sun arcing above
The fret that creeps below us still
Like a brave hand that quietly clears
The sky of its forgotten tears
And sends them down the hill.

It times itself across the mountains:
Tre'r Ceiri's nine o'clock, at three
The middle mountain, dusk the quarry.
It hangs upon the promontory
And sinks into the sea.

It's no surprise to find the sun
Intoxicating: we drink deep,
A summer's depth, a draught imbued
With every idle summer mood
Of love or wit or sleep.

Imperious season! It calls us up
In our unusual calm and fitness
Willingly to mount the stand
And take our future by the hand
In unreliable witness.

As though we just might go on living,
Our testimony never waver
And our condition be the same,
Always to have a right to claim
The judgement in our favour.

But summers come and summers go,
A flourish on the signature
Of the year's cheques, and we the claimant
Of punctual everlasting payment
Have no right to be sure.

A voice is calling down the field,
A trick of the light, or in the ear
The slightest shift, a distant saw,
A sudden rapping on the door,
Brings that familiar fear.

As harvest bends beneath the wind
Or trees are stirred or grasses bowed
When it disturbs the valley's surface
From the chilled wood to where the turf is
Darkened by a cloud.

Until the darkness that our lives
Will unavoidably arrange,
We have this pact to keep in peace
Our favoured landscape till time cease
To hesitate from change.

And Never is a world away
From Now, as Other is from Me.
The solipsist can hardly find
That time weighs heavy on his mind,
Self is eternity.

As on the mountain starry moss
Lies open to the sky unseen:
Proliferating radials are
A perfect mockery of star,
Pale on the darker green.

And yet those systems so like eyes
Are wholly inward, slow to change:
No observation, no reflection,
No intercourse and no connection,
Sightless, profuse and strange.

Is mind to be compared with these?
An accidental peal of bells?
Astronomy's congratulation?
Random organic integration,
A colony of cells?

You will not find the elusive mind
By cutting up a living brain.
As well might fronds of wire be seen
To sprout up from a grey machine
Or grasses rust in rain.

Our new computer in the eaves
Copes with the problems we have set it.
It finds square roots, defines an arc,
Plays asteroids or J. S. Bach
Or anything we let it.

Between the keyboard and the screen
Lies hidden electronic finery
That turns what either of you says
Into electric impulses.
Its simple code is binary.

It makes with anyone who chooses
Its Mephistophelean bargain
To help you to achieve your goal
Provided that you lose your soul
And use the proper jargon.

But I am not with those who fear
Such speed and rational procedure,
For as a model of the brain
It's much superior, it is plain,
To such things as Ouija.

The only problem is, the thing
Is motiveless, immortal, neuter,
You look for something like a mind
In vain, for all you'll ever find
Inside is a computer.

And what it does is limited
To what its program makes it do.
The power of the computer buff
Can only prove, alas, enough
To see his program through.

And that elusive element
Beyond determination still
Eludes. No god could tolerate
A being that he must create
In bonds, without free will.

A tool then, not a creature which
Is appetitive though obedient
Through recognition of its good:
It lacks that one misunderstood
Mysterious ingredient.

What do we call it? Nature? Life?
Where do we find it? Beyond the stammer
Of electronics freely move
Millions of nouns that seem to prove
An independent grammar.

326

Beyond the slavish rigmarole
Of subroutine and variable,
The soft world's at its nightly ruses.
The tiniest midge still somehow chooses
To find itself in trouble.

When all the sun there is touches
The sea, and grey invests the green,
Eater and eaten flitter by,
A demonstration to defy
The passionless machine.

Horny and muffled moths whir through
The window, summoned by its glow,
And in the park of its display
Quizzing each Goto and array
Stroll stiffly to and fro.

The moon itself, the light they think
It is, is no less readable.
Its hieroglyphics are the history
Of an unfathomable mystery,
The grave celestial pull.

What wonder that the dandy moth,
Preening itself in its fur collar
And muttering in its whiskery muzzle,
Ignores the lesser luminous puzzle
Of waiting Inkey$?

So it might wait for ever if
No one could see its flashing cursor,
In a vast emptiness, unfree,
Deserted by humanity
(Or perhaps vice versa).

For if a desert is in question,
It's possible machines will make it.
The world, which has not lasted long
And may not, is going for a song
And no one wants to take it.

Should we bequeath it to the moth?
It needs some strange nocturnal creature
Like the gowned bat that haunts the house,
A crucified aerial mouse,
A tiny baleful preacher.

A world of bats and cold machines!
I do not find the thought endearing.
Programs survive though current fails,
Inscrutable as the bat's wails,
Voices unheard, unhearing.

The universe is full of noises
And rather fewer ears. The gift
Of sight is rare enough for stars
To die unseen. We can touch Mars
But galaxies go unsniffed.

It is our aim to use our senses
Rightly, senses of every sort.
Computers are a harnessed force,
No revolution; they endorse
Traditional ways of thought,

It's hard, though, not to feel that when
I play a game of chess with one
It has a personality.
It gives a bleep to welcome me
Whenever I switch on.

Two pairs of OOs move up and down
As though, while pondering, it scanned
Visible possibilities.
God knows, though, what it really 'sees'.
Nothing that's not been planned.

Those tell-tale traits I find attractive
Mean all that its instructions mean.
Its program tells it what to do.
Nothing it does is really new
Or entirely unforeseen.

It doesn't joke. It plays five games
Straight off and doesn't mind five more.
It won't admit a move is clever
Or make illegal moves. It never
Offers me a draw.

It doesn't like a glass of something,
Ignores all flattery, loves to play
The French Defence and risks its neck
Through ignorance of discovered check
More than a move away.

Losing the endgame makes it most
Like a person, least inert:
It gives up the defence, plays wild,
Moves distant pieces, like a child,
Hopeless, defeatist, hurt.

And such, perhaps, we really are
If mind is only an illusion,
A more or less determined process,
Part of itself, a true hypnosis,
A triumph of confusion.

Arraigned in our material being
The sentence of the court is binding:
Mind is the evidence we show
Of knowing that we do not know,
Of minding, and not minding.

It is the evidence and judgement, too:
Our mindfulness reminds us of it
At all those times when ignorance
Of what we call our loss, by chance,
Might turn it to our profit.

Fatal cognisance! As though
A frown in the flower means it fears
The absence of the bee – instead
Of some decision to be red
Until the bee appears.

Or yellow, plain, fantastical,
Long-lived or short, but never knowing
The pride of colour or the term
Of life, nothing beyond the firm
Root and the grip of growing.

For flowers, mind is only touch.
Green in the colour that began it,
Green the sign of the cell's toil,
A touch of sky, a touch of soil,
The ladder of the planet.

Green is the negative of stars,
Green is the mirror of the sun,
Green is the cooling of earth's fire:
A height from which we have reached higher,
But the best thing earth has done.

A daily hunger tells us we
Are planet, too. That is our root,
Ingesting green. Our meals should prove
We have a root at a remove,
A liberated root.

The body is not user-friendly
(Examples of it we have hugged
Show that its program, though involved,
Still has procedures to be solved,
Commands to be debugged).

Perhaps too liberated, then,
A simple hunger turned to greed?
Imperious inorganic lives
Inform us that mere being thrives
Without that cycled need.

Enchanted earth already turned
To stone, the mountain feels no lack
Of purpose when it is demolished:
Granite is patient still unpolished,
The grey that turns to black.

Grey still undynamited, grey
In crumbled boulders, grey half-grey
Half-ground to that swart glassiness
That graced the dead's last known address
When their souls had flown away.

In amphitheatres of absence
All the machinery is rust.
Slabs, kerbs and banks' façades,
Half-turned curling stones and shards,
Loose gravel, grit and dust

Remain like broken toys to show
What men destroyed a mountain for,
What sudden hunger or excuse
Used it, and left it after use
Half-eaten to the core.

And on the hillside older stones
Make other spaces out of grey:
Windows and doors are holes that show
The light that it may come and go,
A man that he may stay.

The walls are plastered white inside
To veil the stone from scrutiny:
As to a squared-off globe all four
Meet the horizon of the floor
Like a descending sky.

Tiles mimic earth, and rafters boughs,
Curtains are clouds against the sun.
Roomscapes to be conventional
Require a foreground: pastoral
Upholstery for one.

Quarryman and farmer lay
Their arms along its arms and doze.
Its back confers upon the skills
And elbows that explored the hills
Its purpose of repose.

A chair affords its occupant
A sense of being offered to
Some present prospect of content
As though a god, forgiving, sent
A slumber or a view.

As though its seat, through being
Raised from earth, diminished its
Compelling gravity, conferred
On its incumbent, like a bird,
A freedom where he sits

And takes his ease after some pleasing
Labour, motionless, coeval
With the hills in everything
But age, taking their shape, taking
Their air of past upheaval

That lends a present dignity
To their resigned deliberate
Collapse, as if outlasting what
They have outlasted brought them not
Too early or too late

Into their own identity;
When grey retirement's turned-down page
Looks back upon a hero who
Has long desired to pass into
An unperturbed old age.

A mountain is a mountain is
Itself, lasting, indifferent, proud.
The poet on his human throne
Has often wished that he were stone,
Or fluid, or a cloud.

Grasping the palpable, he feels
All that is vagrant in him lift
At the touch. A single fragile link
Offers an anchor he can sink
Into the friendless drift.

And now even the thought of these
Completed peaks, purpled above
Their green and still-grazed shoulders, brings
The shaping calm of well-loved things
Outside our human love

Whose blessing is unspoken like
An institution's is to those
Who freely seek in its employment
Their chaste hopes and loyal enjoyment
So that it never goes

But stands for all time in the shape
Of what it is and has been, till
Its fond dismissal sets us free
From it, and life, and all that we
Might be and never will.

So in the shade of the three mountains
I sit from day to day and teach
The inward eye its signs: from ledge
And scree they run, from slope and hedge
Down to Will Parsal's beach.

Mushrooms put tents up in the field
Where lofted thistles sail and spill.
Three horses come for sugar, late
Against the sun, and by the gate
The lane leads down the hill.

We are at peace here, where the grass
Extends however far we roam
And we can be, without having crossed
A road, tired out and almost lost
In a wood, but nearly home.

It is the world, and so it should be.
And it is ever so, once seen.
For the mind has caught it in its season
And there it is, and for no reason:
The grey among the green.

IX

1981–1988

Breakfast

Mornings restore us to the physical
With the clink of familiar slight purpose,
Toying with a log-jam of All-Bran
In milk almost blue, like a wrist.

The spoon has the weight and arched curve
Of a torso prepared for pleasure or pain,
Reminding us of dreams where we hunted
Free spirits down infinite spaces.

But the bowl, though endless, is finite,
A perfect white circle, with deceitful flowers,
A shape matched by the defining zones
Of our weakest spots: collar, belt.

Dead clothes

Dead clothes tell us what we have outlasted,
Weird surfaces of the self, less hardy
Though more prominent, projections and transmissions
To a world that requires sartorial mnemonics,
Since nudity is the one disguise that discreates our Selves.

I have worn some ridiculous clothes in my time,
Not least in boyhood, to say nothing of later years:
Leggings with buttons done up with a button-hook;
A grey beret with a stalk; a ginger suit
In which I was especially roguish
Behind a hot-plate in a hotel ballroom
At an annual party for the Deaf-and-Dumb;
Separate collars, with a stud to bruise the throat;
A long green overcoat, done up at the neck.

What went on inside clothes like these has been mostly lost,
And my memory of the clothes will not last for ever.

Blow up

That colourless unmoving world again!
The old contact pushing at its edges,
Not only the strain of sphere to contain square

But the unaccustomed size, re-creating
A periphery like absolute annihilation,
A new reminder of the fatal limits of vision.

The unconsidered detail proves to be part
Of the design: beyond an arm, beneath a chin,
Things appear to be about to happen.

We were there? Did we once know? Was
It *our* one eye that squeezed its flat world
Into the random history of a paper wallet?

Or maybe that is us, after all, in the picture,
Unrecognisable. We were all young once,
Strange faces, the dead light from stars.

The art of forgetting

Swivelling from a damp duvet at an hour
Too late for sleep, too early for work,
I wonder if sleep and its rapt drenchings
Are part of the art of forgetting or remembering.

Since whatever grips the mind in these dark hours
Is distinct, pungent, but elusive as smoke.
In the morning it is there and it is not there.
Who knows what it meant or what it means?

Writing this, it occurs to me to recall
A prep-room thirty years ago: Lister, owlish
At chess, scornful of fooling; Campling cutting card
For trains; brown Ryback laughing, tamping a rocket.

All is gone, the room, the house itself gone,
To allow for a widened road easing the traffic
Into and out of the seething heart of dreams.
Forgetting? Remembering? It seems to be all the same.

Equation

A perfect ease of conversation!
I have never managed it so well!
   The eyes sparkle, appraising
Other eyes, like an equation.
   The answer is amazing!
Where will it lead? Who can tell?

And then there is the insistent question
Of what the images can mean
   That come at times like these
With their perfectly decent suggestion
   Of impossibilities,
Wonderful things that have never been.

There's never time for a decision.
Life is made of sterner stuff!
   So, friends, dismiss the thought
That this is a constructive vision:
   As always, as we've been taught,
Life itself is quite enough.

And so goodbye: we'll save for later
The moment when these things are faced.
   Goodbye, dear friends, goodbye!
Goodbye to life itself, creator
   Of that self-serving lie
That life is good enough to waste.

Bud

Mildest of winters keeps the heart
Stirred once again to make a start
   On the old things.
A file of letters like a trap
Gapes. The mind draws on its sap
   For some new rings.

The slumber of the wasps is ours,
Dying in carton, far from flowers,
   Or so we reason.
But now the sun shines through a tree
Across my desk, enticingly,
   Out of its season

As though the year forgot its drift,
Discovering within its gift
 A strange remission
From cycles of that long disease
Which every estimate agrees
 Is our condition.

And so I stretch and seek the air
In the dead garden, finding there
 Something like you:
One paler and intense ellipse
Signals a bud among the hips,
 And one will do.

To each other

Not the calm centre that you think me,
 Not quite there,
Perhaps quietly struggling to be different,
 To be elsewhere
In some sense that you would find absurd
 Or vaguely resent
As being not, when you wish me moved,
 Quite what you meant.

Well, who cares? Life drains away
 Despite the weight
Of hands, eyes, custom, design,
 And it is late
To establish reasons for preferring
 The things we prefer
When now it seems grotesque to imagine
 That they might occur.

Light

Flat looks, flat smiles, dead things:
Ordinary purposes
We follow like a smell
To root, to snuffle up.

But all the time there is
This light, oblique, refracted,

Falling on this and that,
Falling as if by chance.

This light translates the world
Until it does not matter
When and where and how
The final darkness comes.

The light is compelled to gather
Like tears in a ghost's eye
In a long desperation,
And the ghost is you, is only you.

Disappointments

All over the city they are waiting for the night
Like a courtroom hoping for a popular verdict:
The longer it seems, the less likely the pleasure.

Or rather, the pleasure belongs to that whim of authority
Which insists upon the pronouncing of a prearranged sentence
And forbids all freedom of association.

Who *is* that spoilsport, querulous, ancient, severe,
Writing down the fatal words in his book?
It is our condition, first and last judge, who condemns.

At the centres of passion they queue without protesting.
Attendance is frequent in the offices of desire,
But interviews granted are few. The post is unfilled.

When disappointments feed upon themselves
Who dares to say that the diet is quite unsuitable
For the strapping lads they might become if they chose?

Must our delights, then, fall like fruit from a tree
That impatience shakes with the hand of fulfilment?
Shall we grow to relish the small, the stunted, the bitter?

341

Longing

Have you, too, been aware
Of a sort of something inside you,
Something uncertainly there
Like something you never tried?

And its claims are not defunct
Like hopes that age has cancelled,
That the passing of time has junked,
Like many old hopes and plans.

It isn't really dead:
It stirs like a slow April,
It gathers to a head,
It takes some sort of shape.

It's like a faculty
Unused, an eye in hiding
That senses it can see.
That comes to life inside.

Through all the ridiculous hours
It angles for attention
Like the clamour of spring flowers
And their innocent stench.

What is it that we most miss?
What do we have and have not?
In the last analysis
It's what we need to have.

And can we create what we miss?
Merely the fact that we sense it,
Merely my writing this
Is a kind of consequence.

And from these words there flows
A surge of strange fulfilment
Without its object. That goes
Outwards, and where it will.

Gone

Gone, gone, all gone,
Blown, and the gloom is towering:
Remains the dull, the civil,
The patient, the put-upon,
The chill roots that shrivel
After the first flowering.

Now for the decline.
Beauty speeds away
From the seed of our creating,
Following the line
Of its own accelerating,
The simple growth of play.

Often there is this sense
Of being beaten flat
In order to make the past
A kind of recompense.
Some things that we outlast
Were worth much more than that.

Wednesday

Wednesday, black rabbit, seven years old,
You were silent all your short life as though
   Entrusted with a secret
   You could not be sure of keeping.

Easily started, you would never turn your head
But stared in a still alarm through creepered brick
   Into that missing meadow
   Where danger would be a delight.

Not the eyes, a cloudy lidless brown,
But scissored ears positioned like microphones
   Brought the imaginary
   Misty horizons near.

Sometimes you dashed in joy from bed to bed
Like a comedian with surprises in the wings,
   Feet avoiding the fronds
   With a fastidious flick.

Not so many abortive burrows were yours
But the same one, not serious, under the rose.
    Your preferred occupations
    Were transporting paper

Or making circles around our wary heels
When on dewy evenings we trod
    With purpose or excuse
    Into your green domain.

Sturdy little president of the lawn!
We ignored your private moods; your gaiety
    Was at most a flourish
    In our casual moments.

And when you were found, a stretched effigy,
A hard object so much like yourself
    But weirdly without motion
    And feared like an impostor,

The ensuing sorrow was the strangest thing,
A conscious grieving in a larger happiness
    That seemed designed to absorb
    Its choking negative.

Whatever strange lessons of death we learned
Touching your flat still body or pushing turf
    Into impromptu place
    Above the disturbed earth,

We prefer to make of you a remembered image
That accords with our myth of perpetual contentment,
    Of life as an unfolding
    Towards an unseen horizon.

And now at evening in the summer air,
With wine and fruit unfinished on the table,
    The candle sculpts a soft
    But meagre circle of shadows.

And as night comes, the garden is suddenly empty
Of a black shape in the blackness, coming from nowhere,
    Coming at an idle call
    Though never making a sound.

Suppose

Suppose your future is to be
Too little and too briefly loved,
   Though not by me.

Suppose that you discover how
The things you most regret are those
   About you now

That seem so easily achieved,
So lightly kept, and over which
   You will have grieved

Thinking that they would last and last
As now the present seems the perfect
   Gift of the past

And tells of feelings handed on
Like sounds in consort, link by link,
   Till they are gone.

Suppose all this: would knowing where
And when the change occurred do much
   To make you care?

Hardly, for you'll remember such
A wealth of missing things it will
   Not matter much

And even if a day brings pain
It will be gladly worn in its
   Unbroken chain

And grieving is a joy, my dear,
That you will sadly soon discover,
   As I do here.

Daughter

   Once inside my head
The thought is hard to get out:
   Another daughter.

   You were never ours.
Photographs showed you missing
   And no one noticed.

Intention was blind:
How near was your conception
   We shall never know.

The disqualified
Candidates can't believe the
   Office is unfilled.

You don't exist, but
Nobody can take your place:
   That space has been booked.

Three faces suggest
The fourth: compass points of the
   Parental axes.

Words like little loves
Presiding over a map
   For future journeys.

Prospero's secret
Sadness: I had peopled else
   This isle with daughters.

Only the subject
Of unuseful poetry:
   What never occurred.

Lawn games

The rose shoots again
On its dead stump: there are things
   Not to be thought of.

Rambling blue flowers
Fade on the stone: bottle and glass
   Exchange their inches.

A heel on one knee,
A slight air cooling the sleeve:
   The eyes are restless.

Each grass blade aims high,
Each green corner joins arms with
   Its neighbour: a lawn.

Hoops turn the lawn to
A lucky six: the sun looks
  Down on a red ball.

  Palace of pleasures:
Beauty is ignorant of
  Being imagined.

  Five doves on the lawn:
Celestial fingerprint,
  A kiss from earth's lips.

  Nape, elbow, instep:
Her rug settles after a
  Smooth flight from Turkey.

  Ten toes, heels lifted:
Ankle bones like buds of wings,
  Eyes shut to the sky.

Names and faces

Late afternoon sounds:
The laughter of friends,
The filling of water
And kettle-lid's clatter
Heard across rooms
That forget their names
Like rooms that are haunted
Until they are entered
With tea and talk,
At which they wake
To lamps switched
And trays fetched
With steaming cups,
Cake, and perhaps
New contact prints
Of faces like saints
Staring in surprise
(Or smiles, or unease)
Over and over
At one-eyed lover –
Matter for grimace

Of pride, of course,
And tall tales
Of broken rules,
Of friends charmed
And things performed:
Another bundle
Of camera scandal.
Evening extends
Like desert sands,
Darkness comes up
At every sip,
And now the room's
Alive with names
Like an oasis,
With names and faces
In a lit space.

Emily's Chopin

Beyond the bedroom wall
Through which a knocked goodnight
Sounds like the cheerful call
Of an escapologist
To his charmed audience
Who only dimly sense
That once out of their sight
Already from his wrist
The playful shackles fall,

Beyond that boundary
Where brilliant high-fee'd sleep
Is willing to act for free
Who here takes nightly bribes
For cases that he bungles,
Her dreams are thick as jungles,
Precipitous and deep
As falls, down which lost tribes
Row chanting to the sea.

But first upon the air
Drift the pale thunderings

From muted record-player
Of Chopin in a tragic
Elevated mood.
Melodies, we conclude,
Are yearning wraith-like things
That offer prescriptive magic
The sleepless gladly share.

Two galleries

Strolling these stuccoed chambers walled with dreams
What is it that you like? You come and go
With news of Rubens and Correggio
And Jove's outrageous rapes, Ovidian themes
Of revelation where the lover seems
By being a bird, or coins, or cloud, to show
Indifference to that process which we know
Requires in girls a sprawl of pinks and creams.

Pure theatre, wilful, impossible!
I linger in a room of Bruegels, lost
To turnip children stout in winter clothes
Whose gods do not descend in poses full
Of lewd intent, but live in games and frost
And peasant weddings with their clogs and oaths.

Lucy's daffodil

Poorly finger, it didn't know
What it was doing. Now cut in water
It preaches from the tumbril of spring
A last speech on survival. It leans
Into a mysterious angle of beckoning
As if for inspection or attention,
Turning all sound green.

Chill flower, its ribbon pumped
With air, one jewel on the stem
Like a lost bathysphere,
It reaches from the rattling window as if
Hammered from what little light
Winter has admitted, scared
To be reclaimed by the wind.

349

Tissue lifts from the stalk knuckle.
The baby bell is haunted, nowhere
Else to turn. Its silent yell
Is like a gasp for oxygen
Claiming the whole room in the name
Of an emotion still to be invented.
What does the sun say? I can't hear.

Avoid contact with the eyes

You are safe here, in a protective envelope
That stays the shape of your body, warmer than blood,
A horizontal cubicle with a levitated
Door of water, a flooded sarcophagus
To revive in, anointed. If you cut the cord
The life will leak away again. If you sing
Someone will rush in, pretending alarm,
To see for one steamy moment two big eyes
And meringue hair. He will rush out again
For fear of being involved in your inviolable
Voyage and its exciting but innocent islands,
For though in that amused instant you lie
As still as art or geology, there on the edge
He will see the dangerous potion in sudden close-up
And the instructions are quite clear on the bottle.

Synopsis for a German novella

The Doctor is glimpsed among his mulberry trees.
The dark fruits disfigure the sward like contusions.
He is at once aloof, timid, intolerant
Of all banalities of village life,
And yet is stupefied by loneliness.

Continually he dreams of the company he craves for,
But he challenges it and bores it to tears whenever
It swims uncertainly into his narrow orbit.
Meetings, however relished in their prospect,
Seem only to be arrangements for departures.

Exemplum: the spruce Captain and his vampire wife
With her token fur hat and veil, like a bandage
Extemporised by a bat. It seems that exercise

350

Keeps the Captain's horse in a permanent lather.
The wife suffers from a disabling ennui.

What more likely than a harmless liaison?
At their first meeting the scenario is as obvious
As a cheese. Her eyes, half-lidded, turn away,
The cup lifted to her lips. The Captain has questions
About the flooding of the water-meadow.

A furious but undirected energy governs her soul,
Listless as she seems on the surface. It is
A libido on auto-destruct. Opportunities
Occur, but the Doctor, in complacent rectitude,
Bows himself off the stage of further meetings.

He devotes himself to his patients. They, however,
Begin to avoid him as if he has some dreadful disease.
When the Captain is lost on the glacier, his horse
Riderless, returning to graze on the bowling-green,
The Doctor is suspected. It is most unfair.

Meanwhile, his orphaned cousins go ahead
With their threatened law-suit. At first he is amused.
He meets their legal representative over
A schnapps in the Bahnhof Buffet, and is compromised
By the leather luggage of the absconding wife.

He claims to have found a cure for the epidemic of goitres
But only succeeds in killing two maids and a barley farmer.
The Captain's wife is staying at Interlaken
With the Schoolmaster's wastrel son. Her insane letters
Are read out in court, evidence of the Doctor's malpractice.

Only his good old Nurse refuses to disbelieve him.
On her death-bed she grips his fingers tightly
And mutters inaudibly about the lost diaries.
There is nothing now to prevent the red-haired cousins
From taking complete control of his estate.

The Doctor has lost everything and gained nothing.
At the back of his mind there is still the slight hope
That time will explain to him his crucial role.
He becomes a cutter of peat, and realises
That it is never quite easy enough to disappear.

The curable romantic

1

Returning from the encounter
He finds the room excited:
Walls flash mirrors like glances

That require the intended meeting of eyes,
And furniture is eager to be married
To the restless shapes it was made for.

Chess pieces go off quietly like pistols
In the irregular rhythm of a *paso doble*.
Lamps blaze, and books somnambulate.

One of these, settling in his hand like another hand,
Tells him insistently of a reckless love
And closes shyly with a sigh.

When he puts it back on the shelf
The room subsides at last into calm
And he is left alone with his remembrances.

She is in them still, but smaller.
The eyes close in weariness and containment.
The room waits for her.

2

The curable romantic has written five letters
In three days. He knows he will get answers
To none of them, because he has not sent them.
And because it is in the lines between the lines
That everything to be spoken remains unspoken.

3

Let him, like the classic poets, take
An eyebrow here, an opinion there
To assemble his dear impossible.

That way of pausing, this of smiling,
One habit of turning the chin to the shoulder,
Another of looking up from a book in surprise.

No doubt there are more intimate features,
The blind creases that open in the dark,
Nipple, wrist, nape and tongue.

All the relaxed and extended surfaces!
The stretched skin and hair of dreams!
At such times the features are blurred.

He must abandon these choice catalogues
And maintain his friendly relationship
With the actual, the possible, the ordinary.

For it is here, after all, isn't it,
That the ideal features derive? Here is
Imperfection, the truly lovable.

4

The curable romantic is lying in his bath
Having displaced the customary volume.
He is stripped of all his illusions except one:
That this finally which he is lumbered with
Is too solid to be anything but a permanent burden.

5

But then, it is simply waste and rehearsal.
The conversation leads nowhere, drifting
Short of the evening.

Groomed for companionship, the practised faces
Speak against the drawing of the curtains
With fatal fervour.

Doors open and close, and the rooms
Are emptier. He finishes a half-inch
Not his own.

Is it, he wonders, at all different elsewhere?
Above the roofscape a restless flock of birds
Gives no answer.

6

So we know that the hand
Reaches half in confidence
Half in timidity
For its due happiness.

There is a respect for souls
Who seem to share the quest,
A glee with them, and yet
Perhaps no ultimate trust.

Suppose, then, a silence
Not damaged but rueful,
The hand reaching out,
Not grasping, not retreating.

Maybe this is also
Your quiet satisfaction?
A face flowers in beauty,
In absorbed isolation.

7

Looking again on this face
He abandons all resolutions.

Reassumes the illusions
That yesterday he resigned

As he pedalled vigorously,
Hunched at a snail's pace

Towards the dead familiar
Landscape of his life

As he certainly will again
Tonight, and every night.

8

The curable romantic has thoughts of becoming pure spirit:
He waves all clocks away and scribbles incessantly.
His meals are still-lives and he smiles as he talks.
What good is it to say to him: 'Tomorrow you will be hungry.
Tomorrow you will sit down to the feast of your own heart'?

Eloge des gammes

You think you've come far enough for better answers.
For the bitten thumb, the shirt riding over the hip,
And dancing in up five steps at one bound

When the sun first goes behind the trees
And the host is opening bottles. For a hand
On the arm, the fingers splayed like a difficult chord.

For the conspirator's laugh, saying: 'Wait. No, really,
Wait there in the hall. I've something to show you.
You won't believe it!' For the visit already begun

At the hour of committees which is intriguingly
Advanced by the time you arrive. For the square letter
Which came after you left and is still there.

For the glance from parted hair thrown towelled and damp
Behind the ears, and a cigarette put out
Which is still smouldering, you notice, the next day.

But of course (of course!) you will find that there is still
Much travelling to be done. The indefinable
Eludes the contained excitement of its seeking

As from an upstairs room the scales ascend
Farther and farther, regular, luminous, distinct,
And every note is perfect, and still more perfect.

Space invader

Each little thing is arranged. The hotel key,
Numbered like a convict with its ball and chain,
Is slipped inside a folded *Sunday Times*.

The prisoner is allowed one telephone call:
An insistent ostinato devours his money
As plausible devices are capably launched.

Fidel is polishing glasses with the motion
He used for grinding pepper on her squid.
You time him as he turns back to the shelves.

You miss the unread paper and wonder about
The DLY NIGHT O under her arm. It takes
Four minutes to appear to enjoy a strega.

Fidel stares and yawns, a silent Wotan.
It's eleven all the way up the creaking stairs,
A crude conspiracy of brass and carpet.

The rooms are meaningless as an index entry
To a name you forget even as you look it up
Because you are tired or know the search is useless.

She is already waiting, a lump in the bed
You do not know which side to get into.
The light switches are conjuror's apparatus.

And now the program begins. It is a version
Of the familiar, with an alien object. A makeshift,
Though with arcade features. Worth every penny.

Voyage

From meeting on pavements
With raffia weals from the shopping
And a grin for news

To lips on places
Formerly merely admired
And nothing spoken

Is to wake on board,
To slip below the horizon,
To steer by stars.

Who knows what happened
That fateful night in harbour?
A complete blank!

One thing is certain:
There's miles to travel yet
And no going back.

Little mouths, little ghosts

Mouths make shapes like ghosts
That do not know if they
Are space or skin or

Something between surprise
And hope and restlessness,
That nomad harvest of

Fine hairs, exhalations
From the blood, the lips'
Sebaceous pasture where

Orations of protest
Are starved of the air
That could deliver them,

The throat locked between
Urgency and denial
Like the engaged tone,

Alive with pleasure
At the perfect pressure
(5 lbs per square inch) which

Launches these ambassadors
Of the spirit, these spooks
Of the tongue, themselves

Haunted by time that will
Uncreate them, and by silence,
And the nearness of a face.

Eyes and lips

Reading the lesson of the eyes
And paragraphs of lips,
Hands need only touch the face
As if to keep their place

And eyes have nothing at all to do
But speak to other eyes,
And lips absorb their own reflection
Without objection.

Eyes move guiltily, uncertain
Of their coordinates.
Lips receive distinct impressions
In lengthy sessions.

These faculties communicate
With freely borrowed roles
When the whole skin surface goes walking,
Good looking, small talking.

But then, as if such paradoxes
Were not enough, consider:
All this was simply what eyes did.
This was what lips said.

A surprise

All day the window squared off sky
With half a bare ash tree in it,
Grey clouds inching across shut glass
In a wind that made outside sounds,
Nosing slate and cold stone as though

Our mysterious shelter drew
An inquisitive animal
Back again to its frustration.

All afternoon we construed our
Books as cracking logs shifted in
The black grate like restless sleepers,
Never looking up as time slowed,
Till suddenly we sensed the wind
Had dropped and there at the undrawn
Curtains to surprise us was clear
Dusk. And Hesperus, like an eye.

The visitor

How can I begin?
And who will let me in?
I lean upon the far side of your mind
As if a door could learn
It had a hinge to turn
And, opening, disclose what was behind.
I whisper the appealing word
You claim you do not wish to hear, but surely heard.

Windows, as windows must,
Yawn on their jaws of rust.
Their catches snap, their webs are stretched and broken.
Curtains on their rings
Stretch like the folded wings
Of some dark-lidded bird too soon awoken,
For whom a gently sleeping wood
Makes restless sounds that it would fathom if it could.

And now a little air
Stirs in the rafters where
Tied sprays of leaves and herbs are slowly turning.
It wakes the drowsy fire
And makes the flames leap higher
To tell the silent room that they are burning.
It corners rugs with its embrace
As though by folding down a page to mark its place.

You find me in the gloom
Of the chill morning room

Before the fire is stirred or curtains drawn,
And through the ticking day
As hours slip away
I shadow small things struggling to be born.
I am the chimney and the mouse
And all the little noises of the midnight house.

The cat before the coals
From which the smoke in scrolls
Describes the movements of the massy air
Knows that I'm inside
And have a place to hide,
Although her blinking will not tell her where
And motionless her paws lie curled
About the dreaming suburbs of her tabby world.

On and about I go,
Carefully to and fro,
To keep the bedclothes you threw back in tangles.
Silently I explore
Your papers on the floor,
Arrange the furniture at curious angles
In rooms to which you are returning
To find a pan still simmering or lamp still burning.

And now you are aware
That I am living where
You notice these familiar surfaces,
And though I am unseen
You know where I have been
And understand what secret motive is
By now implicit in that being,
Impelling you to this necessity of seeing.

I am the secret print
Of fire within the flint.
I am the sleeping spark that dreams of tinder.
I am the wood that sings.
I am the tongue that springs
To sudden life upon the dying cinder.
I am the burning in your eye
That sets the world alight and will not let it die.

Swimming at night

Swimmers intend to be born again. Their laughter
And purpose bespeak a creature of consciousness

Even when descending a mad path to the night sea,
Stumbling at a damp curtain of black air

When the blackness itself has secret shades of black:
Purse black, space black, the black over the shoulder.

The eye that has no need to see looks nowhere,
But hands reach out for the bond of touch

Whose intention is some sort of commitment to the elements,
Linked and cautious on the delirious gradient,

Elements which perform their nuptials like a great drama
Proving an expressive bond of contraries:

Clouds heavy with the charge of a ready storm
Bounce their energy from the fused ceiling of air.

Thunder in a flickering jumble of light in the hills
Exposes the sea's swirling danger and glamour

And the damp is distinguished as an insistent fine rain
That joins sky and tide in drifts of forgetting.

This is a ritual where nothing was known beforehand,
Urged by the meteorological preamble.

Pleasures must be insignificant beside the attention
Of like to like, salt blood, salt water.

Clothes are bundled from the drizzle, a stub
Of candle flickering in the dredged hulk,

A dead boat beached in the invisible sand
That dwindles, though groined and lantern-steady,

Tiny along the shore as blackness reassumes
The crawling skin like a vestment.

And now hands break the sea as thunder breaks again,
And diving shocks the depths to a response:

Turbid with lit plankton like spokes and clocks,
The salt galaxies are bruised into being by our bodies.

Little fitful beacons of dull watery light
Sharpening the dark as the gallons glop about us

And the air splits and cracks and the rain falls
Alive on the blind surface of the sea.

It was not what we intended. It is not us.
It is something quite other. It is the first thing.

This strange submarine light is a hoarded scattering
Like the earliest seeds, like the touch of kisses.

It is damaged stars, like blotted lightning,
Like points to be joined that would give us wings.

Being born is a gasping and drenching.
It is cold and clean as the dead centre of night.

We have no thought of returning,
Consciousness switched off at the source.

Reckless of gravity, the candle lost,
We strike in light and darkness from the shore.

The cry

You heard that noise in Louis's wood?
Was it the creature that he heard
Three times one night and was afraid
To go much further than the gate
Because it was so late?

The pines that took his life to stretch
Above the skyline try to touch
The sea-westering sun and catch
The reddening light of its eclipse
And break it in their tips.

The wood's partitioned still by walls:
It used to be six fields. Old skulls
Of sheep that can no more (or else
Don't care to) penetrate the trees
Are placed like ivories.

A mushroom casts a shadow now
On pasture where grey thistles grow
That is as long as they. A ewe
Profiles the light, as singular
As the first and bleakest star.

Day dwindles. And then again
That sound, exultant and unclean:
Something that utterly alone
Drags from the foul air in its throat
A bestial strangled note.

Our ears are tuned now for the third
Rehearsal of that cry, agreed
It was no wonder he was scared
By darkness that grew up with him,
Survival's synonym.

If beast, not less for being unknown
And its feared features never seen,
What comfort could there be from one
Glimpse of its tormented flank,
Jaw dropped, point-blank?

For as we more than willingly
Turn from the tied gate, we know
That there will always be some cry
To break our cherished self-esteem
And every civil dream.

And now we're listening inside
The world that is our living head
For what the worst is that the wood
Hoards to remind us of the night,
That failure of the light.

The hand that reaches to the switch
Is not restrained, and nothing much
Inhibits casual questions which
Put up the falling gate again,
Put off the cry of pain.

Branches forever meet across
The paths where once was grass
And we revisit less and less,
When all the space is overhead,
Those spaces where they led.

And all the sky holds all the light
That ever was and we must wait
Until it fills again with what,

As valid as a watermark,
Illuminates our dark.

And the sun that hissed into the sea
Flares briefly on us for our share
Of days and casts its shadows to
And fro across the nibbled fields.
And the darkness yields.

A sudden hail

Once again it is up and over
The stone stairs, parabola
Of ascent for its own sake.

Such climbing is a kind of entry,
Keeping at a distance like
A courtly petitioning.

Laboured breathing is the guilt of a
Restless creature captured by
The supremely immobile.

The head is lowered and eyes are raised
In deference to altitude
At its purest, crest on crest.

At the top the sky starts to open
Like the drawing of curtains,
Fine veils, a theatre scrim.

And an attic hail sprinkles on moss
A careless largesse, cloud stuff,
The hand of the jeweller.

Up and over: the giant presence
Of what, when we are conscious
Of it, becomes endurance,

Something to be lasted that is there
Still when we find it will not
Last, and looms behind us like

The cruel deliberate legends
Of a mountain race for whom
The sky really is a god

And whose future falls like the seasons
On a receptive landscape,
Short shadows, too soon cut down.

We know it is scattered at random.
We know it is our brief gift
Like the snow's lifted waters,

Like the hail's rough milky diamond
Resting a moment against
The tiny feathers of moss.

After that it is all a downward
Tread, tread on tread, the loud heart
Lifted frankly like a face

That attends to its ordinary
Business in a warm valley,
Living cries, level dealing,

And for whom weather is common talk
With other faces and is
That delight faces can bring.

Lines for a 21st birthday

The odd year, like interest
Accumulating slowly,
Adds its decisive value.

How can you celebrate it
For whom, for two-thirds of it,
Guineas were no fee or bet?

A score and a year will not
So easily multiply
Into full three score and ten.

But if years were guarantees
Of that distinctive wisdom,
This praise of yours would founder

And Rosalind be fooled by
Touchstone's prattling, Eva by
Sachs's self-important song.

You with clasped palms and a skip
Will soon be departed to
Whatever your prayers pose

But the future is not here
And wherever age drags you
Will always stay out of sight.

It is the happy Kingdom
Of Ago to which you will
Almost certainly return:

The student city with its
Afternoon breakfasts and slept
Deadlines and parked suitcases

And the whole population
Taking in seven-league stride
This dated majority!

To me, though, it is a real
Achievement, a mystery
Of significant numbers.

Think of the pontoon kitchen
On a Gwynedd mountainside
Falling apart: three sevens!

So think, maybe, of these lines
Which like most art do little
But refer back to themselves.

The poem finishes like
Life itself: before you can count
It it is almost over.

Rook blitz

Once like Crécy tents they pegged the field of battle,
   Cover for prudent or cowardly monarchs,
Setting their long sights down half-obstructed files,
   Biding their time, or gladly exchanged.

But now they have met and agreed on their supremacy.
   Now they patrol their grids at speed.
They control rank upon rank mercilessly,
   Advancing alternately like musketeers.

Being trapped by them is terminal and absolute.
    They steal spellbound pawns like doorknobs.
Their only weakness is at their corners, yet they are perfect
    Turrets, and no one gets in. Or out.

Furies

I see you in your short stride
Aloft in deaf weathers
By sheep-path, ghost-gylls
And the sufficient berry.

Dreaming a distance above
The light tread of your age,
You walk in a charming shadow
Those dreams unwittingly cast.

Alone on your mountain
With the trickling voice of water,
Listen to the maligned Percy,
Damp on his marble page:

'The poet's self-centred seclusion
Was avenged by the furies
Of an irresistible passion
Pursuing him to speedy ruin.'

What better reason, then,
As the mist comes down,
For a considered descent
Into the visible world?

And to claim stability,
The best and surest virtue
For some peace and survival,
Earth-haunting, impartial.

But don't think you are ever safe
From those attendant furies
Who never seem to obey
The beautiful commands of dreams.

For the commands are theirs
And the power is theirs within them,
And every beauty is theirs
And is all your beauty.

For the veil is rent in those dreams
And we without changing are changed,
Pacing a staggered planet,
Powerless, uneasy, awake.

Past

The wind is never freer
From having hair to blow
When we have left the mountain
Before the early snow.

The grass can grow no taller
Beneath our absent tread
And flowers are never wasted
When all the flowers are dead.

The night comes as it has to.
The moon and Wilbur kiss.
With no one there to see it,
What memories will we miss?

The seasons have no hunger
To please us with their sport,
And only words as restless
Betray what we have thought.

And even those emotions,
From being once exposed,
Are like the closing chapters
Of books forever closed.

Goodbye

One by one they say goodbye.
The plans and promises, like sky,
Are for the moment perfectly clear,
But wait till tomorrow:

A little cloud no bigger than
The parting handshake of a man
Who promises he will be back
Thins on the zenith

And there above the roofscape drift
The gloomy greys that never lift
On friends who calculate their hope
In single figures.

Their lips meet like equations of
Elaborate formulae of love
Which founder on some trivial error
And won't come right.

And so they draw away, unequal.
A gradual goodbye's the sequel
Of yet another episode
That came to nothing.

You are the one who's left behind
And tell yourself you must not mind.
You are the hub of all dispersals
But where does it leave you?

Goodbyes like particles define
Their centre with a random line
That only points back to a past
Hypothesised.

And that event becomes your whole
Existence. It is like a role
That keeps you waiting in the wings
For something to happen.

The play itself, although you wrote it,
Would need another life to float it.
The dialogue is dust, the curtain
Not rising or falling.

Yes, these are the goodbye years,
As though the second of three cheers
Has caught the guests with glasses raised
But horribly empty.

The smiles are fixed upon their faces,
The printed names in all the places,
Someone hands flowers, the cameras flash,
But no one is looking.

You've got just one more red to pot.
You've got to make that crucial shot.

You move up to the table, ready
To take all the colours,

And when you see the ivory fall,
A futile trickle of your ball
Leaves you tucked in behind the black,
Lost to the yellow.

As, high and dry on narrowing land,
You look about your spit of sand
To see who cares to take the odds
And share it with you,

And what you find is rising tide,
The sun gone down, nowhere to hide
And birds that gather in the air,
Dismally calling.

Yes, this is the time that kills.
The losing shot. The empty skills.
And the wild sense of saying so,
Over and over.

X
Europe
(1992)

Europe

1

That swirling from Archangel to Gibraltar
Signals the sort of weather we are under.
We know that maps, like institutions, alter
And sticky days give way to evening thunder.
The globe turns round and countries shift their borders,
And satellites observe the tanks and clouds.
Only the rain will not respond to orders.
Only the sky will not break up like crowds.

The wonder is that Europe can survive:
Like a great dinner-service, chipped and cracked,
Reconstituted, lost, its use unlearned,
While all the guests are flushed by half-past five,
Mindful of precedence but not of tact.
The talk too loud. The odd chair overturned.

2

The plains swept them in from Asia like a wind.
It was the hope of water, where their star
Sank to refresh itself. But they had sinned,
And their forgiveness always seemed too far.
The mountains held them in suspense like breath,
Thick forests haunted every settlement,
Night told them stories of a living death
And exile nursed them everywhere they went.

And they were Europe's first romantics. Rome
Had bequeathed a stoic temper, and the cross
Made pleasure something it was worth forgetting.
The sadness of the Slav was different: home
Neither law nor heaven but a state of loss,
Songs full of sobs, the sun forever setting.

3

Borders that roads made into mountain passes,
Cultures that visitors admired and bought,
Languages acquired in language classes,
Religions carefully preserved and taught,
Quarrels converted into fear by taxes
And wars that art made into monuments
Became the rim of a great wheel whose axis
Turned on no more than mythical events:

The sky that speaks, a hero who can fly,
The founding father suckled by a bear,
The wandering race that finds a home at last,
And other lies: the lie of destiny,
The lie of law, and then the lie we care
About the most, that lies lie in the past.

4

Consider the slow gains of the settled life,
The bargains and the prizes of the soil,
Herds of the mother yielded with a wife,
Walls of the son rewarded for his toil
And questions they decided once by fighting
Across a stream that only said 'Perhaps'
Turned in the sharper certainties of writing
To powerful dogma in their deeds and maps.

But there's no argument that will not suffer
From being the point at which the bloodshed starts.
Law is the prior possession of the land
When hate was understood and justice rougher,
And law will sink its claws into our hearts
Till there is nothing left to understand.

5

At their first sight of it they came to know
Pure terror and for once were quite alone.
Earth had no larger absences to show.
This restless emptiness was like their own.
Their souls were mirrored in its treeless spaces.
Its livelihood became a game to learn.
The ownership of routes instead of places,
Horizons that you head towards not yearn.

So, following the darting towns of fishes,
They named each current as they named a peak,
Observed the tides and were surprised no more
To know the stars and compass of their wishes.
This was the blessing they had come to seek,
And paused in prayer when they stepped ashore.

6

We have this image in our politics
Of calm republics of the self, sand-hot
Oases of dreaming, where the mind can fix
Upon its fruitful hatreds, writing what

The Crusoe of our conscience calls its legal
But guilty hoarding of a dwindled stock,
Alphonse with his lighthouse and his eagle,
Or Pincher Martin on his saving rock.

Islands of preaching cormorants or nudes
Are all our castles now. What the king said
Ordered the verbs to venerate his noun,
That most unwelcome of all solitudes,
Exploited islands, islands of the dead,
The dirty rascals always getting down.

7

Islands have better secrets than you think.
The gnarled and rearing shoreline drives you back
A bobbing distance on the cream and ink
To sink a hopeful anchor. Or the track
That winds inland turns on itself again
And simply brings you to a different bay.
The mountains disappear. It starts to rain,
The march put off until another day.

But at the heart the fires still smoulder on,
The passes blackened that you need to cross,
The wooded valleys glowing in their embers.
And if there once were roads, the roads have gone,
And stones in villages record no loss
That anyone has witnessed or remembers.

8

The Turk at length withdrew like a tired lover
And all Vienna breathed into a waltz,
Informers blown to pieces with their cover
And emperors forgiven with their faults,
Religions left on rocks like prison islands
And borders argued over like old toys,
Resentment manoeuvring in utter silence
And townships breaking up in dirt and noise.

It seems the sentries never left their posts,
Their weapons barely sheathed. The information
Whispered in hatred by their tribal ghosts
Contained a single word: a lie, a nation.
Now it is Europe's stinking armpit and
Unravelling sleeve. And clenched, uplifted hand.

9

That's him. There. Arrogantly in our sights,
Strolling upon the ridge. It's easy to
Adjust the barrel's angle as he lights
A cigarette, and shakes the match. For who
Believes a war is started by one bullet?
Or that the slight resistance of the trigger
Could urge the curling forefinger to pull it?
Who would believe his enemy a figure
Whose very insignificance would then
Become a symbol of a natural process
By which the logic breeds that in all men
Has been a prior condition of psychosis? –
Steeling the will until the heart is stilled
And knowing only this: kill, or be killed.

10

The age of empires is forever passing.
The ancient centre of administration
And all the roads that led there slowly grassing
Over, every province now a nation
Blooming uniquely like a grafted flower,
Enthralling as a hostess who dismisses
Her soirée at an unexpected hour,
False as the seal of diplomatic kisses.

Nations in turn exist uncertainly.
Their delegates, like guests, arrive too late
In shabby suits for all-important sessions
Where simply how it's spelled will guarantee
That torture takes the name of a new state,
And maps are issued in minute impressions.

11

Suppose I cut your head off with a saw?
People wake up remembering what I did
With eyelids, folded stumps of ears still raw,
The filthy nose swung open like a lid.
How did those features ever once compose
A face? And gaze in fear or in reproach
At blood still welling deeply like a rose
Or crusting on the shoulders like a brooch?

Before she died, a shadow in her eyes
Entered my eyes, lodged in their caves of bone.

The head became a thing of curious size
And tumbled damply to the meadow, as
A foal drops from its mother. Like my own,
That head contained what guilt the body has.

12
And then the creatures spoke. To some the question
Of whether the bear was sleeping or awake
Simply depended on the bear's digestion,
No likelihood of slumber being fake.
Others voiced miscellaneous objections:
They were not jackals. Despite their best endeavour
The union was bound to cause defections.
A Balkan winter would not last for ever.

Remember what the actual jackals said:
'The interest of jackals everywhere
Lies in the pack. The jackal who doesn't run
With us betrays us, might as well be dead.'
And what the bear observed: 'To be a bear
Takes not the slightest effort. I am one.'

13
Not an unbroken landscape where a dreamer
Might wander with an idea for a day,
Coming unharmed at last to what will seem a
Friendly village, having lost his way;
Not an undifferentiated language which
Strange men on lonely roads could use when meeting
And neither of them end up in a ditch,
Having conveyed a threat, intending greeting.

For lines of speech are like horizons where
Something lies hidden that might blow apart
The frank, the open-armed, the undecided,
And dialects and borders will not spare
The best intentions of the mind or heart
To act as though they'd never been divided.

14
Within the architecture of effect
Fear has compiled its special regulations:
A system of repression to protect,
Façades as grimly closed as occupations.
Outside the towns the track runs as it must

Between the innocent and wooded hills.
Fields stretch for miles and crops grow in the dust
Where man and weather work their separate wills.

A state reveals its nature at its border.
A nervous guard, his eyes like thumb-tacks, glancing
Briefly at passports, moving correctly down
The train, everything more or less in order.
Just yards ahead, in Greece, singing and dancing.
Behind, for every pair of boots, a frown.

15

So little difference. A length of bread
Or wire can separate the living wraith
From the no longer miserable dead.
A length of lip, an accent or a faith
Is like a signature upon a warrant,
The certain failure of some nightmare test
That proves your very choice of life abhorrent
To those who wish to see you dispossessed.

The sunny street you learned to cycle down
Is closed this year. The girls have gone away.
The purses of your fig-tree will not split
Their gold with you. The buses heading into town
Won't stop. And all the time, day after day,
It was to be. Though no one mentioned it.

16

That shape beneath your arm. Is it a gun?
What are your fingers turning over there?
What is that object glinting in the sun?
Dodging for cover, there's no time to stare,
Only to fire. As you would fire on me,
Unable to let that crucial moment pass,
If only to restore the strange normality
Of running doubled over dogs and glass
To reach the safety of an alley's shade.
And there are many more where you have been
And some are still alive and some are dead.
I cannot see the loaves and coins, afraid
Of what I know: the difference between
A line of snipers and a queue for bread.

17

In many ways a meaningless event:
A slight misjudgement, the last hurdle dented,
An unexpected Greek by accident
Winning in games her country once invented.
But who could not detect in her elation
A pride that utterly transformed her face,
Made her both individual and nation,
The dual champion of her lucky race?

Precisely these emotions and this cheering
Deafens elsewhere the hated and the humbled,
For pride itself is double, and is reckoned
Upon the finest calculations, fearing
All common excellence. The girl who stumbled
Condemned to weeping shame by half a second.

18

The map is like a cloudscape lit by flares,
And Serbia, Kosovo, Albania, Greece is
Like a chess position where the squares
Are haunted by the shadows of the pieces,
Where every possibility contains
Too many other possibilities
For any certain outcome, and the brain's
Exhausted by the lines it thinks it sees.

And policy is only what will prove
That there were very few alternatives.
Or that, though different, they were much the same.
The move you end up making is the move
That you were always going to make. Which gives
Excuses to the losers in the game.

19

To be the powers! To sit with microphones
At tables gently circular as the
Great globe itself, speaking aloud from thrones
Disguised as sofas, turning photography
Into an hourly ikon of their trust,
Their rage and their responsibility!
The powers are never threatened. If they must,
They will react to power. And agree.

But hearts are fragile to enforce a bond.
Not a blade's fineness but its fore-edge weight

Counts most, they say, in the cutting of the knife.
Only at length, and wearily, they respond
To the pert brandished arguments of state,
Never to something broken like a life.

20

A resolution will not force compassion.
Pain makes no contribution to ballistics.
No interested government can fashion
Occasions of weeping out of cold statistics.
And though the silent headlines keep accounts
Of all these dispossessions to be faced,
Two million, three, impossible amounts,
Europe again impossibly disgraced,
There's nothing after all we can afford
More easily than easy opinion,
That there is only sympathy to give
The homeless, when the least to be restored
Is somewhere to return to when all's done,
Not very different from a place to live.

21

'Yes, they are saved, and all they have endured
Forgotten. The smallest, dangled on my arm,
Reaches the flight of mercy, will be cured
Of life. These others death will never harm.
They will be children always.' Still we ask
Why have they stopped saving the children now?
Hasn't it only just begun, this task,
Now that we know it must be done, but how?

The sky is silent, and a wind blows through
The smashed windows of buses. Somewhere a child
Crouches behind a gun, his finger curled
Upon the trigger. Children soon learn to do
What must be done, their bodies raked and piled.
If we could save them we could save the world.

22

Stretched in its coastal slumber in the sun
The full length of the continental shelf,
Paws round the captured Mediterranean,
Europe continues to admire itself.
The painful tongue of an immense devouring
Opens the foetid wounds of its old age.

380

The smell of wickedness is overpowering.
We hear the slamming of its summer cage.

We are its willing keepers. Every day
We speak the soothing words it likes to hear:
Whoever is dead will stay for ever dead,
Whatever happens, happens anyway,
Whatever we do, we do it out of fear,
Whatever is said, there's nothing to be said.

XI
Star-gazing
(1993)

Star-gazing

1

This glass is open to the sky
And gives the spaces overhead
(Which only never seem to die
Because they are already dead)
Their bright particularity.

They terrify us with their roar
Of silence and their sprawling lack
Of definition. They ignore
The names we give them as they pour
Their startling shapes against the black.

And in its quivering circle they
Return our gaze with unconcern
As though they only had to burn
And burn, and might not even stay
Till all their light had burned away.

It is a stiff and heavy glass,
Turning within a thread of brass.
It is an eye to frame at night
The airy meteors as they pass
And read their signatures of light.

It has no legs on which to stand
But must be shouldered and then panned,
The eyepiece steadied with one hand,
The other acting as support
Until the looked-for star is caught.

And this is how, in any case,
We tend to use the tilted face:
The naked eye a searching cone,
The straining neck leant back, alone
Or on a shoulder not its own.

Star-gazing is a friendly thing,
When eyes aware of other eyes
And other arms on which to cling
Seek fires of a different size
And arcs that colder clay supplies.

And that discrepancy of sense
Restores us to each other, hence

To our exalted littleness
From which we dare thus to address
The neighbourhood of the immense.

Remember when the season bid
Us wander up and down the hill,
Blinking against the sky until
Its blackness bore a Perseid,
A little spark that seemed to spill?

The dizzy heavens tried to weep
With stars, the night was nearly gold,
We clenched our fingers counting, told
Tall stories till at last the cold
Conveyed us to the house of sleep.

    2
The telescope's one dusty eye
Was found beneath my father's bed,
Coffined and latched. I don't know why
He kept it there. He might instead
Have let me point it at the sky.

We could have looked for every star
Named on his little planisphere,
Making the scattered singular
And with a word bring strangely near
The very farthest of the far.

For language is this human trick
Of simply daring to presume
Upon the contents of a room,
Distinguishing, quadruple quick,
A chess queen from a candlestick.

Since we have words for the unseen
And places where we've never been,
It's not surprising we know how
We can discriminate between
Cassiopeia and the Plough.

The I and Not-I is another,
Learnt by the baby from its mother
When first it predicates the Other,
But this is going too far back
Into the Freudian zodiac.

And anyway you will recall
How Freud declared that after all
Our devious minds turn everything
To something else: imagining
A breast, we dream a piece of Ming.

Are things the same, or different?
We take our pleasure in the trope
Of metaphor, where what is meant
Is not what's said: a star is hope,
And longing is a telescope.

That sort of thing. Or maybe it's
A poem made of separate bits,
Joining the lid and narrow box
By means of hinges and of locks,
Inevitable opposites.

Or it's the closing of the light,
A deathbed of its own, the pen's
Last stroke, the useless oxygen's
Retreat, the stopped watch in the night
Sharing the darkness of its lens.

Or it's a symbol, if you'd rather,
Of the essentially unknown,
The door that opens with a groan
To leave me standing there alone
In terror, and without a father.

3

Most of us eventually
Are orphans. Now that I am one
At fifty-six, it's real to me
But is a state with which no one
Could really have much sympathy.

For when our story's almost done
The plot is clear, it never thickens:
No deeds turn up, no bastard son,
No cruel change of fortune, none,
Nor tight-lipped guardians out of Dickens.

No shocking secret brings relief,
No birthmarks, sapphires or debentures,
No equatorial adventures,
No cousin with a handkerchief
Or pretty lips to blot the grief.

The twin events were feared and fated
And they were not long separated:
After the closing of his door,
Although my mother watched and waited,
Life could not go on as before.

And so she suddenly departed
And finished what her parents started.
Her final face was broken-hearted:
That mask we never rearrange,
The one expression we can't change.

Less of surprise than resignation,
The mouth almost in supplication.
I looked in vain at that inert
Abstraction, trying to convert
It to rebuke, or love, or hurt.

And his: likewise a spurious cast
Of some imposed solemnity,
A hollow mockery, the last
Gaunt face he pulled to frighten me,
One I could never bear to see.

For all the warnings and the fuss
Death is an instantaneous
Incompetent photographer,
The moment always wrong, a blur
We never could admit was us.

We'd always go back if we could
To that authentic unrehearsed
Expression that we had at first.
We may have thought it not much good
But hadn't then foreseen the worst.

And so my orphaned task is to
Redeem that album of the living
In memory without misgiving.
The lens of death is unforgiving.
The shutter falls for me and you.

4

Perhaps the entire universe
Is something like a camera
Within which matter can rehearse

Its unconvincing poses, star
By star, self-satisfied, perverse.

An endless film is moving through
Its darkness, a grey pantomime,
A shadow of some ballyhoo
That we are bound to misconstrue:
The film is us, is mind, is time.

How can we see and understand?
How can we see and be inside it?
We haven't yet identified it.
We think it is immensely grand
Yet need to hold it in our hand.

That particle that we observe
Appears to take a likely curve
And yet we doubt its path and distance:
Is it the same, or did it swerve?
Has it position *and* existence?

We slave to see electrons glide.
We like to watch the cells divide.
We'd put the sun beneath a slide,
Even our own observing eye,
To try to see our ignorance die.

Forgetting that we found the comic
Ages before the subatomic,
Forgetting the philosophic glories
Of the wise Greeks, observatories
Showing them systems that were stories.

No theories do it half so well
As what the lifted eye can trust:
The sky itself that longs to tell
The fable of its mortal dust
That falls and burns because it must.

Now Sol inflates his fiery chest
And drives his chariot to the west.
Beneath the burning wheels and hooves
The glittering sea grows large. It moves
More slowly now, and takes its rest.

Night loses all her inhibitions
Upon the sleeping of the sun.

The dome is opened, one by one
The stealthy stars take their positions
And act as they have always done.

Their dances formally presage
The entry of the real star,
Nude Artemis, the singular
Pale presence in this theatre,
Striding across her silver stage.

5

In every sky she knows her place.
In Corsica she looks just as
She does in Wales. (In Wales the face
She sadly leans towards us has
The old Oxonian grimace).

Perhaps it's something she forgot?
Her one good eye is vacant, more
Like a bruise, a cobweb or a blot.
And we stare back. But don't know what
On earth she can be looking for.

Something immeasurably lost,
Like innocence? Or something hunted?
Does she look savage, or affronted?
She chose a vagrant's path. The cost:
Millennia of dust and frost.

The tides are at her heels, and she
Reflects a special gravity
On water. Easy then to claim
She has a longing for the sea
From which initially she came.

Here on this plio-quaternian coast
The wind has hollowed each exposed
Piled boulder to a standing ghost,
A gargoyle or a weathered shell,
A sort of lunar sentinel.

So the *tafonu* haunts the rocks,
Bathed in the very light it mocks,
A gaunt subspheric demilune,
A meteorological cartoon,
A granite version of the moon.

It takes no time for the grotesque
To normalise its strange aesthetic:
It constitutes the picturesque,
Its likenesses are energetic
And are essentially poetic.

How readily they can disarm,
These sculptures of the Notre Dame
De la Serra or Calanches de Piana!
Configurations of Diana,
Wrecked symbols of her power to charm.

They are the metaphors of change;
Of matter's endless vacillation
And dogged differentiation,
Its power to seem forever strange:
Analogies of alienation.

So we stare down the littoral,
Just as we calculate the night,
For stalactite or meteorite,
Behaviour of stone or light
Departing from the usual.

6

For we have stripped away the year
With grief and work, and found its heart,
Something with which to persevere,
Something with which to make a start,
Something we knew we might find here.

The summer shows us at its core
A state of being that might save us.
What we have lost we can't restore,
But know we have, and need therefore,
The bodies that our mothers gave us.

Our eyes, grown heavier with all
They've seen, need lifting up towards
The light. We need those major chords,
That full acceptance of the sprawl
Of nature in her free-for-all.

We need the sea's oblivion,
To dive below and gaze upon
The coloured life that knows no clocks,

The *oblade* and the *sparaillon*
Playful beneath their crusted rocks.

And where the water meets the sun,
Burnished when the day is done,
The sea and sky appear as one,
Rare stuffs laid out that no bazaar
Could sell: faded, crepuscular.

The late sky's only silhouette
Are hills that few have crossed as yet
Or wish to cross, for on each side
Are valleys where men lived and died
And never were unsatisfied.

The tumbling bat comes out to eat
And crickets open their salon.
The lizard poses at your feet,
Then moves with practised flourish on
The dust it owns and signs, Anon.

Again we light the candles and
Make shadows of our contraband
Of herb and shell, and once again
We pour the pink wine of Sartène
And hold its pebbles in our hand.

At which we come to feel, of course,
With vacillating Arnold, 'Ah
Love, let us, etcetera . . .'
But feel it with unusual force
Beneath the heavens' *feux de joie*.

And wish for it beneath their beams
And watch the orange iris burn
To black against the sky and learn
Again the names of stars and turn
From the flickering terrace to our dreams.

7

Our dreams are how the past arrives
At compromise. They come in clusters,
Like jostling men concealing knives;
Or singly, the strict loss-adjusters
Of over-accidental lives.

Just as distressingly, they go.
Whether unique or in a series

They do not, like a video,
Record the things we ought to know
Or illustrate important theories.

They are not baleful like a spook
Or tie things neatly like a suture,
They do not speak about the future
In riddles like the Pentateuch,
Issue no warning or rebuke.

Yet sometimes out of our obsessions,
Our cautiousness, our indiscretions,
Our dreaming minds intently make
Surprising symbols of repressions
They can do nothing with awake.

Here we sleep long, remember more,
And our unconscious when we snore
Stands open like a friendly door
Revealing our individual isness
Struggling to sublimate life's business.

The frequent dream we never doubt
Or think to ask what it's about
Takes on new certainty, its theme
Acknowledged in the general scheme
Of what we recognise as dream.

That hidden staircase, undetected,
Leads to a half-remembered room.
The smouldering timbers, long neglected,
May breathe each cinder to a plume,
And break into a fiery bloom.

And yet I climb excited there
To find some sort of foothold where
I might do something to reclaim it.
I know I do not need to name it:
The stair's the thrill of being a stair.

And it is almost less surprising
Than the reality around us.
When in the morning fish surround us,
This is because we swim on rising,
Yet still our equilibrium founders:

Half-asleep we glide, mistaking
The weedy rocks for grassy vales,

393

See distant sheep instead of snails
And crows for the black scissory tails
Of *castagnoles* we know on waking.

8

And if we wake up in the night,
We easily feel flabbergasted:
Our dream had such vast scope, despite
Our knowing that it must have lasted
No longer than a meteorite.

A whole Victorian triple-decker
Is there, the scientists have reckoned,
All the emotion of *Rebecca*,
All the excitement of *The Wrecker*,
Contained within a miscrosecond.

Our dreams burn up on entering
The atmosphere of real life.
They snap shut like a pocket-knife,
Are delphic, tiny, maddening
As prisoned birds that will not sing.

What was it that my father said
To my cocooned and dreaming head?
He sat there, dazed, and I was not
Surprised to see he was not dead.
I talked on like an idiot:

The multitudinous happenings
Since he had left us, publishings,
Memorials, his personal things,
How I'd looked after their removal,
Hoping I met with his approval.

And yet all this was to protect
Him from the certain ill-effect
Of his decline, the little chance
Of permanent deliverance.
His face took on a radiance.

With all my silly chatter done,
I put my arms about him, knew
His real dying had begun
And knew this miracle was true,
Occasion for a last adieu.

But what he said, or what I made
Him say, was lost. Was I afraid
To hear, or even make the attempt?
Perhaps that moment was undreamt,
A kind of deference to his shade.

And I awoke or I was woken
By a strange consciousness of tons
Of falling stardust fired like guns
Above me, and my dream was broken
By midnight and the weight of suns.

The bright stars flipped like shuttlecocks
That lurch and fall. Each left a mark
Upon the retina, a spark,
A sudden match struck in the dark
That spurts and dies against the box.

9

Alpha Centauri in the night
Look down and tell me what to think.
Pour out unstinting, as I write,
Over my intermittent ink
Your steady undistracted light.

You are the starting point of what
Has been an idle whim of ours:
To draw a line from dot to dot
In the right order, thus to plot
A secret picture of the stars.

Of light you are the principal
Among the many lights that blaze.
You are the entrance to the maze,
The illuminated capital,
The hidden theme of the chorale.

And all we need is your immense
And unconcerned magnificence
Turning and turning unrevealed,
A random point of reference,
One intersection in the field.

I mean, we simply need to start
And all else follows, part by part:
The heavens turn, and through the art
Of imitation we can feel
Them turn, and so invent the wheel.

Then nature's spiral yields the spring,
Whose impetus from tightening
Controls the otherwise hotchpotch
Of random forces. Then a notch
Upon the wheel invents the watch.

Never so simple, but forgive
An argument that goes slipshod!
My real intent is figurative:
In Lilliput it wasn't odd
They thought his watch was Lemuel's god.

For when our hour of death arrives,
We all admit it's time that drives
Us on and that our only heaven
Has been the less than thirty-seven
Million minutes of our lives.

We can't contrive perpetual motion.
Alpha to Omega is more
Than we shall ever have. Three score
And ten concludes our self-devotion,
While the stars dash upon the shore.

Forgive this clockwork replica
Of what we do not understand.
And let our fretful cells disband
In peace beneath each stopped spread hand
And still heart of our Omega.

10

Strange how our jealous star conceals
From us all other stars as though
Their coded clusters, spokes and wheels
Might point us out a way to go!
Empty and blue are his ideals.

And he intends to lull us with
A spurious sense of being free,
Dazzling the senses with his myth
Of a benevolent coppersmith
Burnishing the sky and sea.

But when the sun has gone to rest
The scenic blue gives way to night.
The constellations reignite,

Harmonious, ordered, self-possessed,
The ancient *mécanique céleste*.

Which of their portents can be true?
For me, perhaps, as well as you
There's nothing much they can foretell
That isn't just our point of view:
Stars shine *away* from us as well.

For certain, even while we're gaping,
Their light is rapidly escaping,
So which events they may be shaping
Is much in question: light doesn't last.
The present soon becomes the past.

So all our history is sent
In light-waves through the firmament,
Continuous record of mishaps,
The most extemporised of maps,
The very picture of Perhaps.

And as one scene succeeds the other,
Each generation is distinguished,
Father and son, daughter and mother,
One by one, the bonds relinquished,
And the long lives in turn extinguished.

No pattern there, except in death,
The stubborn drawing of a breath
After breath after breath that perseveres
For all of our allotted years,
The sixtieth, seventieth, eightieth.

So when we look up at the sky
And claim the interest of the stars
And when we weep our au revoirs
We know it is our turn to die.
The next black-letter day is ours.

We even know there's no reprieve
For our own daughter's generation,
Beautiful in their vocation
And individualisation.
And this is what it is to grieve.

XII

1985–1995

The mechanical body

Lifting a curl of its hair mounted on gauze,
Inserting the key into one ear oiled with its own wax,

You were at first surprised by its yielding and weight,
The way you could wind it to a pitch of response.

The whole mass trembled with released springs,
A shuddering at the heart of it like laughter.

It stunned the player with its fringed opening eyes,
Making the onlookers instinctively draw back.

But it was all surface and expedient dollwork,
With hidey-holes for soul and coils for motive.

Unfinished the canyon of the stitched chest,
The mirror fragments, the panels of easy access,

The lacunae (. . .) (. . .) behind the knees,
The temporary leather, the hinged armpits,

Stencilled flowers on the linen ribs,
Your hands disappearing into glue.

Its sentiments worked on pulleys and punched rolls,
Tinny between bellows and horn-membrane.

The first hummings and trillings eased into
A pert sotto chirrup: 'Now then, Bertie!'

Little fans spun above the turning cylinders
And, with a tilt of the whirring chin and a slight click,

'Do it again, do it again, do it again' modulated
Into deeper, more thrilling pronouncements,

And whatever you cared to say came flatteringly back
From a library of teeth shining and uplifted

As the vibrations of the throat sang out their triumph
Of elocution: 'Tonight – cherry tart!'

That face was all-important, the ivory jaw
Traced in one chisel-sweep from lobe to lobe,

The nose a guardian of resonance, vellum temples,
The powdered cheeks borrowed from mandarin hangings,

Best was the mouth, embroidered minutely,
Hidden the hooks and wires that trembled it into motion.

401

Their working went deep into the busy centre
Of emptiness, as from the flies of a theatre:

Oiled strands trundled from a central gear
Slung between the rolling pivots of the hips.

The sounding vibrato of the belly concealed
The whine of its continual working.

Its long strings leading to that simple ring
Through which they fanned, the ring contracted

And its webs and skeins diversifed into
A pursed amusement or a moue of disgust

Or turned inside-out like a cat's-cradle,
Offering its watered-silk tapestry for kisses.

How the onlookers cheered! The thing was rooted,
Statuesque, a third larger than life.

It was gaunt with dust and tulle.
Bits of it glittered, even in the dark.

Great springs slowly lifted the padded knees,
Whiskery skirts leaking oil on to the floorboards.

And all the time was this ripple of felt and enamel,
This little jabbering of hammers and pulleys:

Its talking might talk you through till morning.
Your back was bruised from its attentions.

You thought of figureheads and oceans.
You thought of young mothers in their milk.

You thought of the egg-smooth backs of eyeballs
Staring unknowingly into the smoky caves of the future.

You thought of your life as a cheerful wager,
As a torn ticket of entry, a key to be used once.

You thought of cog turning cog turning cog,
The perpetual motion of the Last Chance.

You thought of the questioning of beauty in eternity,
Your hands at the controls, and celestial signs.

But as it wound down, its fingers barely twitching,
A tell-tale ticking from the ratchets of its joints,

There was nothing in the business but a blush,
A scattering of applause, a stillness.

And in that stillness, the postscript of a last
Creaking inch of clockwork was like a hollow laugh:

Hollow as the likeness of truth to a skull.
Hollow as the starlight pull of the doll.

Silhouettes

Sister, when I saw your toe whiten
Beneath the blade I thought it was already
Parted from pain and ready to be pitied.
I thought the business done, detached for ever,
Drained of the salt source we share, mere lump.
But that was only fear. The thing was still
Alive, though tensed and bent, like a small man
Almost used to being hurt, the arms
Clasped over the head, flinching from words.
And the scissors, for a moment, still had the skin
To cut. And, look! your hand still held the scissors.
Who said we had to be the shapes we are?
Or that those shapes are not desirable?

Sometimes in the lamplight I could think
Myself not more than shadow-deep from beauty.
Noses and chins on walls are graced a little
And get on terms. I could hug anyone
And never feel ashamed, or if refused
Refused with interest, fondness or respect.
Just a little does it. Like a cabbage:
Each leaf of such a thinness as you strip
To the heart, but that small centre is soon reached.
I think that everyone has once at least
Woken and wept themselves to sleep upon
A restless bed, alone and half an inch
From being hideous. Much more then, we.

When I heard your intake of breath, and the low
Growl of pain from your throat, I knew it was done,
Though cleverly you concealed that new object,
That part of you so like a grave of itself

With its grey little tombstone of a nail.
And you walked so proudly before the prince
As if in glory, with a baleful knowing enticement,
A smouldering glower as if bearing down on his mouth
With your determined mouth, and a small swagger
As without limping you placed each foot on the tightrope
Of the flagstones and no one to notice the slight
Leak at the gripping apron of the slipper.
O sister, though envious, how I prayed for you!

To fail is to want followers. But I
Was by your side, as sisters always are.
I took the scissors and put them in my sleeve.
(Were you to keep what you had seemed to win,
I knew that there was evidence to hide.)
It was not love, nor being a bride of blood.
It was not kingdoms, but a kind of justice.
For there was a fairy creature at the dance
Revolving by the beat, her skirts aflame.
The orchestra was hers, and hers the pulse
Of the night's bodily music, and the stars
Came out for her and for her tiny feet,
And I was wholly with you in revenge.

She took the perfect hours her shape allowed her,
But that was all. The truth has times that are
Unwilling servants of their wilful master
And if she changed her shape again, who knows
What spate of goblin nuzzlings might ensue?
Just once she could be goggled at for being
All she might ever want to be. The rest,
The future beyond the hours, the hours beyond
The future, are nothing but a demi-mask:
Blank as to insight, but cut out for speaking
As speaking is the staying of those hours.
Behind it is the dark we always face,
And silhouettes a dangerous game with scissors.

Now is my time. The crystal slipper wiped
And once again presented on its cushion.
The ceremony is a dream repeated,
Our whole life winding down, a second chance,
The last and only chance, the lifted mask.
What do I risk? I shall go down again

Into the hall with perfect staircase paces.
It might be nothing more than a raw place
At the heel, a scouring, a deliberate blister.
We lose such linings by the moon. A triumph!
For after all I am the elder. It is
Fitting. I am called. My foot is treading
For ever in its liquid sock of skin.

Needing fear

Have we always lived in the castle?
And how can it really be
That the dry moat is sufficient?
Two black ravens flapping
And the practice
Of bractice?

Danger has no future
And never had, whose spears
Rust in the rain outside.
Nor sneaking in of snakes,
Nor the defiance
Of giants.

And when the storm gives tongue,
Flickering from the mountain,
We may from walkways shout
Our answer, slam gates shut
With the clamour
Of a stammer.

No password hears its echo,
No secret touch through walls.
No one makes assignation
At postern for a parley
Nor bribes a sentry
For entry.

Whatever drenches towers,
Whatever grey skyscapes
Inch past the slit windows
It will be sunlight and singing
In the courtyard,
Like an orchard.

Walking there unthreatened,
Forgetting the man-thick walls,
It might be the playful ocean
That surrounds you sleeping with
The hot silence
Of islands.

But again, how can this be?
And must it always be so?
Surely one day we will wish
This sleight of stone we never
Quite intended
Could be ended?

Become uneasy with
Our quiet? Needing the fear
The walls were for? Needing
Their siege and (with whatever
Indignation)
Capitulation?

Lesson of the master

His vision was titanic: the little we enact
Of comic calamity is at his whim,
Every misunderstanding, lack of tact,
Miraculous obtuseness, foretold by him.

Here are the maps of transatlantic drift
And dangerous friendship; the calculated stealth
Of evil, where culture is power and the gift
Of beauty a disaster, like ill-health.

He knew, as we do, how the physical
Acquires significance from our attention to it:
The wet boot held towards the fire, the full
Black hair. We come to see his meaning through it.

Fiction for him was, as for God, like playing
With the helpless questors of Eden. His face the face
Of Mrs Assingham, or Mrs Tristram saying:
'I should like to put you in a difficult place.'

If a charming vulgarian intended to strike
Some bargain with a snob, he would insist:

'You say you are civilised? Very well. I should like
To make you prove it.' He was an empiricist.

If pleasure beckoned, we could never follow.
If ghosts should appear behind the protective glass,
They too would prove our conversations hollow
And, like desire, would never come to pass.

Innocence is always shocking. It resembles
A clumsiness to which our heart goes out.
And we are stupefied. The hand trembles.
It is, we suppose, what love must be about.

Surely we realise that we have lost,
Way back, the path that might have led to joy?
Behind us is a threshold we have crossed;
Before us, other simpler lives we must destroy.

For after all, his humour comes down to this:
Betrayal is licensed by Bradshaw, and the sexed
Admirer foreshortens his future with a kiss
That leads, alas, to the closure of the text.

The grave at Rarogne

He wanted to be buried where he first
Admired the wind and light of the Valais
That like a perfect wine aroused a thirst
To satisfy that thirst, day after day.

Now from the south-west a different wind appears,
A disaffected spirit, randomly clad
In a fine red dust that shapes our seasonal fears
Of migraine, thunder, lost love, feeling bad.

Its visible robe is a hectic model of ours,
Shiftless, sly, or suddenly excited;
Stirring the fields that else would be making flowers,
Roses perhaps; turning up uninvited.

Were poems like red roses, made of earth
To be a moment's thought and then returned there?
Where did they shine, and speak of that strange birth
As though it were a purpose that they learned there?

'Will you not come? Oh, but the human soul
Craves joy and craves a deep eternity!
(That is philosophy.) No other goal
Can tell us from the brutes, or sets us free.'

Will you not come? You are the night sky
Beyond the peaks, containing all the stars.
Things wait for you, these roses that may die
For the unpromised containment of your vase!

The graveyard, like a chattering balcony
The moment that the curtain rises, saw
The mountains as a wonderful wish to be
The thing that hushes us in sudden awe.

And every slab is silent now. Above,
The snows assemble. All the flowers hide.
It is the end of summer and of love.
The little church was honoured when he died

And handsome women came in furs and gave
The poet, as a token, one supposes,
Of all he'd given, dropping them in his grave,
(Although it was the depth of winter) roses.

Dear Brutus

So you will start to count up to a hundred
And we will never know how far you got.
It is like the beginning of time. It is like time ended.
We don't know if it's real for you or not.

Had he already, then, begun to lose
You there among the shadows, knowing so well
The intimate and sexless role he chose
For both of you to play? We cannot tell.

We might think it disastrous, however pleasing:
You with no history, learning what to feel,
He with his dream, his easel and his teasing.
Perhaps it's not for either of you real.

Crack-in-my-eye-Tommy! It's real all right!
Just when you talk of putting up your hair
He has this strange distraction for a light
Like windows in a wood that isn't there.

408

How awful it would be to wake and find
You'd never been alive. That somehow Dad
Had simply imagined you. Yes! in his mind:
The thoughtful romping girl he never had.

But no, that can't be true. You feel it lift
Within your body like a branching tree.
It is the assembling blood. It is your gift.
It tells you you are Margaret, and free.

You didn't think it would embarrass him.
One, two three, four . . . Hurry, Dad, come back!
As the spots fade behind the bosky scrim
There will be nothing for you both but black.

But who imagined whom? Who dreamed the child
And who the father? Was it a sort of pact?
Something within that wood is reconciled.
And now begins the terrible third act.

Photograph

The image of a possession, possessing and being
Possessed by a mystery, stares from this face,
One finger at the cheek, the eyes searching.
There is a double distance: hypothetical
Space, our space; and the studio's.

Light blinked into the brass and guarded chamber:
A faint perception of the curious way that
Something rehearsed could still be unexpected
Showed in the equal distance of her mouth
From either recognition or repose.

It might be almost words about to break
Out there, a smile's postponement of itself
In puzzlement, amusement half-dispelled,
Before the settling of the lips in trust
That ceremony is a silent thing.

And we have nothing but our privilege
To share this silence and its lineaments:
Low forehead, heavy brow and rueful chin,
Young as if for ever and the leasehold
Of its occasion's awkward fragile beauty.

She was not often much like this and now
Can never be again, but over and over
Looks through and at us from the knowledge that
This mystery has thought to touch her with,
A face outfacing all its history.

What has just passed is like the tree above
Her grave where birds shrilly debate their break-
ing from the clamour that they make, until
They burst from leaves and flock about the sky.
The moment afterwards is still to come.

England

Falling towards the map is a controlled illusion,
The text scrolled to the cursor. It is England down there,
Tilted like a display. It is a living space
   Screened for observation,
A gravity-haunted logo, a significant shape
   From which there is no escape.

The shires are whitened with snow, old ploughing
Turned to Aztec friezes and museum crochet.
Between the rafters of weather and the granite flags
   Is a simulated surface
Of plot and portion that we only ever know
   As landscape from below.

It implicates our wish to be welcomed, our resolve
To enter the dull story and to make it remarkable,
To order the memory like a WAAF croupier
   Pushing her heroes across
Inches that are clouds and tiny villages recalling
   Our fear of falling.

At the heart of England we are pursuer and pursued,
Where frozen footprints are the history of that hunt
And towns we think we never visited are like
   Both past and future,
Tremendously distinguished in the willed notation
   Of our imagination.

At the heart of England the drivers are silently crawling
Bumper to bumper, the exits sealed off, the route
A duty to some present but long-forgotten intention

410

And the lights are flashing
As if to warn us to keep to the dogged pace
    Of a wry acquisitive race.

At the heart of England we listen to old stories
With an amusement that guarantees their lack of any
    power
To direct our attention to what they may be saying
    And off we stolidly stump
Past the gingerbread cathedral and the factory blur
    To the scenery we prefer.

There the eye is of course directed upwards
As paths respect the mossy boulders and outcrop
Of the heights that induce their steady winding and
    climbing
    Until some point is reached
Where we see that heartland sprawled as in a lap,
    Half-asleep, half-map.

For the most part they are nibbled humps or great ledges
Swathed in rolling mist like experimental theatre:
It suits us to shade the eyes, to stare for coasts.
    From that isolation
On either side adventurous streams agree
    To part and find the sea.

We never join them. They are unjoinable.
And there is nothing much in the end to be done
Except to return either the way we came
    Or to find some other route,
Which with a monument or some woody confusion
    Maintains the illusion.

And time itself is like this, an elder dimension
Whose fondness for a particular country may turn
At a stroke to a sly or bullying disregard,
    Who knows that place is never
The involving predicate that something meant,
    Simply an accident.

And is after all where we truly belong,
Its present moments less comfortable than sofas
And the presences scattered on tables before them
    That say: 'We are England.

This memory. This book. This headline. And all the things
  That such belonging brings.'

As the very first move is the very first mistake,
Even the king's pawn, the dry kiss, the sinister
Lunge of the baby's toes like Johnson leaving
  The room when all has been said,
As what we are today depends on what we have been
  And all that we have seen,

As the bell while it rings has not ceased to summon us
Though we lose count of the strokes, as one match
Added to the whole becomes the Tower of London
  And we come to the end of the chapter,
As what we are today depends on what we are up to
  And all that we try to do,

As fingers reach where fruit must be before they know
The fruit is there, as the deafening tapes babble of love
And mothers not long out of childhood stitch shrouds
  At the cradle, as our star
Will give us short grace when it finally disappears
  And we know the prediction of tears,

As we find ourselves again in places that made us happy
And like bar-haunting actors on tour forget our cues,
As we rise in drowning with Greek cries of discovery,
  As we scribble our lucky numbers
And believe the oracle so that the hair lifts from our head
  As we shiver down in bed,

As time itself is unable to build its little Durham
Against anointed oblivion, and we are acknowledged
Its fool servitors, bearing enormous covered dishes
  Into the hungry hall
Where we overhear the talk, seditious, immensely grand,
  That we hardly understand,

So we are left at last with only the hopeless instant,
The newborn innocent or wandering dressing-gowned
    victim
For whom the past must be a fable or abandoned
  Like an exhausted quarry,
For whom the future is that breath beyond the breath
  Taken at the moment of death,

So we are left in the thick of all our extended pleasures,
Hearing in the distance the popping guns moving over

England, and saying quietly, one to another:
    'Something is running for cover,
Something has nowhere to hide out there and likely as not
    Something is being shot,

'Such as the refined but shabby fox, left to die
As a gangster dies, arguing with balletic rhetoric
That when in the paleness of dawn the certainty of pain
    Is fully recognised
There will be no reasoning with it, no arguing at all,
    And we shall lie where we fall.'

The shires

Bedfordshire
A blue bird showing off its undercarriage
En route between our oldest universities
Was observed slightly off-course above Woburn
In the leafy heart of our sleepiest county:
Two cyclists in tandem looked up at the same moment,
Like a busy footnote to its asterisk.

Berkshire
Once on the causeway outside Steventon
I had a vision of living in willing exile,
Of living the knowingly imperfect life
But with a boundless and joyous energy
Like Borodin played by the North Berkshire
Youth Orchestra in its early days.

Buckinghamshire
A goose in the garden of the second-best pub
In Marsh Gibbon was busy doing its dirty toothpaste
And noisy, too, when a woman staggered out
Of the lounge bar into the deserted car-park
Saying: 'I could never think of the child at my breast
As anything other than a penis with a mouth.'

Cambridgeshire
The bird arrived. Nothing so stately-exciting
As Handel's dusky queen that was unspooling
Perhaps too loudly from a scribbling student cell,
But looped between the trees, a flash of green:

And only the having chanced to look just there
Could tell you it had ever been away.

Cheshire

There was a young woman of Cheadle, who wore her
  heart
Upon her sleeve, bright chevron! Oh, the keen-eyed
Men of Cheadle, as in the jealous month
When the registration numbers of new estate cars
Change all over wealthy suburban Cheshire,
And they picked out her heart with a needle.

Cornwall

The very last cat to speak Cornish had a glass eye
And kept a corner shop, selling shoe-laces and bullseyes,
Brasso and Reckitt's Blue. My great-aunt remembers
Buying postcards from him as a girl,
When George's profile sped them for a penny.
Aching to talk, he died of pure loneliness.

Cumberland

They play bezique in Threlkeld and they play
For keeps in Shap. And all the shapely clouds
Roll through the streets like weeping chemistry
Or cows escaped. And tea is served in the lounge
Over a jig-saw puzzle of the Princess Elizabeth
Beneath wet panes, wet mountains and wet sky.

Derbyshire

Once upon a time, in Derbyshire's leaking basement
Where you lie back in boats and quant by walking the
  ceiling,
A strange girl in the dripping darkness attached
Her damp lips to mine fast, like a snail's adherence
To cold stone in dusty nettles, and all unseeen
The bluejohn slid by me: yellows, greys and purples.

Devon

You will never forget the fish market at Barnstaple:
Wet gills, double bellies, gleaming scales,
Shells like spilt treasure. And the cream there thicker
Than a virgin's dream, and Devon's greatest poet
Born Gay, on Joy Street, taught by Robert Luck:
It is the paradise of all fat poets.

Dorset

When the old woman entered the sea at Charmouth
And the great waves hung over her head like theatre
    curtains,
I thought of the sibyl who charmed the rocks to yield
Their grainy secrets till history bore down
Upon her and the liquid world was fixed
For ever in the era of the fossils.

Durham

At the end of your battered philosophical quest,
The purity of Durham rises like an exhalation,
Like the stench of sulphur in a barrel. Birds
Build in the walls of the cloisters, disappearing into
    holes
Like black-robed devotees. Inside it is quiet,
The oatmeal crimping distant in grey air.

Essex

I had a vision in the dead of night
Of all the kitchens of commuters' Essex
Alight like the heads of snakes; and down them slid
The bored wives and daughters of the managers
Who were at the identical time arriving
On the ladders of their power and fatigue.

Gloucestershire

Armorial memorials reduced
To leper stone, forests to hedges, hedges
To sickled stumps where perch the songless birds
Of Gloucestershire, and vans require the roads
Before them in their headlights. No one speaks
In the time it takes to cross the greenest county.

Hampshire

Driving at evening down the A 34
Like a ski-run, the sun a deiphany,
The car-radio a percussive Russian insistence:
Pure pleasure, pure escape! Past Winchester,
Unseen its stalking scholars, past everything,
Driving through Hampshire, driving for the boats!

Herefordshire

Alone between the Arrow and the Wye,
Wales to the west, keeping its rain and secrets,
I wandered in cider country, where the shade
Beneath the trees is golden red and noisy

415

With the jealous spite of wasps: Ariconium,
The poet Philips, his long hair combed out!

Hertfordshire
Hertfordshire is full of schoolmasters,
And archaeologists who are part-time poets.
Together they apportion past, present
And future among their imaginary admirers
In the form of examination papers, foul
Drafts, and labels of dubious information.

Huntingdonshire
Herds of deer are moving through the trees
Of Huntingdonshire noisily and rather
Slowly. An idle hand sweeping the lyre
Brings tears to the eyes of the moderately rich.
They will dip their hands in their pockets, gently dip
But not too deep. You've got to keep money moving.

Kent
Old men coming up to bowl remember
Other old men who in their turn remembered
Things that were hardly worth remembering
Through long still nights in Ashford, Faversham,
Sevenoaks and Tunbridge Wells and Westerham
Where even now the fields still smell of beer.

Lancashire
All the oven doors of Lancashire
Swing open on the hour, revealing vast
Puddings. After tea, the lovers stroll,
Their hands in each other's back trouser pockets,
Feeling the strange swell of the flexing buttock.
The sun sinks, and the Ribble runs to the sea.

Leicestershire
Cheeks of angels, lips compressed, donate
To brass invisible impulsions of
Purely material breath: a county's children
Gather to create an overture,
While brothers and fathers leaping over hedges
Wind horns to their alternative conclusion.

Lincolnshire
M1, M18, M180: the roads
With their bright and bowline intersections sweep

North to Scunthorpe. Go further if you will
To where the Trent meets the Humber and Lincolnshire
    ends.
There, at Alkborough, you may draw breath
And if Nicky's at home she will give you a cup of
    something.

Middlesex

Middlesex is mostly roundabouts, the bright
Voice of five p.m., insistent infotainment:
Fingers gallop irritably on the steering-wheel;
The nails make little clicks. Down the line
Of fuming stationary Volvos boys bully with headlines
That tell the drivers all about the place they have come
    from.

Norfolk

Norfolk is somehow inverted: it's all sky
With clouds as bulky as castrati or lines of Dryden
Sailing out above you, tinged with sunset.
Get as far as you can, but not too far,
Say to the Tuesday Market Place at King's Lynn
Where all the conveyancing is done in verse.

Northamptonshire

Once half-lost here, when only a map of sounds
Or smells could lead us from a wood, we came
At evening to horse-brass and low-timbered beams
Where the world had evolved to its great public state
And the men and women of Northampton, being
    counted
And with amber drinks, found themselves to be happy.

Northumberland

Traitors' county: from one end to the other
You can walk bright-eyed with never a second glance
From a stocky frowning people who move slowly
And mind their own business. For they have seen it all:
When the mist clears over Northumberland
It leaves squat towers, valleys scarred with lead.

Nottinghamshire

There is one red door in one slightly curved
Street in one nameless market town
That contains behind it for a moment an image
Of the planet's destiny: a girl stooping

To a hallway mirror, making her lips move
Into a theatrical kiss, a self-kiss.

Oxfordshire

The kingfisher has long flown. Along the Cherwell
The biscuit of bridge and college wall is blank
Of its image, but with a passing presence
Like a photograph taken with an open shutter.
This, we reflect, is just the sense of our life,
Aware of something the very moment that we miss it.

Rutland

Rutland is large enough for you and me
To stumble into as into a wood without being seen,
To tread its moss-starred carpet, enchanted
By the chipped china of the russulas,
Pink, grey, grey and green-grey, and red,
Peeping beneath the oaks, not far from Oakham.

Shropshire

Shropshire Blue, still made, the Lord be praised,
Tart veins that kept the Romans here and Housman
From the rope. The iron bridges lead you to it,
Farms knee-deep in cow. And if you stop off
In red-earthed Bridgnorth, that vigilant town,
Be sure your pint is not ungraced with cheese.

Somerset

A thousand airy harps! We hardly dare
To let out breath, for our imagination
Responds to these full-throated sounds as though
To the ranks of the ever-delighting dead, our wise
Visionaries, and this is the county of dreams
And of the moon's occult praesidium.

Staffordshire

Staffordshire is where you almost came from,
Darkened beneath burnt clay, perpetual dusk.
It is the housewife's dream, twinkling hearths
Bright with Zebo, scrubbed pumice steps
And, in the bathroom, a finger on the nozzle
And little lavender farts to begin the day.

Suffolk

I've had Leigh and buried St Edmunds,
Stowed Felix and Market and Upland,

I've been shut up in Boxton, found it painful in
    Akenham
And felt totally stupid in Assingham:
Carrying around one's valuable despair like a fleece,
To live in Suffolk is to suffocate.

   Surrey
Flying in perfect formation above the sleeping
Cul-de-sacs of Surrey, you observe
The blocked pairing of houses, each with a garage,
Like epaulettes. What whisperings behind
The party walls! What eavesdropping, and what
Bad timing! Well done! Sorry, partner! Boom!

   Sussex
Chalk pie, a quality of sun like laughter,
Distance predicted in hoof-beats: everywhere here
Is vigilance as well as cruel amusement,
That tempered island quality called sardonic.
From Rye to Selsey Bill, something is on offer,
A glittering spread, the bottom drawer pulled out.

   Warwickshire
Driving to Wales I crossed a corner of Warwickshire
That seemed to be hardly space at all, the home
Of Dr Hall and his famous father-in-law
Or of magic woods where lovers were lost and found,
But simply the minutes that it took to tell
An unimportant story, now forgotten.

   Westmorland
Once again the skies are open over the whole county:
From Clifton to Burton, from Grasmere to Brough,
The pubtalk steaming with anoraks and orange parkas.
But I can remember one solitary eye
Raging in silence in the dripping marsh,
Its dewy lashes spooning aphids from the air.

   Wiltshire
In Wiltshire they are sending extra-terrestrial
Signals: what will the Venusians think of us?
Four-footed creatures who like to move in circles?
Let's hope they never noisily discover
That we are only half the men they thought us,
Stumbling at tangents from our glimpsed perfection.

419

Worcestershire

Oh darling, come to Broadway: there we'll take
Tea and scones and jam made from the plums
Of Pershore, perfect, pitless, palate-pleasing.
A stroll in the model street, a browse at Gavina's.
Then it's right foot down in the Volvo, plenty of Scotch
And the largest bed we can find at the Bull in
  Worcester.

Yorkshire

The brown teapot is always warming here
For there will be a time when you must come home
Though you be unknown except to the flowered dead.
On the moors the diagonal smoke rises
Like a bitter smile, tight but welcoming:
Cousin country, extra places for tea.

Masks

One brumy night in early November when cheeks
Were cold to kiss and mist all loose in the grove
At the height of a coffee-table or a craven Jack Russell
So that you could not think of running there
Without dog-slobber or barked shins or simply having
Mysteriously missed your legs in the flooded field
We came back panting and laughing to a book-lined
  world

And you knelt on the rag-rug in your chimneyless room
Till the gas-fire played steadily like a small
Ceramic organ, the curtains not quite drawn.
It was at that moment when you reached for me, your
  hands
At my waist like an iris vase too heavy to hold,
Worth the admiring and nowhere to put it down,
That I stiffened and put one finger to your lips.

'Not now!' I was suddenly unreasonably distracted
By the thought of an expressionless face staring in
Like a guy, like the window's misty breathed mask
But without breath, the mouth and eyes mere slits,
Like a hooded face, both torturer and victim.
I said: 'If we pay him will he go away?'
But you said there was no one and you looked severe.

420

I couldn't keep up my appeal to this admonitory
Absence, or appease a self-induced scare
As though it were an eager High Street drunk
Stiff with dried spillings and a crooked smile
Leaning from the wall: 'Miss, a word with you!'
An old guy, who smelled of need and sorrow,
Sad adult, little father, burned father!

When you poured two tiny gins I was aghast
At the mockery of that painted mask's beseeching.
'Make it three!' But your lips smiled and tightened
In a weary ironical grimace and you tidied
The curtains' corners like a cloth on an invalid's tray.
You had seen real faces staring in – as so often
You stared, serene in thinking, stonily back.

Perhaps the face was your own reflection or
The result of a longing of mine too often repressed.
As the evening lengthened our eyes no longer met
At the explosions and my thoughts survived their
    puzzlement
As they lifted brightly up the chimney of the dark,
So many brave little wayward twinkling smuts
Skittering in smoke towards the hanging moon.

Off the record

Three months to clear the creeper, twined about them
Thigh-thick in places, the amorous grasp of nature:

Pedestals in slime, and obelisks,
Great bevelled diadems and shafts, worn domes.

Most were tiered, sky-reaching, monumental.
Some lay tilted, overturned like idols.

Playthings of the gods, we called them, towers
Stubborned with iron, beasts and pinnacles.

Stone carved into frond-shapes that the skin feels
Inside it, stone blood or nostril, stone like sand.

Stone carved into space-shapes that the sun makes
On eyelids, stone shell or earlobe, stone like pearl.

So intricately carved that, when we hacked,
Nestlings escaped in fright like clouds of spice.

From one, tugging at tendrils we were surprised
By dripping from its lip a muttering of monkeys.

To civilise, that is our mission's purpose.
We have a name for everything we do.

Yet that deep vale now shorn of vegetation
Seemed more especially immensely sad,

A place designed for some forgotten purpose,
A place of energies, of interruption,

A place of understanding and of struggle,
A place of blank unusual namelessness.

Years in that dismal cirque, with knotted ropes
Charting relationships and distances.

We crushed new ink, and in the Record wrote
The names we gave, recording their positions:

Red: Empress, Cardinal, Rhinoceros,
Talia, Talia, Cardinal and Terror.

White: Elephant, Dabbaba, Concubine,
Talia, Champion, Talia and Terror.

Red: Mann, Mann, Mann, Giraffe and Mann.
White: Empress, Rhinoceros and Cardinal.

From the surrounding peaks (three miles of steep
Ascent) we saw much less, but saw more clearly,

Saw that position was relationship,
That space was time, and form a form of power.

This may be done to that, and that to this,
And something else, though not the first, to that.

The Record taught us so: volumes of love,
Of growth and illness, itemised in codes.

We have a name for everything we do.
We have a code which tells us how it's done.

But what of codes for that strange architecture?
Balm for its captures, charms for its every move?

Without impelling touch it was itself
A code: we knew there were no codes for codes.

Rules for this god-game would describe itself,
Itself be understood outside all codes.

No reference to wrestling grips, the shrill
Cries of the breathless, or the stop of blood.

No round O's of surprise, the failure of
Attention, the missed opportunity.

No slackening of attack, the vertigo
Of daring irreversible decisions.

No sensations down the skin, collapse
Of knees, surrender of all tender surface.

From that pure height the pillars still outfaced
The morning mists and our interpretations.

After a week, forced to descend for water,
We closed the Record, all intent abandoned.

Of neighbouring tribes, flushed from the dwindled jungle,
There was nothing for the Record, little to say.

For some of us (too tired now to return
To fame, or bargaining with emeralds)

There was the prospect of a sluttish future
With their squat stolen daughters, who knew some tricks,

Peering between their legs as if to frighten
Wolves, their smiles turned into hideous groans

And sinewy honey-extracting tongues, so long
The tip could touch their anus like a wand.

Their language was a babble much like any,
With twenty different words for roasted oyster.

They said it used to be a paradise,
But we've no skill to make it so again.

Staring from wormy verandahs at the night,
We only note the creeper's slow advance,

Note pulsing in the neck, cries in the dark,
The sense of life as an unwilled postponement,

Note toothlessness, the monkeys come again,
And tendrils round the bases of those stones.

Unanswered questions: if they belonged to gods,
Then were they left behind through carelessness?

Or were the gods surprised? If so, by whom?
If a deliberate bequest, what then?

What could that war of white and red portend
And what its long unknown abandonment?

Gifts that we cannot handle may be stowed
Somewhere, but these we live beneath, like laws.

To civilise! Indeed. And then to dream
Of paradise, dream of the absent gods!

Perhaps these dreams are what we should preserve,
A way to write, and keep, the code of codes.

Otherwise I shall simply die like this,
Naming the millionth star then turning round

To creep from the verandah to the bed,
There to make love, and other useless games.

Twelfth Night

The last ten minutes of cake
    Stands in its crumbs.
Surviving almonds pose
    Like difficult sums.
Soon there'll be nothing left
    When a friend comes.

Birds on their clipped feet
    No longer play.
Golden fruit is plucked
    For the keeping tray.
The star that grazed the ceiling
    Is put away.

As, too, the tree itself,
    Naked, uncrowned,

424

Like an old phonograph
    Spinning round,
Weeping wax and needles
    Though without sound.

This image of our lives
    Seems pretty rough,
But what it might be saying is
    That all the stuff
That we've already had
    Is always enough.

On the mountain

Grass scars
Of snow.
Drifts blow.
There's Mars!
Cloud bars
Still show
Though no
Bright stars.
Half-light.
A fox
Stilts by.
Then night
Unlocks
The sky!

Blackberries

Sister bramble, sprawled in the autumn hedges,
We think we can escape your wild embraces,
Your trailing skirts unpinned, the ragged edges
Bloodied with fruit like tiny damaged faces.
But always around the corner are those places
That something of stone or water makes you haunt.
We know your staring into empty spaces;
We recognise the shameless way you flaunt
Your secrets at each passer-by and taunt
With sulky mouthings and derisive clinging.
You are the summer's jilted bride, the gaunt

Neglected beauty who one day went singing
Out of the house, mindless of wind and rain,
To live from buckets in the filthy lane.

Bog

Kneeling for marshfruit like spilled
Beads bedded in displaying moss
I notice a licked frog dragging
His drenched fatigues up and through
The barring spears and stalks of orange
Bog asphodel as if in terror
Of unknown purposes, as though
I were a weight of sky, a whole
Universe of beak and gullet,
And not, as I am, a mere slider
And stumbler like him, damp to the hips,
Reaching for tussocks, scrabbling for almost
Nothing: these little speckled fruits,
Chill marbles of a forgotten tourney,
Aching playthings of a lost garden
That has always been mostly water,
A place of utter loneliness,
Terrain of the asphodel and of the frog.

Purposes

They totter heavily by
With orthopaedic necks
And pinched feet for purchase
Like night-wandering patients
Mad on a mountain cure.

Looking neither to left
Nor right they start and stop
And start, with little steps,
As if in 'twenties skirts
On a drizzling promenade.

Dowager-bosomed, blinking,
Determined but unsteady,
Rapt but vacant, they admire

Only their own weight
And inscrutable purposes.

Everything else they ignore,
Night, day, boundaries,
Their white child bucking
And wriggle-tailed and ready
To escape, car-wash rain.

Everything is irrelevant
To their stately progress through
The atlas of nutrition,
Keeping the hill cropped close
To see where they are going

And pausing to raise the head,
Purse-lipped, in the blankness of bliss,
Chewing and pausing and chewing
Like a practised taster of Médoc
Almost sure of a vintage.

It may be that we too have
Such singleness of intent
Viewed from the right perspective,
Some alien lofty observer
Who would find us touching and comic.

Perhaps the knowledge would salve
Our own dim sense of confusion,
Sublime hauntings, pure puzzle.
Perhaps. How thankful we are
That we don't, and never shall, have it.

Stony acres

Something is gaping like a broken wall
In vacant fields. It must be the heart's spillage.
Yes, they've been down and up and down before,
These stones. This fresh collapse will take some clearing:
Migrant pieces needing to be flung back
In flinty protest; muddy chunks, and broken
Trapezoid wedges broadening to the shape
Of plates or blade-bones; wandering boulders; hopeful
Lintels whose weathered foreheads show how once
They coped; hurt shale; careless pebbles dancing

Dark down the hollowness inside; and some
Half-buried in the grass like plinths or armour
From fateful battles, immense in ancient moss.
Stemming this sprawl becomes a timely lesson:
A wall in place may be, like self-esteem,
A discipline of the damaged heart, yet somehow
With nothing much in sight that could escape
Or wander freely in, this dogged keeping
Of well-known lines and formal boundaries
Seems nothing better than an idle pleasure,
Balancing, wedging, stowing every crack
To cast long shadows on these stony acres.

Hauntings

This is the greatest sadness, like Handel
Ascending a staircase to loud tribute
That is already worms although
We have to pretend that it is music.
And other sadnesses: that she
Whose whole existence is an answer
Has questions of her own that strike
Us dumb. Only our smile survives,
To haunt our quiet retreat from life,
And that abundant love bred out
Of loneliness which merely puzzles
Its busy, sensual, happy victims.

Inside a piano in a cottage
A mile out of the nearest village
A spirit in the jangling strings
Practises ascending thirds in
Moments of calculated stillness:
Not Peter Lorre's scampering hand,
Nor the ghost-print of Cage prepared
For his strange business, nor even Handel
Reduced to such vague finger-stirrings
As an ecto-presence might manifest,
Like picking the nose, but a ditsy shrew
To whom is allowed its privacy.

Do all such hauntings have precise
Explanations? Only the failure

That makes us feel pursued is never
Exorcised, for we ourselves
Become the terrible excuse
That it projects, our shadow-play,
Our mirror, our familiar.
Out there, though, every kind of music
Is ready to re-create the worldly
Heartache or triumph it once became,
And having once become it, will
Again do so, and yet again.

The two teapots

The small teapot to the large teapot,
Stewed as a pond: 'When you last spoke,
Chuckling generously from your girth and glaze,
There were many who listened, who were friends.
Where are they now?'

The large teapot to the small teapot,
Clogged to a trickle: 'Peace, brother,
Your words are still warm and waited for
By one who will be loved, though alone.
Be contented.'

The waterspider at Easter

In these blue days between the palm and proof,
Learning almost that any theorem
Is possible if someone says it is
Whose very life is of that consequence,
I spend my time with time itself and you.

You speak of Thor endangering with his hammer
Inadequate heroes, having to be restrained
Like an enraged self-righteous householder
By milder gods. Further, in Isfahan
An eagle this week stole a picnicking child.

Let these be A and B, and now let C
Create the shape we recognise and fear,
A pattern of uncompromising law.

429

I do not find the matching shape about me
(Unless it is a mountain), only you.

And would that strange impelling finger touch
(Like taper to a paper) something so light?
A novelty like coloured fire? I guess
Divinity could never dare to be
(Nor shamed to) anything more than such as we,

An imitation of our ignorance
And little equilibrium. Surely
This is our best postponement, as we take
Our time and riot for our share of beauty?
The very idea gives us pause and hope.

And better theorems may disprove the worse
And what we reason be the milky head
And not the hammer, child and not the bird.
An image of the child, as yet unbroken!
An image of the breaking, not to be!

For even granite never thought of dying.
The pieces scarcely rock beneath the foot,
Cradles for water just before it freezes
And moss like ruined carpet after floods.
From cairns all sides descending are unequal.

Nowhere to go but down. We'll never find
By looking, so they say, but how to know
A way of seeing when the found is there,
A foolproof way to prove the obvious?
The famous answer is to kick a stone.

Here are those spurs and valleys where the green
Is parcelled out by legislating walls,
And stones move freely. The idea is constant,
Just as the weakest child's or hero's foot
Still has some notion of the way to go.

Here argument is only exposition
Of truth like a summary narrative of nature,
The seething wells and the little locked churches
Like steps in logic taking us down the page
As the sun's sleep is aslant and westerly.

I want to trust in that as in the voice
Of the drowsing slabs and the wild echoes

Flying, flying, that catch the evening light.
Some suns will rise again, and we who will
Not last for long may not be discontented.

And by that holy pool, far from the mountain,
Where stooping is to touch, and touching is
A calculus of contiguities,
There straddles in its frail exampled stillness
Across a surface troubled but unbroken

The waterspider, miraculously skating
Upon the roof of liquid, sure as the hoof
Of a deer beats shyly over the nibbled grass,
Carw 'r dwfr, delicate stirrer of dreams,
Deer of the water, carw, deer of the streams.

Surely this is enough and will survive,
An image of the place that I have come to,
The irreducible, the secret source,
When time for three days takes its holiday
And all solutions are extemporised.

How kindly the creed of the actually virtuous
To stimulate no daunting disagreements!
For as you show, the good is to be sought
Beyond all rules that might empower its seeking
And that is all I need to demonstrate.

A carawimple

Sir Cuckoo announces one more hedge birth
Like a pure boy fluting in the sacris-
ty or the priest himself coughing a sigh

Over a slab of dry cake and Malmsey,
'*Carum carui*, a good seed for kissing
And for meditation, *dolor crucis*.'

It passes over valleys: 'Who are you?'
'Who are you?' I do not know who I am.
Come, lend me your slant cheek like a succinct

Aunt for whom a child was what her sister
Did, and pain enough, though breaths were hotter
And the manner of its making conscious,

The mouth neither joy nor grief, the rictus
Of a clown, arms east and west, a circus,
Or a dream merely, a dream of terrible

Howling: 'It isn't mine! It isn't mine!'
A dream of eternity, circular,
Pathetic as a feather in the sea.

Again and again we mime the games
Of our making, perhaps in defiance
Of the very spirits that we raise.

No one believes that he is born in sin,
But do the filthy deed itself? Oh, fie!
Let us bob chastely, wincing hot pippins

With lips that were much better formed for thirds.
That strain again! And at dusk the cirrus
Lifting its lid: nature carried away

Just when something good began to happen,
When innocence at last had learned its notes.
On we scurry round our dwindling circuits,

Little nest successes, blessed recruits.
Even our bad jokes are half-serious:
'Jesus ap cwcw, he gets in your teeth.'

We know that we have somewhere to get to
Further than the next valley, though not far.
Somehow quite revealing, it might be said.

Someone, sometime, knew something about it.
Too late was what they said, the interval
Careless, a trifle smug: 'Too late! Too late!'

Our names in columns will never be missed,
Or noticed once or twice like a common plant,
Or nailed like Icarus, and not much kissed.

Pheasant and mulberry

As to put up with damp in a cave and
Its unremovable jewels is to
Claim the weird cogitation of grottoes

Or against beechmast to take a flying kick
Then stoop to nibble in acquisitive
Content is to comprehend granaries

So within the wild garden of the mind
Reality surely excels itself:
Two pheasants paired beneath a mulberry,

Economical sketch by the sexual
Philosopher, there pacing out a loss,
Or worse, the absence of the never-claimed.

Much meditation may see a design
In the fall of fruit, the pheasants' slow dance,
An imagined labyrinth dictating

Satisfied puzzles, willed speculation,
Maps in flagstones, directions in hedges,
Everything that defines a centre.

Most of us have known these languid moods
When we create and discreate ourselves
In the landscape of our fugitive thoughts.

Grotto, granary, garden, labyrinth
Are pleased to design the impossible
As our sadness at envisaging it

So that every little tread in the grass,
Each stain or husk, is an almost noiseless
Echo of the world we have to live in.

Eating the still life

The wind is in the stove tonight and we
Must not eat the still life. A shuddering
Passes across the chimney. The coals glow.

We made this civil practised silence out of
Thought that dwells on shapes. We know we must
Not eat the still life. Eyes look down and up.

The stove is booming like a basset-horn.
Apples in the basket glow. We know
We must not eat the still life. We draw.

We make these ceremonious shapes in silence
That lives in thought. We know we must not eat
The still life. Beauty is a translation.

Its burning rises into the night. Are these
Apples or faces that we draw? The fire
Leaps, and we must not eat the still life.

At sunset

The fear of everything, the fear
Even to name fear, a kind of content
To sit in the spreading light, to sit
Helpless like an exhausted mother at last,
Amused and perplexed at our most precious gift,
Sitting and watching it go.

No, the feeling is like a child's,
In fact is a child, waiting for a word,
The word that comes at the end of a long day,
At the end of all its ragging and play.

What word is it? Who knows?
Something between rest and a kept promise
All the more valued for the keeping
Known long since and only half-resisted.

As on this very evening, noticing
Such a weird light against the wall:
Forgotten whatever I looked up from,
Forgotten the fatigue, forgotten the fear,
Forgotten in this sense of possession and stillness,
The stream loud after a recent rain
And the sun leaking like fire beneath the door.

In time

Spring thickens the tips
With black-blobbed buds.
Burnt marshmallows at the grate
Is winter's regret
For all its sticky lips
When the stove's heart stops.

The earth's ungatherable
Suggestions of growth

Promise again that they'll last,
That all is not lost,
Winding the year from one spool
To another, reel to reel.

Look again. How they've grown:
On far elder
And bordering hawthorn a mild
Flourishing like mould;
From the warming stone
The nettle's cautious fan;

And these black buds on the ash
Seem to explode
Like a conjuror's device
Or massed voice
When brass and cymbals crash
And the word is made flesh.

Tree fungus

Standing to attention by the wall that once divided
Cottage-ground from field-bits and the beginning
Of steep descent to a rabble of civilian oaks,
It never questioned or guessed what it might have guarded
But grew in girth, eased stones aside, spread boughs.

A gate-place disappeared and corners collapsed.
The wall was nothing much, for what was on one side
Knew it could just as easily be on the other,
And what sheep started continued with digging for buttons
And roots growing through bottles in that littered ground.

Already the ash wore its medals of lichen with pride
And round its base in October the tell-tale signs
Of superannuating *Pholiota squarrosa* clustered,
Yellow pixie fringes sprouting at its coat,
Little insistent fingers probing its weakness.

Then winter, signing off the year with its flourishes
Of slate-slithering wind, delivered its stroke
And the great shape hit the deck in a dead

Faint, thought by many to be its last,
Hinged from its roots in gaping mountainous splinters.

But still it lived, sap flooding through the flap
To send up spindly shoots at what were really
Downward angles from the recumbent trunk,
While the still-sprouting crown, disguised in grass
Offered unusual food to inquisitive sheep.

It couldn't last for ever, this suspended state,
Reduced in leaf-lift and soil-suction, in all
Standing and buoyancy that makes a tree.
Branches that tangled with cables had to be sawn,
Its stumps leaked, its whole scope was diminished.

Well, it is our fate to live with symbols
For just so long as we ourselves persist,
Old soldiers of the paced life, admiring
Old soldierly qualities wherever we find them,
Hoping for nothing beyond the daily horizon.

So when, as ever in April, once more this year
Its buds blacken at the tips of its stretched fingers,
We are pleased to stand on its collapsed shoulders
And stroke its wild clumsy arms with a touch
That intends encouragement, a calming of terror.

It is then that we notice a new growth, the invader,
Daldinia concentrica appearing at the wrists
And pulse-spots in a lavish globular blistering,
Smooth exuded bulges running into each other,
Of a mineral hardness and coppery invalid brown.

Is this to be seen perhaps as a kindly harbouring
Of a vagrant fruit-body by one with weakened resistance?
Or is it pure power, an edging-out of the host?
It's a fungus not seen before, not edible, not lovable,
But whatever a tree does it is still a tree.

Hope and hearts

In the brown garden
Where playing lost its shadow
Among the lonely trees

These pale children of November
Rise from leaves
To forbid the frost and burning.

Frilfralog round the oaks
Tipsy and teetering
Putting up parasols

Skirted and stiff as dolls,
Never so still a dance,
So haunted a step

Till limp they lie down
Spilling their frills
In a lavish sprawl.

Everything goes back to earth
But first it must dance,
Dance to exhaustion.

They are our strangest thoughts,
Music of a mood
That will always create them

A solemn raggedy dance
At the year's end
But still as our own games

Games of outlandish endeavour
Games of promising
Games of hope and hearts

And like their rules
Allowing all they allow
And sometimes unbroken.

Tempo

Tendrils are playing for
Their lives. The squares are crowded.
It seems there's no voyage left
To make. The evening star
Shines on an impasse here.

The creeper's thickening grip,
The pressure on the centre,
Is a slow paying-out
Of time, like a long rope
Never quite tied up

437

That inches through the grass
Or lifts from water, dripping,
The only sign that somewhere
A hull, though motionless,
Will in the end break loose.

The lessening light can find
No space for shapes to fill,
The blocked diagonal
Cannot be seen beyond,
The vital pieces pinned.

And always this slight moving,
Buoyant, invisible,
Draining the heart away
When what we need is loving
With no sense of misgiving.

Much is already lost:
Leaf repeats leaf repeats leaf,
Darkness assails the green
With indistinctness, fast,
And we await the worst.

But even as we despair
We feel the increased weight
That signifies the pull
We have long waited for
Hour after hour after hour.

And it is not too late
To take whatever we have
When taking is more like finding:
The freeing move long-sought,
The flowering overnight.

The Malverns

Loaded like pilgrims who go upon their journey
Simply to be divested of those burdens
    Once the journey has ended,
Slogging our bodies with nature as if to prove
That they are still themselves as natural as once
    We used to think they were,
We find ourselves with a route to read that looks

Like a rough map of hopeful lives circling
   Back to begin again.

Down we plod from the wandering wooded ridge,
Scanning the fields as pages of a volume
   That never fails to please;
Tracing raw furrows, flints turned up again,
Those well-worn characters once lying beneath
   The chapter of a harvest;
Or stumbling by a hedge, a finger in the margin
Of a square of working barley which the wind
   Excitedly describes.

Here in one corner is a bribe of sweet-briar,
Its sprawling tangle of confessional blossom
   Appeasing some wild god,
The laughing enemy of agriculture
And all predictability whose arms
   Rake in the little badges,
The pale petals pinned at the centre, and gather
The illicit grasses in its thorny hoops,
   A sprouting lair of roses.

We take a path left by the tractor's wheel:
Squat incuse treads baked to a bare legend
   The stalks grew up around,
We cross the vale in a whole lake of barley,
The feathery beards brushing our bare arms like
   Insistent regrets or children,
Until we reach the further slope, the last
Before the hills, our eyes distracted by
   Its illustrations of flowers.

The sky is enlarged, and such as hides birds in it:
Birds flattered by the sun; birds emulating
   A single blown cloud;
Birds at their equal ease and distance, drawing
A notional horizon where is only
   An indiscriminate haze;
While nearer, though less visible, the lark's
Hectic credo and the response from a copse:
   'Brilliant! Brilliant! Brilliant!'

Our circuit at last ascends the green worn spine
Of the enormous book whose covers are two counties
   Laid down on England once

By yawning millennia hauled off to their sleep.
And now along the linked and nibbled knolls
   From peak to reaching peak
We pace in five winds like funambulists,
In agreement to take precedence by five paces,
   Windy, not yet quite winded.

When we have become pure vacancy,
Escaped like thin breath from dropped jaws
   Into completedness,
There may be many images to crowd us,
Ungathered treasures, ungathered irritants,
   Many things left over.
But when the spirit is finally finished
With its false hopes and its remembrances
   And is at last at peace

I can imagine its decision, in absolute freedom
(The random and theoretical gift of choosing
   Just one more scene or story,
One last opportunity of self-creation,
A momentary careless embodiment
   For no particular purpose),
To find itself aloft on this ancient turf,
A high place that only once was ours, our bodies
   Almost blown away.

No more

The seal's head in the calm
Turns to inspect the shore,
The road down to the farm
Is grass, is grass.
We've learned to think: no more.

But when the hinges tighten,
When the sea grows rough,
As the waters whiten,
As the chained gate rusts:
One look is always enough.

Heartmelt

The treacherous blue of the hollow snow
And the ancient blue of the gletscher
Are like the flicker of a headache
Or the acid of the etcher
Making transparent what was opaque,
And now the haunting, oh so slow
Beginning of movement, the light of ice
Dripped from a lip of rock, showing
The sun what beacons are, the glint
And dribble of the water flowing
Freely now, falling without stint,
Once each drop has fallen twice:
The danger is past, as we have long felt:
Though mountains are still there, the mountains melt.

Looks

Once or twice, is that an alternative?
One being less, and two is as much as double?
Did we ever settle the question of the green cardigan?

No, but twice does suggest an extended future.
Twice is a shapely word, a sort of portmanteau,
A tendril, a twin, a twined splice.

Once is miraculous enough, out of all
The fatalities and possibilities,
And the actual probability of nothing.

But twice is the freedom of choice, a confirmation,
The careless proof of being right first time,
Of being rightly in our own good looks.

Once, your eyes turned to mine in conjunction
Like a performance of model planets when
The clockwork completes an entire unlikely circuit

And we were explorers staring at the theory
Of an eclipse, not daring to believe
That anything which wire and plaster proved

Could quite convince us of the moment's stillness
In which the dark and day were interchanged
And we were blinded even by our seeing.

Most looks are away. Lashes descend
On the hurt gaze, the averted silent hunger.
We attempt, in turn, the Alec D'Urberville gleam,

The quizzical eyebrow, the pipe-sucking frown,
The bright sparkle of metaphysical challenge,
The doggy slither of friendly supplication.

We may have thought for a time that we believed in
The laughing glance, the boyish twinkle, the stare:
But their actorly attention meets only skin,

Meets only cheek, meets only a strand of hair,
The turn of a head, the bit that we much admired
But having turned is seen only from the side.

What are we left to stare at but ourselves?
Absorbing absences with infinite mass,
Night with no stars that are not out of sight,

Areas of dangerous collapse where we
Are nothing again, as once upon a time
We were and some time yet again will be.

Our looks are sent off into darkest space.
Our orbs go into orbit like brilliant saves.
It seems unlikely that we will get much cheers.

But drink to once. To once *and* twice. For twice
Is twice as nice. We need to believe it. Once
May be a mirage, but twice is a law of nature.

History

In memory of Angus Macintyre

Then came the frost to put its signature
Upon the earth, tight and white as a knuckle
Above a contract that yields whatever is owed
But long before its time, and every creeper
And every blade of grass stood halted and still
As if by some spell that kept them from their growing,
Suspended in the cold ghosts of what they had been,
Preserved for a future that no one could guess.

The miniature angel blowing its gold trombone
Like an unfolded paper-clip announced
The matters arising, that whatever we had expected
Was now to be reviewed, a matter for silence,
Life postponed for this session, a halted process.
Whatever the coloured stars and eggs proposed
Referred back to a body that was powerless
For once to put the idea into effect.

A man is carrying a piece of wood
Like furniture, but to be hurt with it.
These stories, when we think of them, still shock,
Though never as much as all that is not story,
Conditions of being, the general state of things,
Information received, the bald facts,
Experience as it stupidly shoulders past us:
No wonder we have to make such stories of it.

Something at the best of times has almost
Believed in us. It is, like an only child,
The outcome of our passions, and so we tell it
What otherwise we might ourselves forget
Or could never defend unless called to account
By its wide-eyed searching gaze, its absolute
Faith in our own accountability,
Our fear of inheriting an alien world.

And it is always past, before we can know it.
Just as our individual lives, which we see
In daunting or luring prospect, minute by minute,
Make little sense until we are seen by others
As completed fact or anecdote, not likely
To slip out of character, palpably there.
Is this, then, our chance of eternity?
And what would you, what can you, say of it now?

I see you walking gravely through the mist
In the gangster hat and the oiled fisherman's jacket,
Passing the deer with their ignorance of history;
Passing that monument whose yearly ruin
Is a sign of its treasured leafage and renewal,
With its aching shoulders propped in lavish repose;
Passing to that north-eastern corner of Cloisters
Where the young Addison pondered the stoic of Utica.

And pondering yourself the puzzle of how we come
Through all the undetonated chances and mistakes,
Following the mothballed flag of our assumptions,
To this Janus-knowledge of our future and duties,
Of what we must say that is just, and what we should do,
What kind of story we make of the present moment
As without any excuses it simply buggers off.
The right way to proceed, as you always put it.

And I see you presiding over the account
Which history gives of our provisional forgiveness.
Reaching your room, you motion me to a chair,
That ancient leather into which your pupils sank
Gratefully, as into their understanding,
And you take two glasses, and a friendly bottle,
For this is now a dream, or is the spirit
Of the once that tells us who we are.

It tells us twice, two sides of the flipped coin:
It is the once of the unique, the once-only,
The once of happening, of not to be repeated;
It is also the once of the past, the once of then,
The once of story, the once of all that is lost.
It gives us everything, but takes it away.
It says: 'This is for now, and hardly to be imagined.'
It says: 'This has been revealed, but never again.'

I drink to you. In turn you raise your glass.
And all that we have to decide in this quiet place
Must still obtain your approval: 'I think that's right.'
'I think that must be the right way to proceed.'
The gravity of your tone is achieved through full
Consideration of all that might disturb:
The haunting thought of failure, the slight mistake
That would instantly reverse the entire intention.

Or sometimes, with your mouth's severe compression
Giving a dramatic emphasis to some
Fully imagined but quite insane prospect:
'We simply can't allow that to happen. Ever.'
Underlining, as you did, with a sudden gleam
Of the eyes, the solemnity of the prohibition,

444

An awful warning made the more chastening
By the brief ensuing twinkle of a smile.

For you realised, too, the infinite comedy
Of muddle and pride, the occluded puddle of theory.
At the slightest conceit or duff solemnity
Your knees sagged, your elbows concertinaed,
Finger jabbing the invisible victim in glee.
Your laughter celebrated the melting of rectitude.
It was a defence against the grim obsessions
That fuelled the Preacher, or the Flame-Haired Temptress.

It was also a love of the half- or the wholly innocent,
Sympathy for the feckless, a trust in the survival
Of the amiable, the outlandish, the incorrigible.
A disbelief, though without faltering, in the sheer
Presumption of begetting, of passing muster,
Of taking everything on without complaint.
Of our follies as young fathers, of the fallibility
Of senior counsel. It was Bertie's mauve shirts.

How often when you drove up England's spine
Had I taken the other, shoulder road which ended
In the ambiguous rocky arm of Wales,
Forbidding Ireland, or perhaps escrying her,
Or even holding out a hand in welcome.
We left behind our unbiological lives,
We left what is agreed for the agreeable,
We left the shorter for the longer view.

We shared these acres, glosses on pastoral texts
Where civility to survive must prove a truth
Plainer than law and friendlier than estates,
Where the eye travels not across but up and down,
Where the oldest inhabitant is a ruffled sheep
Chewing in the rain or stubborn by a gate,
Dogs to be called in several languages
And the sun lighting up the windows of our neighbours.

Our glasses are empty. The windows growing dark.
There are things that I want to tell you, but the occasion
Forbids it. And if there is anything for you to say,
That chance has already gone. What we take
From encounters like this is finally only the sense

Of how we must salvage everything that we can
From the tide that casts us up on the shore of our lives
At every moment, wave upon wave upon wave.

For you that future has been unexpectedly cancelled
And I must take care to remember your best advice
About history, for in the one chance we have
Between 'Take care, laddie' and 'Watch out, matey'
Lies the always threatening gap of the crucial decision
That is either a one-way bridge or a shared relief.
If there is anyone now whose words we are glad
To listen to, we shall be lucky, uncle.

Interrogations

For Moykeska Maxinnia

1

This business of questioning the world, as though
To question were to establish reliable bearings
And not, as it is, simply a lapse of inertia

Or in mindlessly conniving at the heave-
ho of our pathetic bits and pieces
Through the chipped paintwork of time and place:

It turns out to be a kind of satisfaction,
Pretending that our righteous stab of the finger
At the meaningless small-print of our unread lease

Is a valid case, or something like it, a hope
Of things that require defence by sacred naming
And an odd lift of the mind that would like a response.

2

Indeed, it is, though we never stay for an answer
To our exhausting wrangles, preferring forgetfulness
And forgottenness, our pleasure's dippy sisters.

Looking into a pair of astonishing eyes
(Gooseberry green with pupils like dark doors ajar)
We are reminded that to feel to be on the outside

Is a function of that miraculous otherwhence
That allows love to exist at all in the first place
Or to imagine that adoration is returned

When all that is on offer is an exemplum
Of speechless calm from an accidental being
That cannot plan, and has no sense of outrage.

3

Put the question to her, or on her behalf,
And see where it gets you: the answer is Science Diet.
(We have lived for too long in that one-way street).

The world, after all, has nothing to ask of us
Except that we understand, once in our lives,
The worst fact that the animals do not know,

Offered neither as a startling privilege
Nor a shameful burden, nor even as a riddle
(Like something that might perhaps have slipped our minds)

But as a small reminder of the agreed conditions
By which our lips first learned their empty dance,
Their chattering mimicry of hope and longing.

4

For all of us, death seems something that might occur,
A liminal minuet with stoical bequests
And fear regulated like an environment.

But sooner or later everything is outlaw and absence,
And death for certain is no respecter of persons
And could hardly be said to be an event at all

For events are measured not only by the forefear
And prior judgement by which we try to survive them
But by survival itself and its insistences:

'How did it strike you? Better than expected?
Quite as bad as everyone said it would be?
Worse? Well, at least it can never happen again.'

5

Such questions have no one to attach themselves to.
And therefore are questions that can never be answered,
Since no one directly concerned is there to hear them.

For the world refuses to admire us even though
We speak to it cajolingly and stare
Into its staring and pre-perfected face.

It speaks no solution to our problems, having
Problems of its own. It will die when we do
Is one way of looking at it. No wonder

Its incomprehension has touches of sad rage.
It knows the case is lost. Its names have no meaning.
Its face is merely the other side of our face.

Little friends

Whose little friends were hostages?
Which stared nose to nose, gave up
The ghost? Which little friends were eaten?
Which little friends were those?

What do the wrists around the floor
Buffet to keep in view? The breadbin
Is an accomplice. Who are you waiting
For? Who waits for you?

I do not know which is the worse:
Far from where you belong, to hang
From some unfriendly grin. Or just
Be hiding. But not for long.

Quartet

The Duke String Quartet in Trinity College Chapel

The sound's diagonal, like oars. Its space is
Also made of wood: the altar's square
Geometry of light, the framing faces
Of carved startled children, pair by pair;
The strut of column, urn and cornice topped
By an ascent of drapery and toes.
The pulsing heartache of the strings is stopped
By pressure of the fingers and the bows.

It must be the medium's nature to be profuse:
Grain of rose in its rubbed lake of wood
Offers a panelled ear (or is it an eye?)

To reflect the voyaging mind. Along the pews
Heads are inclined like saints' who know they could
Endure this exultation till they die.

Metropolitan

In cities there are tangerine briefcases on the down-platform
and jet parkas on the up-platform; in the mother of cities
there is equal anxiety at all terminals.
  *West a business breast, North a morose jig, East a false
  escape, South steam in milk.*

The centres of cities move westwards; the centre of the
mother of cities has disappeared.
  *North the great cat, East the great water, South the great
  fire, West the great arrow.*

In cities the sons of women become fathers; in the mother of
cities the daughters of men have failed to become mothers.
  *East the uneager fingers, South the damp cave, West the
  chained ankle, North the rehearsed cry.*

Cities are built for trade, where women and men may freely
through knowing each other become more like themselves;
the mother of cities is built for government, where women
and men through fearing each other become more like each
other than they care to be.
  *South the short, West the soap, North the sheets, East the
  shivers.*

In cities the church fund is forever stuck below blood heat; in
the mother of cities the church is a community arts centre.
  *West the Why-not, North the Now-then, East the End-
  product, South the Same-again.*

In cities nobody can afford the price; in the mother of cities
nobody dares to ask the price.
  *North the telephone smile, East the early appointment,
  South the second reminder, West the hanging button.*

In cities the jealous man is jealous because he is himself in his
imagination unfaithful; in the mother of cities the jealous man
is jealous because he reads the magazines.
  *East the endless arrival, South the astounding statistic,
  West the wasted words, North the night of nights.*

In cities we dream about our desires; in the mother of cities
we dream about our dreams.

Enigma

*Thompson's coup was a bonus for the Admiralty. Poking about the
manuals, bottles of Moselle and other detritus sloshing about, a naval
intelligence officer found the empty box of an Enigma cipher machine
which had been fashioned to accommodate a slot for a hitherto unknown
fourth rotor.*

>Thompson flew out of Iceland
>To enter his own fable.
>He left a Capstan burning
>And cards strewn on the table.
>The sea was cold as pewter
>And dimpled like a shield.
>He saw the U-boat ploughing
>Strange harvests in that field.

O Thompson, Tommy Thompson, you caught them on the hop,
  The Atlantic opening up like Saturday night,
For the sub was scrambling for a dive and certainly wouldn't stop.
      Its situation (let's say) was tight:
  One nudge from you and they'd either drown or fry.
  Die in your head and you never have to die.

>He cursed the sticking Hudson:
>The charges wouldn't drop.
>But for Thompson it was only
>Another daily op.
>So he bided his time and circled.
>His eyes were steely blue.
>He scoured the empty waters
>For that craven Nazi crew.

O Thompson, Tommy Thompson, you knew they hadn't got far
  And the ocean would give her secrets up to you
As the night creeps slowly on the sky and pinpoints every star
      And you knew just what you had to do
  When you saw them breaking the surface, and knew why:
  Die in your heart, and you never have to die.

>Four charges at each compass point
>Fell in a perfect square,
>Their pluming circles lifting
>Into the salty air,

450

Depth-charges at each corner
With the U-boat in between,
Unlikely as the Four of Spades
On a twisted seventeen.
O Thompson, Tommy Thompson, did you ever find it tricky
Surviving with your story and your fame,
Saying: 'They crawled there in the conning-tower, they were waving
the Captain's dickey
And they had given up the game!'
To boys who would repeat it by and by:
'Die in your past, and you never have to die.'

They knew about the first two wheels
And they knew about the third
In the box where the darkness scrambled
The illuminating word,
But Thompson like an angel
Out of the frozen North
Had pointed a careless finger
And found the crucial fourth.
O Thompson, Tommy Thompson, did you stop to think of what
A futile kind of bargain you had struck?
In time they would do without you, since the secret prize you'd got
Would put a certain end to luck
And in the future no machine could cry:
'Die in the dark, and you never have to die.'

Four charges like four gospels
Standing round my bed,
Matthew, Mark and Luke and John
Look on me when I'm dead.
Four wheels undo my meaning
From my parting to my toes,
Four wheels to crack my spirit
And tell me where it goes.
O Thompson, Tommy Thompson, you had climbed the cloudy roads
And the pirates' chest was all you could expect,
For the fourth wheel was perfection, it was the code of codes,
And elusive life itself was wrecked
On the North Atlantic shelf of that great lie:
'Die only once, and you never have to die.'

First day

When she had left his side
Nothing at all was said.
She walked on that first morning,
Her heart in hiding.

For he was upon the slope
Of a deliberate sleep,
Dreaming his single silence
Like a truth unopened.

A simple thing that filled
His mind, fold upon fold,
Number on number, changeless
As a dark building.

While her awakened ear
Knew where the creatures were
Who brought their clamorous being
Within her hearing:

The cock's deflating lung
That greets the light along
The slumbering valleys, speaking
His love and hunger;

What robins announce to have
Other robins behave;
A dove wooing a gable;
The hens' palaver.

She learned that bark and bud
Could sing beyond the bird
And heard under the meadow
The root's shudder.

The babble of the sap
As it begins to seep.
The autumn orchard's chorus
Of thudding apples.

Then came a deeper sound
Running through time, like sand
Invisible in glass,
But pounding, pounding.

A sound beneath the green,
A sound in slab and grain,
The groaning of the gravel,
The tone of granite.

The sky's shout of delight
When all the stars are lit,
The vocal moon performing
For her, nightly.

Then, as the planet sang
So she began to sing,
To celebrate her being,
Her self's language.

What did her body say?
What did heart hope, ghost sigh,
Becoming one with that music
In play and labour?

This day was her new life
As a book is leaf upon leaf
And the world between its covers
Is song's cipher.

So she returned to his side
And everything that she said
Let song into his signing
And became an idea.

She was the day to his night,
To his silence she was the note
That sets the word in motion,
The building lightened.

For light was what she must sing,
And light was what she sang,
Knowing the world is many
And truth not single.

Song is the pain of change,
Song is the body's hinge
When the whole future widens
As window or angel.

Till what you have become
Tells you from where you came,
Your heart-beat loosened from
The earth's drumming.

Hearing the feathered oar
Creaking upon the air,
The glitter on the water,
The reflected fire.

Logical exercises

A1 The tree enters the body in the form of a god.
2 Matter is everything that doesn't matter.
3 Manna is a divine rebuke.
4 Simultaneous was the discovery of crops and of the transmigration of souls.
5 The flower longs to be fruit.
6 The birth of the lamb is also a miracle.
7 The righteous are those who can control their dreams.
8 Nomads learn to expect hunger.
9 Stories are the food of the soul.
10 The tree leaves the body in the form of the planet.

B1 Freedom is an illusion of the organism.
2 Grandmothers hunger for what they already know.
3 The greatest freedom would be to live for ever.
4 Wicked is the god who decreed hunger.
5 Nothing is adored by mistake.
6 The motion of the wolf is the desire for independence.
7 The fat boy is hungry for stories about woodcutters.
8 Longing joins the active molars with the planet.
9 No nomad is a woodcutter.
10 There is no such thing as the solitary life.

C1 Fruit inches through the body.
2 The worm aches to displace the soil.
3 The teeth meet in the bone-marrow.
4 The woodcutter never goes hungry.
5 Gods have no need for stories.
6 The thrush mistakes the udder.
7 Desert food arrives from nowhere.
8 Yeasts adore the tree.
9 The wasp craves for pig cheese.
10 Illusory also is the stitched belly full of stones.

454

D1 Fruit dies into our dreams.
 2 Nothing can imagine a life that is not already its own.
 3 The dreams of nomadic tribes struggle for permanence.
 4 No man is lonely when he eats.
 5 Digestion is the defiance of species.
 6 No god rebukes a righteous man.
 7 The flower squirms on its root like the fat boy wanting to be
   excused.
 8 No god is an animal.
 9 The soul leaves the body in sleep and drunkenness.
10 There are many stories about trees and wolves and gods.

E1 A god would rather be adored than eaten.
 2 The grandmother's words are forgotten.
 3 Illusions are sinful unless agreed to be illusions.
 4 We long for what we know we have no means of imagining.
 5 Men would like to be gods.
 6 Loneliness is nothing but the imagining of other lives.
 7 The woodcutter's wife suckles the lamb.
 8 Killing to eat is an assertion of rootlessness.
 9 God reminds us of our sins by turning himself into a tree.
10 Writing was invented to record material things.

Shape

Edgeways, the ledge
Topped by a cowl
Becomes a chair:
But not quite square,
Like a knuckle.

Lintel of flint,
Spilled marble lap
Stiffened in air:
To reach you were
Too great a leap.

Old swathed shoulders,
Mother hunchbone
With your blank stare:
We don't know where
You may have been.

Birthshroud of earth,
You have become
White in this glare:
Grained, almost bare,
Floating in calm.

Strange stone angel,
You will not bless
Us from up there:
You do not care
At all for us.

Though what you know
Is what we like,
Something we share:
If we could dare
Return your look.

Barbed wire blues

Hear that wild dog hollering?
Keep him out with Two-Staple Wing,
Roll me some Two-Staple Wing, yes, and make it plenty,
My baby has ten fingers and a throat to croon and sing.

No ways he going to reach you, girl.
Keep him out with Merrill Twirl,
Roll me Merrill Twirl, yes, and keep it rolling,
My baby has a mile of hair and starlight every curl.

Roll me Brink Flat, roll me Buckthorn,
Roll me Baker Perfect.
Never know what I'm expecting,
Post and wire is for protecting,
Still more fences to be pegged.

Pray that if he leaps he miss.
Keep him out with Oval Twist,
Roll me Oval Twist, yes, and make it bristle,
My baby has a tongue moves like a contortionist.

What makes him think he's getting down?
Keep him out with Wrap-Round,
Roll me Wrap-Round, yes, and make it double,
My baby has a couple of legs reach right to the ground.

Roll me Old Square, roll me Half Round,
Roll me Haish and Glidden.
Tug it, turn the loop and bend up,
Where I start is where I end up,
Ripped-up hands is all I get.

Tell that dog to take a trip.
Keep him out with Scutts Clip,
Roll me some Scutts Clip, yes, and pack it thick,
My baby has a low-slung rear cracks like a rawhide whip.

How's that wild thing getting in?
Keep him out with 4 point 1 Between,
Roll me 4 Point 1 Between, yes, and nail it clean,
My baby has the tightest little snatch you ever seen.

Roll me Stubbs Plate, roll me Sawtooth,
Roll me Kelly's Knife Blade.
Plugging staples, three days riding,
Skin was never made for hiding,
Still they find her where she lies,
Still they find her where she lies.

Detective story

In memory of Julian Symons

Now you draw us into the circle
In which we are audience
And suspects too. The light
Requires our apparently
Unconcerned attention.
Its shadow is our guilt.

A peaceable scene: children,
Neighbours, wife or lover.
You play with the audience
And its fears. Our guilt
Is a cultivated pleasure,
The price of our attention.

We none of us apparently
Could escape our hurt lover
And we are like spoilt children
Eager for the limelight,

Knowing how to take pleasure
In the tight accusing circle.

Shall we admit it? As children
We adored a grown-up audience
Who took pleasure in our pleasure
At their reliable attention,
And knew how to arrange the light
So we could bask in that circle.

Now each has betrayed his lover
And therefore must apparently
Take the consequence of guilt.
Let us admit it to that audience
Of wise ghosts whose attention
Is all that is left to us of light.

For we must finally forgo all pleasure,
Must step into the centre of the circle
And once again suffer like children
A finger pointing at our guilt.
Each lover blames the other lover.
None is innocent, apparently.

The garden

For my father

Considering that the world needs to be born
Endlessly out of our looking at it, it's no wonder that
We retire here for that purpose in our brief time.

Mappers and model-makers, traffickers
In language's unreliable schedules, all our
Journeying is a nostalgia for this.

The garden bears our traces and becomes
Through them the model of a mind which so
Defines itself: a part, and yet apart.

The world may grow here. All that is left outside
Is unimaginable, all within
So like itself that there is nothing else.

Blossom is rumoured. The mind also prepares
Its own best growth, pruning just beyond
The bud. Though summer is already past.

Leaves that would fly have lately fallen. Lifted
Once in wind, they have now become detached,
Ready to drift. And autumn, too, is gone.

Those purer spirits whose undeliberate music
Also creates a more or less habitual space
Have turned their retreat into a coded return.

These pebbled paths lead only to a point
Which shows where they have come from and that now
To continue is a figure not a journey.

Those walls were built no higher than they need be
And where they join give reasons for joining. Where not,
Is a hinge never still enough to cease to be one.

For to enter is always possible, as it is
To leave, though to do neither is at last
As much a relief as both were ridiculous.

If others care to overlook these long
Endeavours, let them, for after all we are
Contented merely with corroboration.

The solemnest face caught staring in would be
Your own. The reason that it never is
Seems like the reason for almost everything.

We are, possibly, posed this riddle early
In life: which is the likeliest of mirrors,
The face that reflects the world, or another face?

The last is not easily admitted, the first
The one we know. It is a grief that placed
Together they only do what mirrors do.

Reflections of reflections, it is said,
Are a symbol of all desire. And lead nowhere
But endlessly and shallow into themselves.

To see oneself in the garden is the final
Privilege, the last illusion like
The glittering letters in a burning leaf.

To be an image of the thing already
Containing you is surely a fine prospect,
As the fruit is an eager portrait of the tree.

459

And being so requires the greatest detachment,
Function of the philosopher's particular passion
To locate beauty beyond its short-lived shapes.

The garden, therefore, is a signal comfort
To those who fear that belonging is an illusion
Like longing itself, like the desire for desire.

For though it takes no pleasure in itself,
The garden is beautiful while you are in it,
And having once been you are always there.

A cuclshoc

Not the new racquets themselves, strung
To the pitch of drums in that wiry meshed black
Of loudspeakers. Not the crammed tube of feathers.

They are a daughterly indulgence, gear
To stir the sluggish pumps and muscles of our fifties,
Mythical as the breath they need, and tan knees.

Not these, which seem a flattering novelty,
But a letter found later in a dusty trunk
Brings to mind all that I know of this game.

Brings it back across a half century
In a cautious upper case and licked pencil
That once imagined Blackpool for Nairobi.

The signifiers are elementary. I HAVE
GOT A CUCLSHOC. I CAN HIT IT
5 TIMS. What else do I remember?

The cistern drip and chill of an attic Christmas.
The layered curves of the frames, stained maroon
Like spills, and trussed with yellow woven gut.

And the rattling thwung of the wobbly cork tub
Bound with its brittle stumps of varnished feathers
That however hard you hit it, slowed, and turned.

It made me think of the parson's nose, all quills:
When it wavered towards me over the washing-line
It was like getting ready to biff a chicken's bum.

And if I missed, although it had stopped dead
Mysteriously in mid-air, it dropped just too quickly
Out of my reach, like a newsreel commando.

Whatever I might have known about adult love,
About the sacred triviality of letters
Or their conspiracy at a distance about presents,

Whatever I suspected might be uncertain in the future,
In the size of oceans, the licensed irregularity
Of wars and the accuracy of torpedoes,

Cries out from these laborious sentences
With all their childish feeling and now with all
My later tears. I HOPE YOU WILL COM BACK SOON

So WE CAN HAVE SOM FUN. That winged basket,
That little lofted button, forever hovering,
Still hangs in the back yard, beyond my racquet.

The feathers are splayed in the sun, like the fragile words
We sometimes write and mean, which therefore always
Mean and always will be there to do so.

SEND A FOTOGRAF OF YOR SELF. It glints
With the stitching of angels, buoyant in the light,
Never falling. WELL WELL GOOD BY DADDY DEAR.

Sunflowers

The surging of a star
Makes moons of umber
Many-million-grained,
Bowed like dejected dolls
In ragged slumber.

Penitent in their pews,
Their only reason
To turn and turn about,
Tilting up their bonnets
For a short season.

Hope for them was a halo
Of chrome petals
Worn with utter devotion
Till the gaze became a mask
Of the deepest of metals.

461

Impossible to conceive
Of such a hero
Whose indiscriminate eye
Passed over them unseeing,
A moral zero.

Passed, and is passing now
Over the errors
That we have often sown,
Over the stumps of crops
And other terrors.

For hatred in the earth
In neighbour and nation
Grows equally and tall
Though it hang its head
In exculpation.

Though it wept in the dust,
Though it pleaded
For one more second of life,
The fruit has broken open
And the fruit is seeded.

Saint August in his robes,
Praising his maker,
Treads in the burning fields
A passage through each ranked
And guilty acre.

Edward Lear in Corsica

*Is it not unpleasant, at fifty-six years of age, to feel that it is increasingly
probable that a man can never hope to be otherwise than alone, never, no
never more? Did not Edgar Poe's raven distinctly say 'Nevermore'?*
(Edward Lear, Journal of a Landscape Painter)

With its colourful flora and fauna
How delightful to visit La Corse!
There is silence for once in the corner:
Poe's raven has cried himself hoarse.

The terrible word that he utters
Brings none of its usual fears.

In Ajaccio, latched are the shutters
And deep are the hats over ears.

For hope is a buoyant statistic
And here they are used to being free.
You are bound to become optimistic
When you wander into the maquis.

The woods breathe a whimsical vapour
That doesn't compel you to think.
The walks by the shore smell like paper.
The sea is the colour of ink.

The landscape was formed when the planet
Had little but rocks on its mind.
The fall of the coastline granite
Is awesome but not unkind.

When the clock chimes five and a quarter
Already I've fought with the sea.
I rise from the vanquished water
And drip from my beard to my knee.

My pride, like a low-tide anemone
Is sailing at less than full rig
And my otherwise pendulous gemini
Are tight as a Cargèse fig.

I shall live in crepuscular mountains
Where the chestnuts are full of white cows.
I shall drink at the pebbly fountains
And put on a peasant's loose blouse.

I shall draw every day what's before me.
My spirit will put up a fight.
Not a thing on this island could bore me.
I shall map the behaviour of light.

Here's the pichet. Now take out the stopper.
Through my breakfast I'll know who I am.
The honey's the colour of copper.
The wine is the colour of jam.

The fish are the colour of roses.
The cheese is the colour of cheese.
Its smell has found out where the nose is.
The name of it sounds like a sneeze.

In heaven one stores up treasure
From every shifting mood
That belongs to the landscape of pleasure
With its rituals of air and of food.

The host of the morning croissant,
The sacrament of the pêche,
The globulous soupe des poissons
That is almost an act of the flesh.

The tone of a leaf or a petal,
The wind with its breath of intrigue,
The herbs that seduce from the kettle,
The herbs that define the garrigue.

But it's on to the col de Bavella!
Where the mountains are pink in the sky
Like the ribs of a lady's umbrella
Left out in the garden to dry.

The easel unfolds like a table.
There is oil, and fresh pigments to crush.
With a sweep of my hand I am able
To lay on the sky with a brush.

In each cloud, in each pine, in each boulder
You may see that the paint hasn't lied.
Come sir, look over my shoulder:
The hills are like elephant's hide.

There was a young lady of Zonza –
But I cannot come up with a rhyme.
My verse-making skill has quite gone, sir.
I find that I haven't the time.

It was something to do with a corset,
Or was it the shape of her toes?
When the memory's gone you can't force it.
God knows where the memory goes.

The past is a prison. I've tried it.
It is choked up with ash like a grate.
The future has nothing inside it.
The present is hard to locate.

I have made an important decision:
I shall live from now on in my art.
It's a way to achieve the precision
That's dulled in affairs of the heart.

The nourishing zest of the highlight
That glints from a rock or a spoon,
The deepening draught of the twilight,
The rich chiaroscuro of noon.

And then, when the starlight is silent
Above the still murmurous sea,
I shall know I belong to this island
And this island belongs to me.

And I shall have found the haven,
That glistening granular shore,
Where flown is the ruminous raven
And the echo is: 'Evermore!'

Villanova

This sea so clearly exhibits its forms of life
That nothing seems too deep or wet about it
Even as it slowly ladders the hairs of the thigh.

Ever so slightly lift its gently revolving lid
And it drips back into itself like a fountain
Of which for a moment I am the amused inventor

Or a richly nude and indolent Brahma, laying
My knuckles upon the surface of creation,
Remembering to bless it in the middle of a yawn.

Admire the little fishes in the water pointing one way,
So still and pale, only their shadows show.
To be them is to be as cool as may be.

And well might it indeed be better to be them,
For the sun cannot bear to be looked at, angrily
Throwing back upon me my glance and godhead,

Saying: 'Imagine the unlikeliness of liquid rock
Surviving into the insolence of monuments!
Imagine the seething vapours falling like tears!'

I can only think of this: if our desire
For a defining stillness is a memory
Of the unsuffering planet which imagined us

We shall find it here. And in the magnificence
Which is this sea in the middle of the world
There will be some shade, all that is ever needed.

'Prudence dans l'eau'

Far from being a warning,
Today's newspaper horoscope
Is simply a tender description
Of this aquarelle you enact
As if by a maître of 1919

For whom the maillot, beyond
Its masquerading as a garment,
Becomes the tracing of a line
Negotiating a containment
Of convalescent blue.

You may picture the sea
As a requirement of masses:
Here, the caution of shoulders
A shade of biscuit against
A disintegrating wall of wave.

There, the wide wash of azure
With its pucker of cobalt
And unsettling flung creams.
And further, just off-centre,
The teacherly red tick of a sail.

It's not that you're happy to become this picture.
You're happy for once to be yourself,
Cradled in water that moves for ever
Over the stones and fishes of the morning,
Beneath the stones and fires of night.

Canicule macaronique

Heureux ceux qui ont la clim – Corse-Matin (6.8.94)

Heureux ceux qui ont la clim
Pendant la grande canicule.
Heureux those whose culs are cool.
Heureuse her and heureux him.

C'est la canicule qui hurle,
Ready to tear you limb from limb.
Heureux ceux qui ont la clim,
Cri-criant: 'O turlútuturle!'

La situation est grim,
The mise-en-scène a trifle burle.
À chaleur disons donc: 'Ta gueule!'
And keep ourselves amused and slim.

Heureux qui par terre se roule:
Lucky Luke and Lucky Jim,
Edith Piaf, Tiger Tim,
Et le plus divin Poupoule.

Heureux Toccate, heureux Hymne,
Heureux Mouvements Perpetuels,
Heureuses Les Bîches immortelles,
De tristesse sexuelle synonyme.

Je ne regrette rien. I'm full
Of love as are the seraphim,
And plein de bonheur to the brim,
Pendant cette grande canicule.

La vie has satisfying sym:
For every lui there lives an elle.
Finding its level in her well,
La source sauvage is in the swim.

Ni ouragan ni canicule,
Ni pretexte prompte ou assez flim,
Can keep le coeur from feeling imm,
Allègre in the planet's pull.

Let's fly together in a bim,
Au-dessus de la fou-foule
Qui mange ses menus et ses moules,
Impregné de sueur, et prim!

For always I'll have you, and you'll
Have me, and though desire grows dim,
Heureux ceux qui ont la quim,
Heureuses celles qui ont le tool.

Forever through the sky will skim
Le pé-pédalo de Dédale,
Escaladant sans escale
The blue horizon's endless rim.

En pénitence, le tournesol
Beguiné, poudreuz, anonyme,
Turns and turns, and at a whim
Sonne, en sol, son son du sol.

From Chatellerault to Arles and Nîmes
Le visage bronze du tournesol
S'incline comme un pa-parasol
Trouve une épaule coquette, intime.

Devisé dans le banderole:
'Heureux ceux qui ont la clim.'
Across the fields the notes are dim:
Son sol, son sol, son sol, son sol.

Pyrosymphonie

You and I, when our days are done, must say
Without exactly saying it, goodbye.
If we could choose at such at time one free
Embodiment which might, by being the last,
Stand in the account somehow as one
Generous entry putting the whole in credit,
What and where would it be, that final choice?

There are times such as when we have had them
Must serve in their completeness for the fancy,
For they are all we get. As yesterday,
Breathing in the wood, crouching for ceps.
And just a week ago, the eyes narrowing
For twenty porpoises sewing the waves
Beyond West End, not seen for fifteen years.

And then last month, the heart syncopating,
We slipped from a canoe into the shallows
With golden Beynac above us, tall, half-robed.
That wood, that sea, that river, rooted or moving,
Survive in all their changes, year by year
In which we drift through them, seizing on hope,
Searching for our permanent lost shapes.

Perhaps for that moment we could be ourselves
For once, and somehow find ourselves in time
For the Assumption at Calvi, surprised by night,
The whole sky split by fire and dripping stars.

And we should live this passionate postscript till
Those shapes no longer named themselves as all
That they suggest, these mimes of the cascade:

Lamps of the hill town's single street, guiding
Its evening Clios after each other down
To the pleasures of the coast, the pulse of light,
Celestial pinball, instantaneous blooms,
Paper in chimneys, headaches, calculations,
Ribbons, Spanish exclamation marks,
Cringing anemones, the sky shocked red,

A burst of dizzy bubbles in the kicklight
Of the downthrust of an ankle, following
Your swimming shape for ever for this moment
Onwards through weed-flagged crevices, as quick
As your shutter on these artificial fires
That live just longer than we might expect,
Though never giving time to say goodbye.

Index of titles and first lines

479